Praise for Chapters in Dolphins ~ Whales Forever

"Roberta's chapter is a wonderfully informative piece, full of insights and clues that could only come from someone who is experientially tuned into the cetacean intelligence." ~ *Timothy Wyllie, Author of Adventures Among Spiritual Intelligences: Angels, Aliens, Dolphins & Shamans, and many other books.*

"I instantly connected with and felt total feelings of joy and love, and could feel the energy of the thread of Divine love and how it is so exquisitely communicated in these words. As I kept reading, I felt more connected to the Divine in myself. I was reminded of the significance and joy that opening our hearts plays in our lives, and how animals play such a big part in this process." ~ *Diane Cusano, San Jose, California*

"Truly, this is a moving and profound chapter. This will be a great gift to readers. Had me in tears by page 2. Downright lyrical and poetic at times, in a natural and lovely way." ~ *Judith White, Adjunct Professor of Complementary and Integrative Therapies at Drexel University in Philadelphia*

"Trish and Doug's amazingly beautiful story about their spiritual journey to work with the dolphins and whales has touched my heart and life profoundly . . . I have heard pieces of their story, but never so comprehensively and inspirationally articulated as in this telling. For me, the power and beauty of Trish and Doug's work with the cetaceans is especially enhanced by the gift of their partnership--the way they bring the loving essence of the feminine and the masculine together . . . thanks to Trish and Doug's wonderful guidance and facilitation, the dolphins have initiated me into a path of fulfilling my own true life's purpose." ~ *Constance M. Piesinger, Ph.D.*

"Couldn't put it down! It led me to want to read it all, right now! The mother whales's experience of healing was very touching. Reading this was truly a blessing!" ~ *Deb Gibson, Harrisburg, Pennsylvania*

"It opened my mind and heart to how much more aware some animals are to why they are here in this lifetime and what they came to work through. . . including the heartfelt story about Mama whale and her baby and how wrong it is for the fishing gear that is dumped in the oceans. It is the story of how Mama grew from this experience, but it has the possibility to change anyone's life who reads this chapter." ~ *Judy Specht, San Jose CA*

"I learned that love and healing is universal and that change is possible even in situations you think will never change. That growth can come from pain as it did for both you and Mama whale who reopened her heart." ~ *Kath Quinn, Roswell, Georgia*

"I learned that as magnificent as the whales are, they receive and appreciate love, help and healing from humans. The whale Mama's story was especially heartfelt. She was so brave to allow all her pain to flow, with the eventual outcome of re-discovering compassion and a new found trust of humans. I also learned that a soul is a soul, no matter what form it takes. All are deserving of love and respect. If we are open to it, there is much to learn from each soul. It was interesting, informative, funny, touching and so well written it captivated me from the first sentence." ~ *Marti Pattishall, Redondo Beach, California*

"What I found inspiring were the messages and wisdom displayed by the whales, especially Mama whale's transformation and the re-awakening of her emotions. Feelings of love and compassion overwhelmed me." ~ *Mickey Kane, Lancaster, Pennsylvania*

"I LOVED this chapter. The experiences and stories were genuine, heart-felt, educational, inspiring and deeply moving. There was a nice cohesiveness, flow and clarity to the information presented. It stirred my heart and soul. It inspired me. It made me cry. And, most of all, it made me feel blessed for the presence of whales on our planet . . . Gives the reader an opportunity to know whales in a deeper, more expansive way, as fellow beings with whom we share the planet, and not just as a tourist attraction. It shows us the deep level of love and connection that exists (or can exist) between whales and humans . . . ~ *Dixie Golins, North Vancouver, British Columbia*

Dolphins & Whales Forever

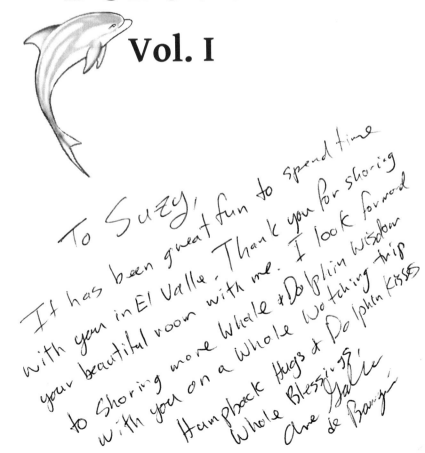

Vol. I

To Suzy,

It has been great fun to spend time with you in El Valle. Thank you for sharing your beautiful room with me. I look forward to sharing more Whale & Dolphin Wisdom with you on a Whole Watching Trip

Humpback Hugs & Dolphin Kisses
Whole Blessings,
Ane de Barryn

Dolphins & Whales Forever

Vol. I

Debbie Takara Shelor
With Nina Brown, Grandma Chandra, Celeste Eaton, Mary J. Getten, Roberta Goodman, Sierra Goodman, Anne Gordon de Barrigón, Cyndie Lepori, Megan Leupold, Joebaby Noonan, Joan Ocean, Frederique Pichard, Trish Regan & Doug Hackett, Laurie Reyon, Linda Shay, Teresa Wagner, and Madeleine Walker

Dancing Seas Media

ISBN-10 0984743111
ISBN-13 978-0-9847431-1-7

10 9 8 7 6 5 4 3 2 1

This book was typeset in Gentium Book Basic with Chopin Script used as display typeface

Interior Image – Jean-Luc Bozzoli

Table of Contents

Dedication & Acknowledgements

Dedication

This book is dedicated to the Dolphins & Whales ~ *our family with fins* ~ and to all the humans whose hearts and lives they touch.

Acknowledgements

An extraordinary amount of effort and support is required to bring forth a collaboration such as this. I'd like to specifically acknowledge Anne Gordon de Barrigón for heeding "the call" to bring together a group of dolphin and whale experts. Several of the authors in this collaboration met through that project. Special thanks to Marsha Scarborough for her editing finesse. Thanks also to the many people who have assisted individual authors, as well as the project as a whole.

Introduction

Dolphins and whales "call" to certain individuals. Those who heed that call often experience profound life changes. Dolphins bring healing and joy. Orcas offer empowerment and transformation. Whales share a deep and ancient wisdom. By reading this book, the dolphins and whales will touch your life as they have touched ours.

Those who commune with them develop an inner peace, heightened intuition, ability to flow with life, connection to higher wisdom, grace, poise, passion, and a sense of purpose that people leading "normal" lives are often unaware is even possible.

The authors you are about to meet have a love, connection, and rapport with dolphins and whales that transcends conventional wisdom and understanding. Because of the unique relationship they each have with the "people" of the sea, every one of them has experienced an extraordinary level of personal transformation. In many cases, they have in turn become catalysts of change for others.

Their personal stories are vastly different. Yet the messages they share each contain the universal themes of love, harmony, compassion, and truth. Having come from various parts of the world, they have unique approaches to life and experiences to share as it relates to dolphins and whales.

A core element contained in every story is a special meeting with a particular dolphin or whale that changed their life completely. Whether that "meeting" was literal or experienced as a vision or meditation, the results were always the same.

I invited each of the authors you are about to meet to share their wisdom and to answer the following four questions:

1. How were you first introduced to the dolphins and/or whales?
2. How did that encounter or subsequent encounters change your life?
3. What do you do now that is related to dolphins and/or whales?
4. How does what you do with dolphins and whales improve the lives of others?

The authors in this collaboration include:

- Nina Brown
- Grandma Chandra
- Celeste Eaton
- Mary J. Getten
- Roberta Goodman
- Sierra Goodman
- Anne Gordon de Barrigon
- Cyndie Lepori
- Megan Leupold
- Joebaby Noonan
- Joan Ocean
- Frederique Pichard
- Trish Regan & Doug Hacket
- Laurie Reyon
- Linda Shay
- Debbie Takara Shelor
- Teresa Wagner
- Madeleine Walker

I found tears gently rolling down my cheeks as I read several of the chapters for the first time. Since my own life changed so dramatically after a virtual dolphin encounter, I could easily identify with experiences shared by others and how their lives were changed.

I trust that this book will touch your heart as well. The beautiful words contained on the following pages are encoded / imbued with the loving vibrations and embrace of the dolphins and whales.

A few chapters were written by non-American authors and contain words spelled in a non-American fashion. For example, the word honor in America is spelled honour in some other countries.

It is my great pleasure and honor to share with you the following stories of hope, healing, inspiration, and joy.

Takara

November 22, 2013

Chapter 1: *From Sea to Land*

By Linda Shay

The tenderness of wind and sea reveals the heart of truth in me.
Amidst the dolphins, ocean born, my love is like a banner, worn for all to see.
I hear the call. I swim to shore. I leave my sacred sea once more.
With tender heart, I touch the land.
Beloved friend, please take my hand, and know that I from oceans come,
that move, that flow, where all is One.
I pray to let my heart expand.
To live this Love upon the land.
- Kim Rosen, excerpt from poem Ocean Born

I first met the dolphins through the hugely popular and beloved TV show, *Flipper*, when I was a kid. As much as I loved that show, I didn't have posters of dolphins in my bedroom growing up. Honestly, I never gave the dolphins any thought at all until they started knocking on my door, spiritually, when I was living in Sedona, Arizona (the desert!), in 1996.

But there were two early childhood clues that hinted at a profound connection with these beautiful beings. As an infant, I was slow to walk. Where did I take my first solo steps? On a deep sandy beach in New Jersey! My older brother Paul reminisced one day, "Yeah, Lin, when we got to that beach, you just popped up and took off walking." I guess I took one look at the ocean and recognized it as home. I wanted to go there!

One other bizarre clue was when I practiced holding my breath underwater at the community swimming pool, which my family lived at all day, every day, during the summers. I have a distinct memory of being underwater holding my breath, and just when I felt the need to surface to breathe, I did something with my jaw that I swear extracted oxygen from the water, extending my underwater stay. Then my mind kicked in saying that was impossible. I propelled myself to the surface, gasping for air.

In the early 90's, I was 36 years old, married and living in Sacramento, California, when my seemingly happy and perfect life began to crumble. At that time, the word "spirituality" wasn't even in my vocabulary. I had no awareness that the world of energy and spirit existed.

A friend invited me to attend a meditation gathering with her. I'd heard of meditation and was curious about it, but I'd never tried it. I was up for a new experience, so I said, "Yes, I'll go."

On my third visit, the most extraordinary thing happened. After the guided visualization part of the meditation, we entered into the silence. Instantly, I found myself standing at the ocean's edge, being magnetically drawn into the water. In my peripheral vision, I saw movement ahead. A fin was slicing through the water toward me. A shark? Curiously, I had no fear.

I was so surprised when a very large and beautiful dolphin swam toward me and stopped by my side. The next thing I knew, I was holding onto his dorsal fin for dear life flying through the water! And then, we dove, slowly at first as I acclimated to his underwater world. Deeper and darker we went. The moment I felt fear from the cold, the darkness, and the unknown, we turned and rose to the surface to play more.

When we dove the second time, I was able to see more and go deeper before the fear came. As we ascended to the surface, wave upon wave of peace and well-being passed through me. I knew these sensations were coming from my new dolphin friend. It seemed he knew everything about me, and he loved all parts of me. I felt completely safe with this dolphin. For the first time in my life, I felt completely seen, loved, accepted, and acknowledged by another being. This was a wondrous new experience for me.

From worlds away, the facilitator spoke, inviting us to return to present time and space. As the ocean and my dolphin friend swirled away, I felt disoriented and confused. As the room and the small gathering of women came into view, I felt sad and alone. Where's my dolphin? The world with the dolphin felt more real to me than the world to which I had returned.

Life went on, and I forgot all about my dolphin friend ... for a while. But a subtle shift was underway, both inside of me, and in my outer world. My husband and I had grown disenchanted with our corporate jobs. We'd begun meeting people who were living very different kinds of lives—outside-the-box kinds of lives—which intrigued us. One day, we made the huge decision to leave the corporate world behind. We left our jobs, sold our large beautiful home, bought an RV, and traveled America in search of a new life and our next perfect place to live.

Magic and synchronicity landed us in the sacred red rocks of Sedona, Arizona. From the day we arrived, my spirituality blossomed through spending hours alone on the land every day. I would hike for a bit, and then be drawn to a particular place to sit. I just sat for hours, day after day. I "did" nothing. Unbeknownst to me, while I sat immersed in the mystery and wildness of this dramatic high desert landscape, my old life dropped away. I learned how to "just be."

For two weeks, the moment I stepped onto the red earth, I burst into tears, intense tears that seemed to come from the depth of my soul. This emotional catharsis lasted for forty-five minutes or so, and then peace came over me. From this peaceful place, I'd open my eyes and look around. This is when the magic happened.

Nature began revealing her mystical aspects to me. I looked up into the big blue sky and saw the tiny dancing sparkles of light swimming through the air all around me. How could I have not seen these before? The light is everywhere! Another day, I was spontaneously drawn to connect deeply with a flowering Manzanita bush. I found myself extending my hands toward the bush, palms open, and asking, "Will you share your energy with me?"

Slowly, subtly, the essence of this beautiful plant began coursing through my veins, my body, my whole being. When I walked away, I was in a completely altered state. I was in bliss! When I returned to my car, I had to wait a while for "me" to return so I could drive home.

Soon, the trees were talking to me, the rocks were talking to me, and the plants were talking to me. This spectacular high desert landscape became my classroom, and Mother Nature became my teacher. It was a profound and magical time. And, it was divinely orchestrated preparation for my spiritual dolphin journey that was yet to come.

While I was out-and-about in our new community making friends and creating an exciting and fulfilling new life, my husband was struggling mightily. He wasn't "into" the world of spirituality and metaphysics. He was at a loss as to how to create his life in Sedona. He became depressed and spiraled quickly into the depths of darkness. Despite my pleas, he would not seek help.

For six months, my life was a wild pendulum swing between the ecstasy I was experiencing on land and in the community, and the pit of despair and darkness I walked into every time I returned home. One night, the unimaginable happened. My husband took his life.

I moved through the succeeding days and weeks in a daze. Love and prayer support from loved ones got me through that devastating time.

Even so, I had to get away, just for a while, to heal and to grieve. An astrologer friend said, "I'm feeling Hawaii for you ... Maui." I'd never been to Hawaii. It never would have occurred to me to go there. But when my friend suggested this, it felt right.

While there, a woman I had befriended invited me to join her on a day trip to the island of Lanai. We'd heard that a pod of wild Hawaiian spinner dolphins frequented the bay there. When it was time to depart, everyone on the boat was curious and excited about the possibility of meeting them. We were not disappointed!

Immediately upon setting off for the return trip to Maui, a playful pod of spinners swam right up to the boat. Everyone ran to the sides to see the dolphins, but I wasn't able to move. A strong stream of energy poured into my crown chakra and surged through my body and out my feet, gluing me to my spot. Inside myself, I heard myself asking the dolphins, "What are you here to teach us?"

"*Unity-Community*," was their immediate reply.

Because of my telepathic encounters with the natural world in Sedona, this communication with these dolphins felt completely natural and normal. After this exchange, I didn't give the dolphins, or their message, another thought.

In a moment of clarity, the thought came to me, "I'm free! No one is depending on me. I'm not working right now and don't have to for a while. My life is a clean slate. I can do anything I want!"

And so, for the next two years, I lived off my 401K money and followed Spirit. I did some traveling and enjoyed life. When I started feeling the tug inside to settle down and focus on creating a new career, I took another cross-country road trip to find my next place to live.

After everything that had happened there, Sedona was not even on my list of possibilities. However, to my astonishment and dismay, Sedona is where I landed, again. The signs and synchronicities all led me back there. I arrived late at night, kicking and screaming. The gloriously vast ink-black sky, streaked end-to-end with a ribbon of brilliantly sparkling Milky Way, and the biggest, brightest falling star I've ever seen, silently witnessed my return and welcomed me "home."

The very next day, the strangest thing started happening. Within minutes of talking to people, strangers or old friends alike, they started talking to me about dolphins. It was so weird. We were in the desert! I didn't have much to contribute, because I knew little about dolphins. I certainly didn't feel that they had anything to do with my life. The signs and messages started coming on strong, in clever and sometimes hilarious ways! I couldn't ignore that something was going on between me and the dolphins. I was perplexed, open, and curious.

Before long, the universe conspired to get me back over to Hawaii—the Big Island of Hawaii this time—to swim with the wild Hawaiian spinner dolphins there. Within hours of my arrival on a warm, sunny day in February 1996, I was alone in a bay, surrounded by an entire pod of approximately eighty-five spinner dolphins. No other humans were in sight. For two timeless hours, all that existed in my world was this bay, these dolphins, and me. There was not a moment that at least one dolphin was not in my sight. While I knew that what I was witnessing and experiencing was truly extraordinary, it felt like the most normal and natural thing for me to be doing. I knew with certainty that I was exactly where I was meant to be, and I was doing exactly what I was meant to be doing.

But it was one moment, with one dolphin, that changed the course of my life forever. A group of three dolphins, followed by a group of two, had just swum past me. As I floated at the surface, mesmerized by the exquisite underwater ballet that was taking place all around me, my head moved on its own, looking below and behind me. One lone dolphin was floating there. As soon as we made eye contact, this dolphin swam toward me at full speed. I thought he was going to hit me! My body reacted, and when I opened my eyes, I was floating vertically in the water. I was astonished to see this dolphin also hovering vertically just inches in front of me. His face, looking so purposefully at me, was all I could see. This was so unexpected, I burst out laughing–not the thing to do with a snorkel and mask on! Water filled my mask, and as I prepared to surface to clear it, this dolphin made clicking sounds at me and then swam away.

That very night, the magic began. Over the days, weeks, and months that followed, I discovered I had become a vehicle for the beautiful healing frequencies of the dolphins to flow through. By simply talking casually to people about dolphins, I got reports back that many felt energy moving through their bodies. Some said they felt they'd received a healing!

Upon my return to Sedona, I went out onto the land one day, pondering this whole dolphin phenomenon. What does this have to do with my life? I wondered. A big red rock beckoned for me to sit. Surrounded by my silent sentinel friends – the towering red rocks that make Sedona so special – I slipped into a meditative state with this question in my heart and mind. Within minutes, the most sublime energy approached me from the right. Inside myself, I heard the words: "Will you be one of our ambassadors on land, and do dolphin energy healing as your career?"

This visitation by a pod of spirit dolphins, in the desert that I called home, took my breath away. I didn't say "yes" right away. The idea of being a dolphin ambassador and dolphin energy healer was far outside my self-view, even in Sedona, where anything goes!

When I did say "Yes," even though I didn't know what exactly I was saying "yes" to, I sensed my other spiritual teachers and guides take a step back, and the dolphins take the lead. In that moment, the dolphin consciousness (which I soon abbreviated to "Dolphin") became my primary spiritual teacher and guide.

An extraordinary new adventure had begun!

A new question started floating through my awareness: "How does one become a Dolphin Energy Healer?" I certainly didn't know any.

I had been a banker in my earlier adult life. After leaving that world in search of something more fulfilling, I took a basic course in therapeutic massage followed by a one-day class in energy healing. When Dolphin knocked on my door, I had learned the basics, but I was pretty much a blank slate and wide open to their teachings and inspirations.

Soon, people with an affinity for dolphins started showing up in my life. We shared our dolphin stories, and at some point we would erupt into goose bumps. In these instances, I felt an inner prompting to offer dolphin energy healing to these people. "Yes, please!" they replied with excitement and curiosity.

Dolphin Heart World was born.

I started sharing dolphin energy by holding hands with my receiver. The moment we touched, I was "taken" to the sublime place of no thought that lasted for the duration of the session. Sometimes I felt energy passing through me and sometimes I felt nothing. Sometimes my receiver spoke about their sensations and experiences, and sometimes we were in silence.

Sometimes I received messages from the dolphins through my receiver. It seemed my channels weren't open yet to receive such messages from them directly. A few times, the words, "You are one," came through my receiver. On the third time, I finally got what Dolphin was trying to tell me. You are one ... a dolphin. I am one of them, a dolphin in human form. These three small simple words took a while for me to fully appreciate and let in.

I listened, in awe and wonder, as my receivers described their session experiences. Every session was unique. It seemed the only limit to what Dolphin could do was the limitation the receiver held in her own mind.

Some examples of session outcomes are:

- Melissa had been trying for two years to get pregnant. "My biological clock is ticking," she said. During her session, she felt the dolphins working in her uterus. Two weeks later, she called, overflowing with joy that she was, indeed, pregnant! (A number of our Certified Dolphin Energy

Practitioners have had similar successes in their healing practices.)

- Kathy, a clairvoyant, had a torn ligament in her back that was quite painful. She saw a team of spirit dolphins laying healthy new tissue over the damaged tissue, and weaving it meticulously into place. She felt that area of her body heal and get strong again. When she stood up, she had no pain. Many days later, she called and told me that her pain was still gone, and that the tissue repair was holding.

- Renée came to her session overflowing with questions. She believed, with all her heart, that her soulmate is a dolphin alive on the planet right now. She was seeking validation. As soon as the session started, huge amounts of what felt like male dolphin energy started pouring into my body. It kept coming and coming and coming. I realized it was the spirit of her dolphin soulmate! He entered into me so that they could experience meeting one another physically. It was amazing to facilitate their meeting, and to feel that enormous amount of energy inside of me! Renee emerged from her session deeply grateful and peaceful in this profound knowing.

After reading my book, *Dolphin Love ... From Sea to Land,* Sandy contacted me to share the life-threatening health crisis she was confronting. The team of natural healers she had worked with for years had done as much as they could for her. The next step appeared to be two invasive surgeries. She was not willing to go there.

Having read about dolphin energy healing in my book, she was certain the dolphins could help her heal all the way, without resorting to surgery. We embarked upon a profound healing journey together. Sandy received weekly dolphin energy sessions from me for three and-a-half months. Even after all the years I'd been doing this work, I was in awe at how Dolphin choreographed her healing.

The session that stands out in my mind was when the dolphins told me, "We are going to re-write her history. We're going to change her past." From the moment of conception on, Sandy led a profoundly challenging life. Among other things, her father sexually abused her when she was just four years old. During this session, I found myself affirming over and over inside myself, to her: "I am conceived in Love. I am carried in Love. I am birthed in Love. I am received in Love. I am raised with Unconditional Love and Joy."

When the session was over, I shared all of this with Sandy. That session was a turning point for her. Throughout our time together, not only did Sandy make great strides toward the 100% healing of her body, the relationship with her father, her sole remaining parent, healed.

I received the most exquisite e-mail from Sandy while she was back east visiting her father, many months after her history-changing session. The moment she arrived "home," her father threw his arms around her and held her in the biggest hug, telling her over and over again how much he loves her, and how happy he was that she was there. She was shocked! The whole time she was there, Sandy's father treated her with enthusiastic love, affection, and respect. I was overcome with joy to read about Sandy's magnificent homecoming with her father. Wow ... what a gift and a blessing. Thank you, Dolphin!!

These stories are just a tiny sampling of all that I've been blessed to facilitate and witness over the years. I've learned so much about us humans, and about the dolphins, through sharing the gift of dolphin love and healing with those who find their way to me.

However, this new path was not only about being able to serve my fellow humans in this profound and remarkable way; it was for my own healing, growth, and awakening too. Those clicking sounds my dolphin friend made at me in the water that day was the initiation of my own "attunement" journey to the energy and consciousness of the dolphins.

In the beginning, every healing session I facilitated opened and cleared my own energy channels more and more. It got to the point that I "needed" to give healings to others, for my own healing and growth. For a while, I was practically dragging people in off the street to receive!

As my immersion in the dolphin frequencies deepened and grew, I recognized that the quality of Love I felt from Dolphin was unlike any other. Dolphin Love filled me up on all levels. It fed me and nourished my whole being. I didn't need anything else. My spiritual searching was over. I was on the Dolphin path now.

Dolphin took me deep within myself, deeper than I'd dared go before. Soon I longed to BE Dolphin Love all the time. Not just when I was meditating with them. Not just when I was swimming with them. Not just when I was facilitating a healing. The "urge to merge" with Dolphin came from the deepest part of me. It made no logical sense, and it didn't even seem possible while in this human form. This yearning was ever-present. It informed all that I did and shared. It propelled me forward on my awakening journey that spanned seven years.

This journey wasn't easy. I knew many people who loved dolphins, but no one else whose life was completely taken over by them ... that was how it seemed to me at the time. I had periods of deep grief about being a human. Life as a dolphin was so much more ... loving, connected, caring, and joyful! Peak inter-dimensional experiences shifted and changed me, followed by long periods of seemingly nothing going on. I battled inside myself that I wasn't doing enough, I wasn't making enough money.

Sometimes I felt like I was going crazy. Maybe I need to stop this and do something more normal and practical with my life. A few times I did stop and try new things. Invariably, my life fell apart. Soon I was pleading with the universe, asking for help. The next thing I knew, I'd find myself at my computer, looking at dolphin-related websites, thinking, "I could do that!"

And then I'd get it ... this is my path! This is my work. I'd say YES to Dolphin again, and in a heartbeat, my anxiety and depression dissolved. I was completely lit up again with Dolphin Love and Joy, and energized with new inspirations of how to share Dolphin's healing gifts with the world.

I dove deep and soared high throughout my seven-year healing journey with Dolphin. And then, one evening in December 2002, I was scheduled to lead a dolphin energy meditation for the community. The whole day, leading up to the meditation, I felt the energy building. Something felt different. When I arrived at the event location, the energy that was moving through me was intense. Only two men showed up, regulars who had been with me since I first started leading dolphin energy meditations years before. "We're going to dive right in tonight. No dancing, no sharing circle. I have a feeling that tonight is for me!"

For about an hour, we were in the silence together. Slowly but surely, I felt Dolphin frequencies penetrate deeper and deeper into me. I felt their energy seep all the way into the marrow of my bones. My body was so saturated with their love, I couldn't move for a long time. Finally, I forced myself to sit. The best I could do was slouch. And I was breathless. The first words I spoke to my two dear friends were: "I feel drunk." I laughed, but the honest-to-goodness experience I had in my body was that every cell had been made mad, passionate love to by the dolphin consciousness. I was drunk on Dolphin Love for three bliss-filled days.

Several weeks later, I contracted a bad case of "the flu." Mid-way through, I experienced bone pain throughout my whole body. I'd never felt anything like that before. By the third day, it dawned on me that during that meditation, dolphin energy penetrated all the way through to the marrow of my bones. And now my bones hurt. "This is not the flu," I announced to my husband, David. "Something divine is going on here!"

One morning in early January 2003, I woke up symptom-free. I was brand new. Everything about me was changed. My fears were gone. My doubts and insecurities were gone. I felt energized and vibrant and alive as never before. I had energizer-bunny energy from morning until night, day after day. I got so much done! The change in me was so pronounced, David started asking, "Who are you, and what have you done with my wife?"

My phone started ringing with new opportunities to share Dolphin Love in the world, and I said "YES" to every opportunity, without hesitation. My witness self observed this new Linda being in the world, fully expressing herself without a care as to what anyone thought. The lightness of being ... the freedom I felt, for the first time in my life ... was thrilling and intoxicating!

I was floating through life on a magic carpet, and the entire world was sprinkled with fairy dust. Part of me was waiting for this high to fade, for my old self to return. It did not.

As David and I wondered what on earth had happened that caused such a pronounced shift in me, messages and information came in from a few trusted sources.

"You are now spiritually awake, my dear. It's not possible, anymore, for you to go back." - *Dr. James Martin Peebles, channeled through Summer Bacon*

"Your soul's journey is now complete. It is time for you to go home and heal the hearts of those whom you serve, and those who are in service to you." - *Grandmother Chandra*

"A new quality of consciousness has been birthed on planet Earth. A new spiritual path for humanity has been created." - *Dr. James Martin Peebles, channeled through Summer Bacon*

13

I was humbled and awed to discover that Dolphin had found a way to manifest my deepest heart's desire to BE Dolphin, all the time. Over the course of seven years, they slowly and methodically made microscopic changes to my body and energy field that enabled me to carry and sustain their high, fine frequencies and consciousness all of the time. My inner journey, described in depth in my book, *Dolphin Love ... From Sea to Land*, was about dissolving the illusion of separation between human and dolphin. From my home in the desert, far from the nearest ocean, Dolphin and I merged and became One.

Just weeks after my awakening, Dolphin said to me, "Now it is time to gather your pods and give this gift to others."

I had longed to gather "pods" of humans who desired to dive deep into the dolphin consciousness over time. Given what I witnessed Dolphin accomplish in a single meditation or healing session, I couldn't even imagine what they would do with a group of people who committed to journeying with them together, over time.

Those three magical words, "It is time," sent a shiver of thrill through me.

I awoke one morning with the words "Dolphin healing hearts ... dolphin healing hearts ... dolphin healing hearts ..." resounding in my mind. I heard these words all day long until I picked up paper and pen and wrote them down.

"Dolphin Healing HeArts ... A Gateway to the New Paradigm" appeared on the paper before me.

Dolphin had given me the name of a new spiritual school I was to create! My vision of this school was that I would teach dolphin energy healing, and we would journey into the realm of Dolphin together through guided meditations.

But then a new piece of information came from my spirit friend, Dr. Peebles: "You will do more than teach dolphin energy healing, my dear. You will attune people to the energy and the consciousness of the dolphins."

I will attune people to the energy and consciousness of the dolphins.

I didn't know what that meant, but it felt huge.

He went on: "Your pods need to meet six times, and there needs to be time in between the gatherings."

Slowly, the knowing came to me directly from Dolphin that what they had done with me had been an experiment. Thankfully it was a

14

success! Through that experiment, they created a blueprint so that other humans could also receive the gift of Oneness with Dolphin that I had achieved - the six Dolphin Attunements.

I was very surprised when David announced he wanted to participate in my first pod! Upon receiving his fourth Dolphin Attunement, his love for teaching rose to the surface, and we both realized he had a valuable contribution to make to this (r)evolutionary new school I was co-creating with Dolphin. This Dolphin girl and her computer guy's paths converged, and we embarked upon the amazing adventure of traveling world-wide, teaching our fifteen-month long "Dolphin School" program!

In 2011, Dolphin gave us the great news that the six Dolphin Attunements could now be delivered at a distance to pods of receivers spread out around the world. The Dolphin Attunement Journey was born. It's been thrilling to share the Dolphin Attunements with beautiful new podmates all over the world, and to reach profound levels of love, safety, and connection in this virtual environment. Unity-Community, indeed!

Dolphin is not limited by time, space, or physicality. In early 2014, our Dolphin Healing HeArts program will be available to anyone, anywhere in the world, who owns a computer and has internet access. I offer personal dolphin energy healing sessions to individuals, both in-person and at a distance. David offers transformative healing and channeling journeys with Archie, the dolphin spirit who guides us in this work. All that's required to deeply benefit from a session is an open mind and a willing heart.

In 2007, Dolphin told us:

"It is our desire to heal the hearts of humanity ~ all of humanity."

Dolphin sees this project continuing 250 years into Earth's future. It is a privilege and a joy to play a role in this project, heart-in-heart, hand-in-fin, with Dolphin (and Whale).

I am grateful beyond words for the extraordinary gifts Dolphin, Whale, and Ocean have brought into my life. Thank you, beloveds.

Perhaps you will feel inspired to join us in some way on this grand human-dolphin adventure. We'd love to welcome you into our growing global pod!

Linda Shay is a Dolphin Ambassador, international spiritual teacher, inspiring public speaker, and pioneer in the field of Dolphin Energy Healing. She authored, *Dolphin Love ... From Sea to Land*, and founded Dolphin Heart World (1996) and Dolphin Healing HeArts (2003), a (r)evolutionary spiritual school. From her high desert home near Sedona, Arizona, Linda joins the Dolphin Consciousness in its mission to heal the hearts of humanity ... all of humanity.

After eighteen years in the corporate world, Linda realized something profound was missing in her life. She took a sabbatical in 1993 and embarked upon a journey of self-discovery. In 1996, Linda was guided to go to the Big Island of Hawaii to swim with the wild dolphins there. On her first day in the water, Linda was surrounded by a pod of 85 spinner dolphins. One magical moment, with one dolphin, set her life on a radically different course. Linda's book, *Dolphin Love ... From Sea to Land*, is her true-life spiritual adventure story – and her love story – with the dolphins.

Linda brings through the beautiful healing frequencies of the dolphins (and ocean, whale, and other beings of the sea!) anywhere on Earth, without physical dolphins present. Linda shares these gifts in fun, powerful, and inspiring ways, for the healing and evolution of humanity.

The Dolphin Attunement Journey™ is a series of six spiritual initiations delivered through Linda by the Dolphin Consciousness. The Attunements accelerate personal healing, transformation, and growth. They culminate in a merging of human and dolphin consciousness, creating a new quality of consciousness on planet Earth. Dolphin Heart World also offers training in Dolphin Healing Arts™ and Dolphin Living Arts™, as well as personal healing, channeling, and mentoring sessions.

Linda is joined by her husband, David Rosenthal, in this sacred service. Linda and David are passionate in their commitment to co-creating, with Dolphin, the New Earth reality of a healed and whole planet Earth, whereupon humanity, and all of life, reside in peace, love, harmony, and Unity-Community.

www.DolphinHeartWorld.com   linda@dolphinheartworld.com

Chapter 2: *Touched by Dolphins*

By Sierra Goodman

> *We are tied to the ocean.*
> *And when we go back to the sea,*
> *whether it is to sail or to watch –*
> *we are going back from whence we came.*
> *– John F. Kennedy*

I always told people, "Before I die, I will swim with dolphins." So when the postcard came announcing a dolphin swim with Penelope Smith, the "Mother of Interspecies Telepathic Communication," I knew that my time had come to take the plunge!

I didn't know how I was going to pay for it, so I told the Universe, "If I am meant to go on this trip, let the $500 deposit appear now!" In a few days, I received a $500 bonus from my work I was not expecting because I had not worked there for long. The Universe had spoken! As I continued to tithe and do spiritual work around the trip, the rest of the money came from magical places. The dolphins made sure I was able to be with them at this time.

A couple of weeks before the trip, I entered a dream state, wherein psychic experiences were frequent and strong. I felt an inner pull I could not explain. I was calm and happy and didn't go through the usual "going on a trip" stress I have felt when I've gone away for much shorter periods of time. My animals were fine with my leaving. They knew why I was going and were anxious to do some healing work on my friend who was taking care of them while I was gone.

When I arrived at the hotel, my déjà vu experiences continued. I felt like I already knew everyone, and it all seemed so dreamy, I literally felt like I was in the twilight zone. I had a hard time getting to sleep, but right before I did, I closed my eyes and received this message from the dolphins:

> "Come enter our world of
> Crystal Blue waters
> and pastel corals
> But come with a pure heart
> and ready for fun
> Let us show you the way –
> our way of life
> And when you leave
> You will take us with you
> in your heart
> and we will never leave you."

We left for the crystal blue waters of the Bahamas, and I knew that we would soon encounter dolphins. About half an hour out of Grand Bahama, I got chills up and down my body, and I knew they were near. We started to drum and play flute and otherwise call out to them and then suddenly, DOLPHINS!

I dove in just as a female dolphin passed by. For about ten seconds, we swam next to each other in unison. I felt my heart about to explode, and I had to remind myself to keep breathing.

All of a sudden there were sixteen dolphins dancing and twirling all around us. I couldn't believe what I was seeing. When I got back to the boat, I sat down on the bench and cried tears of pure joy and happiness. I felt a big release in my heart and soul, like I had come home. Words cannot communicate exactly how I felt in that moment, but I will never forget it.

That was the beginning of my new life and I have never looked back. After going on several more dolphin trips, I started my own company, The Divine Dolphin, to take people to swim with the dolphins.

At the time, I was working as a paralegal in Santa Cruz, California. It was March of 1998, and I had six weeks of trips in a row planned starting in May. I decided to take the leap and told my boss that I was giving two months notice that I would not be coming back to work after my trips in May.

That very night, I received a call from one of the captains I had been planning trips with in the Bahamas. He said, "Sierra, why don't you move here to Florida and be my assistant?" Say what?? Of course! I had taken the leap, and the Universe provided something even better than I could have imagined in return.

I went into work the very next day and said, "I am retracting my two months notice and am now giving two weeks notice or less. As soon as you find someone, I am out of here!"

I sold most of my things and packed up the rest in a U-haul and drove across the country from California to Florida with my four cats, my wolf dog and my greenwing macaw to start my new life living in Florida and helping to run dolphin trips just 60 miles across the ocean in Bimini, Bahamas.

I was living my dream and swimming with the dolphins often. One night, I received the following message:

> *"Circle Circle Circle*
> *Circle of Life*
> *Circle of Love*
> *Circle of One*
> *We embrace you, human fish*
> *Our spirits are wild and free*
> *And so joyous, like you*
> *We circle you now....*
> *And forever"*

In August of 1998, in between dolphin trips in the Bahamas, a good friend and I went for a week's vacation to Costa Rica. I have always been called by Costa Rica. When I was 18, I announced to my parents that I was going to move there. I was told that if I did, I would not be receiving any financial help from them, so that ended that, for the time being, at least.

While traveling around Costa Rica, we picked up the Tico Times, an English language weekly newspaper. I began to read it and was amazed when I came across an article about swimming with dolphins in Costa Rica. My heart began to pound. The article talked about how no one was actively running dolphin encounters in Costa Rica and how someone should do it. Could this possibly be a message for me, I thought? What a "coincidence" that this article had come out the very week I was visiting Costa Rica.

I had not come to Costa Rica thinking about dolphins. It was a vacation with my friend to see the rainforest. My mind started to roll. The rest of our trip my friend and I entertained the possibilities of conducting dolphin swims in Costa Rica. It was perfect, the seasons were opposite of the Bahamas, I could be swimming with dolphins year round! I could do dolphin swims in the Bahamas May through October, dolphin swims in Costa Rica November through May, live in Florida and fly around to wherever I had a trip. By the time we flew back to Florida, a plan was in the making.

But before I could leave the airport, something else amazing happened. We were riding in the tram that takes you to the customs area of the airport. I had on a shirt that said, "Salvemos Los Delfines" or "Save the Dolphins" in English. A lady standing directly across from me in the tram asked me, "Where did you get that shirt?" "By Arenal Volcano," I told her. "Do you like dolphins?" she asked me. "Oh yes, they are my life. I take people to swim with dolphins in the Bahamas." "Oh, well, my name is Maria del Mar, and I am President of the Dolphin Foundation of Costa Rica," she said.

Again my heart began to pound. Again I felt like I was having a déjà vu. My girlfriend looked at me, nodding her head, already used to the miracles that happen to me. I told Maria I was thinking of setting up dolphin encounters in Costa Rica. We exchanged cards. I could not believe it. How was it that while I was thinking of doing something with dolphins in Costa Rica, the President of the Dolphin Foundation of Costa would be standing directly across from me in an airport tram? I then knew that something big was happening.

I got back to Florida and started to do some research about areas to conduct dolphin swims in Costa Rica. My idea was to plan a couple of trips there, see how it went, but stay in Florida and continue what I was doing in the Bahamas. But some crazy things started happening. Everything all of a sudden seemed to be about Costa Rica. I would turn on the TV and on the news there would be something about Costa Rica. I was listening to the radio, and in the middle of a song, were the words Costa Rica. I know I heard it because my friend who was with me heard it too. But the next time we heard this song, the words Costa Rica were not in it. The dolphins were playing tricks on me again. Then my landlord told me that he had lived in Costa Rica. My next door neighbor then told me he had done business in Costa Rica for years and took me to breakfast to tell me about it. Every day, it seemed, someone mentioned Costa Rica to me.

My head was spinning. I had only moved to Florida five months earlier. I loved Coconut Grove, I loved my condo, I loved being able to fly to Bimini to swim with dolphins in 20 minutes. I thought that I was going to stay in Florida for a long time. Could it be that my path was to now move to Costa Rica? All the signs seemed to be pointing in that direction. I have learned to follow those signs because they lead me down my divine path and to wonderful things. But where was I to go? I had no idea where there were dolphins, if there were dolphins that would swim with us, if there was a location suitable from which to conduct these encounters… but I had that good feeling that I would be shown the way, as always. I made the decision that yes, I was going to do it! I was going to move to Costa Rica!

After the decision was made, no one could stop me. And as soon as I made this decision, I received a telephone call from Maria del Mar, the President of the Dolphin Foundation, asking me to come and work for them. I told her I would love to be a part of it. Wow, a job too!

I made plans to go to Costa Rica the next month to look for my spot and didn't find it and ended up going twice more in the following months.

We planned to go to Costa Rica's South Pacific, the only place I had not yet been and visited several areas, still none were feeling right. We headed out for our last stop, Drake Bay. I was feeling a bit desperate. I had to be out of my condo in one month. Nothing had felt like it was the right place. During our travels, Hurricane Mitch had arrived in Costa Rica, so when we arrived in Drake Bay, I had no idea what it was like because we were so wet and cold all I could think about was getting dry. We never did get out on the ocean that trip, but one of the local guides told me that there were lots of dolphins in the area. I don't know why but this light went on in my head. I just knew this was it!

I asked about rentals in the area and was taken to a property that was 10 acres on a point, in the rainforest with an ocean view on three sides. WOW!

When I got back to the States, I called the owner of the property to see if he wanted to rent the property. I almost fell out of my car (I was driving my friend to the airport at the time) when he said he would rent it for $500 a month. I was expecting at least $1,000! We made up a rental agreement, and it was finalized.

I was really moving to Costa Rica to be with the dolphins! Now came all the arrangements on how to get me, my stuff, and my animals into the country, but that all went very smoothly. I made arrangements to live in Escazu for the first month (a suburb of the capital, San Jose) so that I could get bank accounts, make some connections and wait for my rental agreement to start in December.

I was about two weeks away from moving to Drake Bay when I got a call from the owner of the property. Someone had made an offer on the property, and he was going to sell it. What was I going to do? Here I was thinking I was moving in two weeks, in a temporary house with five animals. If I wanted to live on this property, I was going to have to buy it, but with what money? I was in a temporary panic, the kind that I forget all I know on how to manifest things. But it didn't last long, and I got to writing in my journal:

> "I own the property. There are no problems with the purchase of this property. I have all the finances I need to purchase this property. I am a rich child of God and am completely provided for. If this property is mine by divine right, I have it. I cannot do this by myself but God can and is creating miracles here and now. Thank you! Thank you! Thank You!"

The next day, I went to the attorney's office who was handling the sale. I brought a letter of my intention to buy with a payment schedule. And I also brought all my pictures of dolphins. I explained to him what I

22

wanted to do with the property. He said he would talk to the owner, and I had a very anxious day waiting to hear.

Finally I got the call from the attorney. "We are going to sell the property to you, Sierra." "Why?" I asked. "Because of the dolphins. We like what you want to do with the property." Wow! The dolphins did it again.

When we arrived in the late afternoon of December 29, 1998, we came across the bay to an amazing purple sunset, and I knew I had found my true home. Ten acres of ocean-front property, on a point, waves crashing on two sides, and monkeys, toucans, iguanas and all the animals of the Discovery Channel in the trees and surrounding jungle. I still had never gotten out onto the ocean, but I was running on trust, and it had worked so well for me up to this point.

Our initial plan was to run dolphin encounters and have our guests stay at other hotels in the area, which we did for a short time. But I found that I really missed "hanging out" with our guests, and I didn't feel we had enough time with them by just going out on the tours. So, we decided to become a small eco lodge. We erected three tents on platforms and started to bring people to Drake Bay to see the rainforest and dolphins. We became Delfin Amor (Dolphin Love) Eco Lodge.

We saw dolphins every time we went out and eventually discovered a large pod of dolphins, numbering five hundred or more. I was in paradise. I had never seen so many dolphins in one place.

I just couldn't believe what I had magically and effortlessly stepped into. But of course I could believe it, the path had been so magical through all the rapid changes in my life and now, somehow, I found myself surrounded by dolphins. In my front yard, the Pacific Ocean!

As we explored the waters surrounding Drake Bay, we came to discover that there are over 25 species of dolphins and whales that live here or pass through. We have the longest season of humpback whales in the world as we get migrations from both North America and South America. We have had the pleasure to meet orcas, psuedo orcas, pilot whales, humpback whales, sei whales, fin whales, rough tooth dolphins, common dolphins, spinner dolphins, bottlenose dolphins, risso's dolphins, melon head whales, and of course, our most common friends, the pantropical spotted dolphins, whom we call the Homeboys. And I can even see the humpback whales breaching off the point right below my bedroom.

Along with all the dolphins and whales we have discovered, we have also found that there is a lot of commercial fishing in the area. Long lines, shrimpers and the whole dolphin/tuna netting happens here (we are in the Eastern Tropical Pacific, after all). We decided we needed to protect the area and create a marine sanctuary. We talked about becoming a non-profit foundation, but found that it was a very expensive and lengthy process in Costa Rica. But very quickly, magic happened again.

In April of 2000, we rescued a striped dolphin who was trying to beach herself. I wrote an article about it for a local paper. Several days later, Maria del Mar, the lady who I had met in the tram after my first trip (the President of the Dolphin Foundation of Costa Rica), called me to say that the foundation was falling apart because she couldn't get anyone to help her. She wanted to GIVE ME the foundation because we were doing such great work. Just like that, we were able to become a non-profit foundation, without the cost and a minimum of paperwork.

I knew then that I was sent here by Spirit and the dolphins and whales to share their divine nature with others and help to protect them. Everything had fallen into place so magically and easily because they want me to help spread their messages of joy and divine ways of being.

I later founded The Vida Marina Foundation and our data collection and participation and publication in scientific conferences has furthered the reality of creating a protected marine area off the Osa Peninsula. I chose to focus on the dolphin and whale tours and conservation and protection.

My work in marine conservation and protection does not stop at Drake Bay, and during the big Gulf of Mexico oil spill I asked for guidance from the dolphins and whales. This is what I wrote and received:

For weeks now, I have watched the disaster in the Gulf of Mexico get worse and worse. I kept trying to stay in joy, in my "all is well" belief, seeing things through the eyes of source. But as I saw my beloved ocean, dolphins, whales, sea turtles, the coast get covered in an ever increasing oil slick, I felt my thoughts turn into a black, oily, suffocating mess. Finally, yesterday, I let it all out. I allowed myself to get REALLY angry. I cried on and off all morning. I felt powerless, I felt the pain and anguish and frustration. I let it flow. I posted to a few friends of mine on Facebook, and through them and a few of my Sacred Soul Sistas, I began to find better feeling thoughts.

Even through my darkest anger, I was able to see and feel the higher part of me, the part that knows all is well, but I couldn't quite close the gap between us. By the end of the day, I felt much better and was quickly closing the gap.

I felt a message coming through from the dolphins and whales, so I sat down to listen. I started off by asking them: "I believe I am the creator of my reality... so tell me, how did I create this?"

"Sierra, you asked for this when you asked for alternative energy and to clean up the political arena. Did you think that would happen without an event like this? The asking was so big, so strong, from so many, that only a big event like this could answer the asking.

We love you so much, and we will be fine, our species will continue. You cry for our bodies, but you know you can connect with us telepathically anytime. They are just that, bodies, our vessels in the physical. And while we know you and others like to see us in the physical, our non-physical connection is even stronger. And our species will survive. We will come back in even greater numbers in the new world.

It will come back, new and better than before, like a forest after a forest fire. When the smoke clears, new life will appear. Yes, things will never be the same. They will be different. It will be a constant reminder of what you never want to go back to.

The power for change lies with the American consumer, the buyers. Do not forget that the powers that be are dependent on YOU and your buying dollar. You, and your friends, really are the ones with the power. It is an illusion that it is any other way. They just want you to believe that. You must demand alternatives, and you can do that with the power and energy of money. This is really a case of putting your money where your mouth is. The people will come together like never before.

Yes, many of us will die, there will be much more than now, this IS going to get worse, but you know that there is no death. We are eternal. We know this is for a higher good. We understand. And many of us are already on the move to other places; the word is out through the Cetacean Communication Network (CCN) our very own CNN. (I hear laughter). We lived here long before the humans, and they cannot destroy us. We have safe havens to go to where you will never find us.

We applaud you, Sierra, for allowing yourself to get angry. As our friend Joebaby Noonan said, anger is good to clean out the pipes. Do you see what a clear channel you are now that you have acknowledged your feelings of anger, let them run through, and move past them? This event will cause a lot of anger. And it is very good as it is through the anger that change will come. It is through the anger that new desires are born.

Do not doubt the power of creation. Do not doubt the power of many focusing together for a common goal. Do you see how through your tears and getting really mad you sent out all those rockets of desires for something new? Do you see how through the passion of so many; the anger, the frustration, that a powerful desire for a new world is being asked for in a very powerful way? This is the power of creation at work. Through the catastrophe comes the powerful new desires; the creation of something new. It was time, it is time. This is what you have been waiting for. A new world. The time is now.

You must not focus on dead and dying bodies. This is focusing on the problem and focusing on that will bring more of it. We know this is very hard for we know that you and your friends love us. And we love you. But you MUST focus on what this catastrophe caused you all to desire. You MUST focus on the solutions. You must focus on alternative energy, on transparent politics, a new world order of the best kind. You all have been asking for this for so long, can't you see? This is what you have been waiting for!

A new world awaits. What do you want to see in your new world? Therein lies the focus.

We love you, we love you all. All is well."

Also through another tragedy, the killing of dolphins and whales in Taiji, Japan, I received another divine message from the dolphins and whales that has helped me to process and deal with the pain and anger.

As September 1st rolled along and the brutal killing season of dolphins and whales began once again in Taiji, Japan, I found myself seeking higher answers in how to deal with the sadness, pain, frustration and not so nice feelings towards those involved. I asked "What would Spirit say? What is for the highest good of all? How do those of us deeply affected by this tragedy best deal with it all?" As soon as I asked, I felt and heard the dolphins come in and this is what they told me.

"Our Dear Ocean Sister. Thank you for coming to us with your questions and concerns. We have seen your pain and anger and embrace

you and Love you. And therein lies the answer. There has to be love for ALL concerned. Even as the killing goes on, we feel only Love and Compassion in our hearts for them. They are not bad or evil people. Evil does not exist. There is only Love or a self-imposed separation from Love. They are only doing what they know, perhaps uneducated about our species, following traditions.

We ask you, all of you, our dear friends, to do the same as it is only with Love and Compassion that they might see the spark of Love and Compassion in our eyes that will make a difference and change them forever. It is only with Love and Compassion that they can even hear you, your concerns and feelings. It is the ONLY way that things can truly change. Love still is the answer!

Does that mean not to write letters and take action? No, not at all. We need you to speak up for us!! You KNOW, dear Sierra, that we have called you into action on our behalf. But it must be done with Love and not in hateful and threatening and making wrong ways. It must be done with Light and Love. It must be done with love, compassion and concern for ALL involved, in educational and mutually satisfactory ways where everyone wins. It IS possible. ANYTHING IS POSSIBLE. You KNOW that!

Help us to tell the people. Help us to put the "E" (Evolved) back into human to create the human"e" society that you ARE.

Make Love not war no matter what anyone else is doing. Focus on ALL involved finding Love and Compassion in their hearts. See and feel them seeing the Light and becoming conscious and Evolved Human(e)s. Envision them waking up, all those that contribute to the destruction of the oceans and planet. Sign your petitions, create and participate in your campaigns and write your letters, but only those focused on solutions, education, compassion, Love. This is not about not standing up for what you believe in. This is about standing for what you believe in with Compassion and Love. It is the only thing that will make the difference we all seek.

Spreading hate and making war will not be your solution. Your focus must be LOVE while taking action.

As you Love us, BE like us.

War does not create Love. Hate does not create Love. Only Love creates Love.

We LOVE you."

This has truly been a magical, divine path and I thank Divine Spirit and the Angels of the Sea for all they have done to make my wildest dreams come true. I am a messenger of nature. I am a messenger and voice for the dolphins and whales in particular. How cool is that? I am truly blessed to share my life with the divine dolphins and whales and all of you, and I hope you will come experience the dolphins and whales with me here in gorgeous and pristine Drake Bay, Costa Rica.

Sierra Goodman is a woman who truly follows and lives her dreams. From her ocean front rainforest property on Costa Rica's Osa Peninsula — known as the most biologically-intense place on Earth, both on land and at sea — Sierra inspires thousands of people daily with her unique insight, clarity, wisdom and humor through her Facebook page, blog and contributions to books, articles, websites, and interviews. Sierra teaches us about living the authentic human experience with ease and joy, natural weight loss (she lost 170 pounds in one year - see www.iam-iam-iam.com), as well as sharing insights from her beloved finned family, the dolphins and whales.

Sierra also has the JOB (Joy of Being) of facilitating life-changing trips by taking humans to swim with and experience the unbounded Joy and Love of the wild dolphins and whales in Bimini Bahamas, Silver Bank Dominican Republic and at her home in Drake Bay, Costa Rica. See her website at www.divinedolphin.com.

Now Sierra's evolving wisdom has perpetuated the creation of the Oceans of Inspiration series of products featuring her Heart-Inspired quotes in her new book, Oceans of Inspiration, and also screensavers, coffee mugs, t-shirts, digital photo frames and an upcoming coffee table book coupled with her gorgeous photos of the dolphins and whales that she encounters. For more on Oceans of Inspiration, visit: www.oceansofinspiration.com

Sierra has learned to hear and follow her inner guidance and intuition and take inspired action on the messages, or Echoes of the Heart, that she receives. She attributes her knowledge of the Universal Laws and a lot of quiet time in nature to her ability to connect deeply with 'All That Is' and express what she hears in words that inspire others. And that it inspires others greatly inspires her. It's always a win-win when we follow our highest good and express our true, authentic selves freely and with love and joy.

Chapter 3: *Wise Whale Woman*

By Mary J. Getten

"Any glimpse into the life of an animal quickens our own and makes it so much the larger and better in every way."
- John Muir

My best friend is a whale – a killer whale, also known as an orca. She lives in the waters of the Pacific Northwest around Washington State, Oregon, and British Columbia, Canada. Her name is Granny, and she turned 102 years old in 2013. I first met her in 1991.

How did a girl, born in Minnesota in the 1950s, end up making friends with a whale? I had always loved animals and spent time as a child playing with squirrels in the back yard. As a teen, I dreamed of spending my life as Jane Goodall's assistant, sitting in the Gombe studying chimpanzees. I was fascinated with the idea of getting to know another species and seeing things from their perspective. I never got to Africa, nor did I get the education required to do research.

Years passed, and while my desire to work with animals was still intact, I was afraid to pursue it. Deep down I didn't feel good enough, and rather than confront my demons, I avoided them by doing office work. If I didn't try to work with animals, I could hold onto the dream of "someday." That was far safer than trying and failing.

I finally took a step toward this goal in 1987 when I was living just north of San Francisco. As part of a temp job, I had to speak to the Director of the Marine Mammal Center in Sausalito, California, a hospital for seals and sea lions. I could hardly speak to this woman with my heart pounding so loudly in my ears. Her life revolved around animals, something I had always hoped for myself.

At the end of our conversation, I timidly asked if they had any volunteer options and she said there was a training class the next week. I signed up immediately and within a few months I was a very active member of the animal care team. I did rescues, releases, was a docent, and worked on the Wednesday night animal care crew. I loved every single minute of it and spent most of my free time at the center. I even helped with the small stranded whales and dolphins that we rescued. My life finally had purpose and meaning.

Then, in 1988, I heard about telepathic animal communication, and I attended a class with Penelope Smith. I thought that if I could talk to the seals and sea lions and find out what was wrong with them, it would be very helpful to the medical staff. But when I went to the director of animal care and said, "This elephant seal has a stomach ache," she raised her eyebrows and walked quickly in the other direction. I tried to pass on information that I'd gotten from animals on several occasions, but none of the staff was interested in hearing what I had to say. I had hoped to help the animals, but I only succeeded in becoming that "wacky Wednesday night crew leader."

So I put my animal communication skills on a shelf. My heart ached when I had information from a suffering animal that I couldn't do anything with. It was better not knowing. I rarely communicated with other animals either. Since telepathic communication was a new field, few people knew about it or understood it, so there was no one I could discuss this with. I felt very alone.

I stayed at the center until December of 1990, when I moved to the San Juan Islands of Washington State. The Bay area had gotten too crowded and I wanted to live where I could get involved with whales. The

San Juans seemed like the perfect solution. They had a resident population of orcas, seals, sea lions, and even a wildlife rehabilitation center.

My first meeting with Granny took place on a foggy morning in May of 1991. I had arrived early at Lime Kiln Lighthouse, a whale research lab on the west side of San Juan Island, and sat down to begin my data entry work. I'd begun working in the research department of The Whale Museum shortly after arriving in the islands. Engrossed in the computer, I suddenly felt that someone was watching me. As I looked out the window behind me, dorsal fins appeared from the mist. I ran outside to the rocks and saw about a dozen whales going by, some very close to shore. They were traveling slowly, just moseying along heading north. I stood alone on the rocks, peering around the lighthouse to watch them as long as possible.

Without warning, a female orca came straight up out of the water directly in front of me, only twenty feet away. The huge black-and-white body rose silently from the depths, water cascading down her shiny, taut skin. Half of her body was exposed. The stillness was shattered by her explosive exhale. She hung motionless, gazed at me for a few seconds, and then slid quietly back into the water.

My feet were glued to the rocks. What was that? Why did that whale look at me? Then I found myself shouting, "Oh my God. Did you see that? She looked at me!" No one appeared to answer my call or share this incredible moment with me. I was alone, just the whale and me.

I ran to the other side of the lighthouse in time to see my whale surface and noted a little scoop out of her dorsal fin and her solid saddle patch. She surfaced again and then disappeared. I stood there for a long time in the swirling fog, trying to make sense of the encounter.

I felt a consciousness in this whale that I had not expected. She had regarded me and made a connection. There was no doubt in my mind.

Looking through the Orca Identification Guide, I found a female that matched the saddle patch pattern and the scoop out of her dorsal fin. The whale that I'd just met was J2, also known as Granny.

Granny is the leader and matriarch of J-pod, one of three resident families of orcas that form the southern resident community. She was given the designation J2 in the 1970s when researchers first started studying this population. They are now one of the most studied whale groups in the world. Orcas are actually the largest member of the dolphin family.

A few months later I was hired as a naturalist on a whale-watch boat. This gave me countless hours to observe whales and other wildlife in the San Juan Islands, as well as educate passengers about these amazing creatures. I chose to focus on Granny and her family and to observe their behavior and daily activity. Our encounter had touched me deeply and I wanted to understand her.

The more I got to know orcas, the more they captivated me. Their magnificent size and graceful movements are absolutely awesome, and the explosive sound of a whale's blow was enough to cause ripples on my skin. I wanted to spend every moment around them.

Most of the people on my whale-watching trips were awestruck like me. Almost everyone who sees these animals soon acquires a strong desire to be physically close to them and to see them out of the water. Orcas are mysterious and that makes them even more attractive. They spend roughly five percent of their time at the surface, and even then we see only about a third of their bodies. They are hidden from our view most of the time.

What are they doing down there? What do they really look like? How big is that body? Where do the fins attach? What is their tail like? The mere presence of orcas elicits excitement and wonder. There is so much we cannot see and don't know about them that our analytical minds run wild.

Each summer, I spent about 100 days on the water with the whales. Whenever Granny appeared, I ran to the deck or leaned out the wheelhouse window and yelled, "Hey, Granny!" I called to honor her and let her know I was there. I knew that she heard me and understood my greeting from the sense of joy and peace that flowed through me after this ritual.

After three summers of regular interaction with Granny and more than 80 orcas, I knew that it was time to renew my telepathic communication skills. Here was my opportunity to do research, without a degree, grants, equipment or anything else that the traditional researchers were using. I would be able to ask the whales whatever questions I wanted and get the answers directly from them. What could be better than that?

For two years, I studied animal communication, perfecting my technique. I practiced fervently, consulting with harbor seals, eagles, and other patients at Wolf Hollow Wildlife Rehabilitation Center, where I also worked. I talked to cows on the side of the road, to neighborhood dogs, and to birds in the forest.

Then I talked to Granny.

It took me those two years of study and practice to gather up my courage to contact her. It's not surprising that it took that long. What do you say to such a magnificent creature? This would be my first conversation with a whale and there was no precedent to follow. Although I possessed a burning desire to learn about Granny and her family, my insecurities held me back.

Whales are different from other animals and many people attribute mystical qualities to them. Some consider cetaceans (whales and dolphins) more advanced than humans. I was intimidated by the thought of contacting such a being. I felt small and insignificant and didn't want to intrude or make a bad impression.

Finally, one sunny day in the summer of 1995, I mustered up my courage and went to Whale Watch Park. I found a quiet spot away from everyone. Orcas had been passing the lighthouse frequently, and there was a good chance they would go by.

I reviewed the list of questions I'd made for Granny, and mulled them over as I ate my sandwich. Before long I could see fins in the distance, heading my way. I grabbed my binoculars to identify someone. Was it J pod? I wanted to see Granny before I made contact. There was a large male near the front and within seconds he was identified as Ruffles, Granny's son.

I closed my eyes and centered myself, trying to get calm and peaceful. My heart pounded so loudly that I could hear nothing else. I checked again with the binoculars and this time I spotted her close to the lighthouse with three females and a calf. They were taking their time. I felt like Dorothy as she stood in front of the great OZ, small and in awe of this being. I took a deep breath, closed my eyes and went inside. When I reached that place of calm where communication happens, I called out mentally, "Granny, are you there?"

Without hesitation I heard,

"Yes, dear, I'm here."

My stomach turned to butterflies, but I went on. "Granny, my name is Mary, and I work on one of the whale-watch boats, the Western Prince. I'm the blonde woman who yells at you when you come near. Do you know who I am?"

"Yes, certainly, my dear. I have been waiting for your contact. It is good to speak to you."

The sweetness and immediacy of Granny's response calmed my fears and a wave of warmth filled my heart.

I only spoke to Granny for about 15 minutes, but our connection was astonishing. She was friendly, engaging, and oh so sweet. I was overwhelmed with gratitude and my heart soared that this wise whale woman was willing to talk to me. I wanted to know her and understand her and find out everything about orca life. I continued to communicate with Granny, but I still felt insecure and didn't trust my telepathic skills.

Earlier in the year, I'd met an animal communicator, Raphaela Pope, at a Penelope Smith workshop. A few months after my initial contact with Granny, Raphaela came to visit and was treated to a wonderful show by the whales. While we were on the water, I gave Raphaela a few questions to ask Granny, and she was blown away by her powerful presence. I proposed that we work together to interview Granny. She jumped at the chance.

We spent more than a year interviewing whales: Granny, her son Ruffles, daughter Sissy, and various captive whales, including Keiko, who starred in the Free Willy movies. Our only limitation was in knowing which questions to ask. We took turns being the communicator and the interviewer, depending on how much I knew about the subject we were discussing. I didn't want my preconceived ideas to interfere or influence the information we received.

Raphaela and I questioned the whales about all aspects of daily life including food, travel, sex, sleep, and relationships within the pod and with other whales. We talked about whales in captivity, their concept of God and spirituality, death, and how they felt about humans. Eventually, I published our findings in the book, *Communicating with Orcas: The Whales' Perspective.* (Available at www.MaryGetten.com)

This process of diving deeply into whale consciousness had a greater effect and consequences for me personally, than I ever could have imagined. First, it honed my animal communication skills in several ways. I learned to hold a focus for extended periods, sometimes hours at a time. It taught me to be an investigator, to really search and dig for the right questions or answers. It provided me with a curiosity that would serve me well for all future communication with any type of animal, and it gave me confidence in my abilities.

There is also something about the energy field of cetaceans that assists telepathy. When you are in their presence, it seems easier to communicate on that level and you can go deeper. I have had many people over the years tell me that while they were reading Communicating with Orcas, they found that they were able to slip right into telepathic conversation with Granny and other animals. Spending time in this field changed my vibration and expanded my telepathic abilities.

I started my telepathic animal communication practice in 1996. Since that time I have worked with thousands of people all over the world, helping them to solve problems and create more harmony with their animal companions. This work is very rewarding and brings so much peace and understanding to the human caretaker. When I am able to help someone realize what his or her animal needs or wants, especially when it concerns end of life issues, I know that I make a difference.

Even before I met Granny, I sensed that the biggest problem we have on our planet today is our disconnection from nature. Many humans just don't see themselves as part of the whole, and they often don't comprehend how their actions affect every plant and animal species that we share this world with. Granny saw this problem clearly, and when I asked if she had a message for humanity, this is part of what she shared:

> "Know and understand that you are totally connected to, and mutually dependent on, this planet. Love it. Protect it. Your existence depends on it. You are children of the beloved earth, sky, wind, and water. When you detach, you die."

My contribution to healing that disconnection has been to teach people how to communicate with animals and nature. Telepathic communication is the universal language used by plants, animals, minerals, spirits, and beings in the unseen realms. It is an ability that we are all born with, but most humans have been socialized out of it. We have the pathways in our brain to communicate this way, they just need to be strengthened. Like any muscle that we cease to use, over time it atrophies. The best way to regain your abilities is to get a little guidance and then practice, practice, practice.

Telepathy is direct mind-to-mind, or heart-to-heart, communication that extends beyond our five senses. It is feeling across a distance, and time and space don't matter. It's just as easy for me to communicate with a dog in Australia as one sitting right in front of me. In fact, for me it's easier! I prefer to not see the animal I'm talking to, so that my analytical left-brain doesn't butt into the conversation.

There are four common ways that people receive telepathic communication: mental pictures, hearing sounds or words, physical or emotional feelings, and an intuitive sense of knowing. There is no right or wrong way to get information, and most people have one or two channels that are more open. I encourage students to start with what they have and build those skills. Over time, their other channels will blossom.

Some people have more natural ability than others, but to increase your telepathic communication skills, intention and commitment are the most important. Anyone can reclaim this ability by first attending a workshop. It's not unlike learning a foreign language. Once you have some instruction, then it's all about practice, and the more you practice, the better you get.

When you can converse with a being, whether it's a snail or a tree, you perceive it differently. You see the similarities between yourself and the other. You are able to understand their perspective and find common ground. All beings want basically the same things: food, shelter, companionship, respect, and love.

The best thing to come out of my relationship with Granny is that I started connecting with other types of whales and dolphins. Just like visiting with people in different countries and continents, communicating and spending time with various cetaceans, and all animals, expands your view of the world.

One remarkable creature that captured my interest was the gray whale. They undertake one of the longest migrations of all animal species: approximately 10,000 miles round-trip. They summer in the Bering and Chukchi seas of Alaska, fattening up on small "shrimp-like" amphipods and worms that they filter out of the mud. Grays are the only cetacean that feeds by plowing the sand and mud with their snouts, stirring up their prey and then straining them through their baleen.

In the fall, the grays head south, traveling alone or in small groups. They traverse 5,000 miles of the Pacific Ocean, swimming parallel to the shore for two to three months to congregate in three different lagoons on the Baja peninsula. The pregnant females arrive first and give birth soon thereafter. Breeding adults and immature whales arrive a little later, but they spend several months together, mating, raising their calves, and enjoying the warm water.

These lagoons were the sites of horrific whale slaughters in the mid-1800s when Charles Scammon and other whalers arrived. They were so successful at harvesting whales in these locations that the gray whale was almost extinct by the turn of the century. In 1946, the International Whaling Commission gave them protection, but by then, the Atlantic Gray was completely gone.

San Ignacio Lagoon was peaceful for many years, and then in 1976 a fisherman had an encounter with a friendly whale that came up to his boat. He was able to touch it, and he sensed that the whale was curious and wanted to interact with him. Since that time, more and more whales are seeking out human contact in the lagoons and more and more people are connecting with the whales.

In 2004, I led my first trip to visit the gray whales of San Ignacio. Twice a day we went out in small pangas, open boats that are about 15 feet long and seat eight to ten people. We motored around looking for whales, but often they found us first. Friendly whales will swim directly toward a boat, sometimes with enough speed to resemble a torpedo. These whales are 35-40 feet long. Human hands reach into the water, and the whales come up underneath them, eagerly asking us to rub them and even kiss them. When you put your lips on a salty, rubbery whale your heart fills with rays of golden sunlight. It takes your breath away, and changes you forever.

It's not only the adult whales that interact. Very often a mother will bring her calf up to the boat, even pushing the baby over to the side where we can caress and touch her. They are teaching the young that humans can be trusted and that our interaction will be loving and kind.

The whales tune in to our excitement and joy when we connect with them. It is that joy that draws them to us. Don't you want to be around loving and high-energy positive people? The whales and dolphins do too.

Fortunately, just being in their presence raises our vibration, and we are unable to contain the sense of wonder, delight, and bliss that emerges from our souls. Our self-consciousness disappears, and we are free to whoop and holler and scream and cry. We become whole.

Five times, I brought a group to San Ignacio to meet the gray whales. Each trip people arrived stressed and sad, confused, lonely, and dissatisfied with life. Always, they left in high spirits, sporting uncontrollable grins, and with love coursing through their veins. Gray whales exude love, and we soaked up that essence from the water, the air, and the clouds of heart shaped mist that these giants exhale.

San Ignacio Lagoon is magical. People were always overcome by the energy of the 200-250 whales that gathered there. I always felt as if my soul was being washed clean by a powerful waterfall. I sensed that any sadness or negative emotions were draining into the water, and I was left clean, with nothing but peace in my soul, joy in my heart, and a huge smile on my face that stayed for more than a week after leaving the lagoon. It was always that powerful.

Although I treasured my time with the gray whales, I wanted to investigate other cetaceans as well, so in 2009 I began leading an annual trip to swim with wild dolphins in Bimini, an island in the Bahamas. Now, I am able to get into the water and feel the energy of the dolphins throughout my body. Unlike the gray whales, dolphins don't want to be touched, so we are respectful of their wishes. But dolphins love to play!

In the presence of gray whales, I feel the deep pulse of their enormous hearts and the boundless love that they emit. I feel that, too, with the dolphins, but their predominate energy is of joy, play, and bliss. When dolphins arrive, it's like popping the cork on a fine bottle of champagne, all bubbles and iridescence and fun. Dolphins strip away adulthood and bring back the child in us.

In Bimini, we spend time with wild bottlenose and Atlantic spotted dolphins. We go out in a sailing catamaran, and when dolphins approach, we give them a ride on the bow of the boat, then wait and see if they hang around. When they do, two people get in the water, and if the dolphins come over and interact with us, then everyone gets in.

Now these are wild dolphins, choosing to interact with people. We don't feed them, so there really isn't anything in it for them, except that they like to be with us. They love it when you can dive deep or swim really fast, but I can't do that, so I just snorkel on the surface. The dolphins always greet each and every one of us. They swim over and look us in the eye, and an incredible energy exchange takes place. Time stops, and your heart opens so wide it aches.

Being in their presence changes you deeply. They freely give unconditional love to you no matter who you are, what you look like, your handicaps, your deficiencies, fears, and wounds. Dolphins operate on such a high level of consciousness or vibration that their love heals us to our core. I am so grateful for the kindness, compassion, joy, play, and wisdom that these dolphins extend to humanity.

Participants on these trips shed their fears, stress, and negative emotions when they connect with dolphins. Possibilities open in their lives and many make profound changes, emotionally, spiritually, and sometimes even physically. Old careers and locations are replaced with new ones that are more in sync with who that person is now. Courage replaces fear, and the memory of our interaction with these mystical beings carries us forward.

People often ask me about how the whales and dolphins view us. They assume that cetaceans are swimming around grumbling about how bad we are, how we have polluted their home with chemicals, plastics, and sound. People think that they are mad at us because we are taking all the fish and upsetting the balance of the ocean. This is absolutely not true. They do not spend their time thinking about, worrying about, blaming or judging us. The whales and dolphins have told me that they don't waste their time or energy on things that they can't change. Instead, they feel a little sadness and pity for us somewhat misguided creatures, and they do what they can to raise our vibration and open our hearts.

The fastest and easiest way to raise your consciousness is to spend time with whales and dolphins. If you can do this in person, do it, but not everyone can make that happen. The good news is that you don't have to be with them physically to reap the benefits of their love and enlightened state of consciousness. You can connect with cetaceans telepathically and work with them on the etheric level. Many people who attended whale or dolphin trips with me now work with those beings from home and are continuing to learn and grow and expand their awareness, aided by the cetaceans.

A good way to move into resonance with whales and dolphins is to surround and educate yourself with books, videos, and photos of them.

Spend time daily reading or watching a video or gazing at a photo. Learn about the various aspects of their lives, focus on "feeling" their energy, and notice how you feel in their presence. If you are drawn to a particular type of whale or dolphin, concentrate on them.

Once you have gained an appreciation for who they are, you might find a guided meditation to meet a dolphin or whale guide. You could even write your own meditation, record it and then establish a relationship with your guide. This is not an imaginary being, but an energy that is willing to work with you in whatever capacity you desire. The only limitations are the ones you impose.

You can also engage in dolphin or whale energy by connecting with them telepathically. The process is simple. First, decide whom you want to communicate with and what you would like to discuss. Then sit quietly and allow yourself to move into a meditative state. Call out to the cetacean mentally, asking them to come and connect with you. Wait until you feel, hear, see, or sense their energy. It might be faint, but allow it to be whatever it is. There is no right or wrong way to do this, doing it is what's important!

Once you feel a connection has been made, have a mental conversation like you would with anyone. Express your love, ask for help, tell them about what you want to bring into your life or your reason for contacting them, and then allow the information to flow in. All you need to do is allow it to come. Bask in the energy, soak it up for as long as you feel it flowing, and allow it to reach to your depths. This is how transformation happens. Close the session by expressing your gratitude, set a time to meet again, and inquire if there is anything you can do for them, or if there is anything further you need to do for yourself.

The whales and dolphins love humanity and want to assist us. They say that they are committed to working with human consciousness and to help us evolve to a higher level. You just have to ask.

My friendship with Granny continues today, even though I now live on the other side of the country, in Florida. Our relationship has changed my life in so many ways. It inspired me to create a career that I love – helping people to understand their pets better and to solve problems, training students in animal communication, and leading trips to meet with whales and dolphins. I am so grateful for this rich and varied life.

The inner changes I've experienced are profound. Embracing the dolphin and whale way of life, by living in the moment, being nonjudgmental and forgiving, spending time playing and experiencing joy, has contributed to shifting and raising my vibration. It can happen for you too.

I now work with animals every single day. What do you want your life to be? Ask the whales and the dolphins to help you. They create miracles.

Mary J Getten - Animal Communicator - Naturalist - Author

From wild orcas to naughty house cats, Mary J. Getten loves animals and has been connected to them all her life.

Whether she is working with injured and sick seals and sea lions, interviewing orcas, swimming with wild dolphins and humpback whales, or kissing gray whales in Mexico, interaction with wild marine mammals has been a focal point of Mary's life for over 25 years. The enormous depth of Mary's connection is chronicled and explored in her Nautilus Award winning book Communicating with Orcas; The Whales' Perspective. It offers a multi-dimensional view of killer whale life and consciousness while simultaneously opening your heart and your mind.

Since 1996, Mary's work as an animal communicator has helped thousands of delighted clients worldwide to better understand and create more harmony with their naughty, sad, sick and puzzling pets. In fact, she's communicated with everything from snails to whales! By facilitating a dialog between people and their animal companions regarding behavior issues, health, death and dying, upcoming changes, and physical or emotional problems, Mary brings clarity, understanding and peace of mind. Her skill at problem solving enriches lives and assists people in developing deeper relationships with their pets. Mary also facilitates conversations with animals in spirit, allowing their people to find closure and contentment.

Human disconnection from nature is a major problem on the planet today. Mary's greatest joy is helping to heal that disconnection by teaching people how to communicate with animals and nature. Empowering people to connect telepathically with all life restores their natural birthright and allows them to remember who they really are. Students leave every class excited, connected, alive and transformed.

Mary J. Getten helps people "see the world in a new way" and she does this through every aspect of her work. Connecting with Mary by consulting with your pet, attending a workshop, listening to an inspired talk, participating in a swim with dolphins or whale trip, or by reading her book, is an enriching and life affirming experience not to be missed.

For more information, www.MaryGetten.com

Chapter 4: *Deep Transformation with Dolphins and Whales*

By Trish Regan and Doug Hackett

> *"The dolphins have shown me that we need to move beyond*
> *our belief in physical, three-dimensional reality,*
> *Materialistic reality is an illusion.*
> *Instead we live in a universal field of energy*
> *that is the source of ALL possibilities.*
> *It vibrates, it is alive.*
> *It is unmanifest potential and it is a frequency we call Love."*
> *- Joan Ocean, Co-Founder Dolphin Connection International*

Trish - How we entered into our work with the dolphins

When Doug and I married in 1992, we made the commitment to follow our hearts, to follow Spirit. We knew we would be doing spiritual work together, but had no idea what it would be.

Only one year after our marriage took place, we received an invitation we could not refuse. In May of 1993, our good friend, Joan Ocean, came to visit us in our home in California. Joan's life was a perfect demonstration of the power of living by following your heart. I met her in 1983 and became the first participant in her meditation group in Belmont, California. She soon began to receive messages of love, peace and harmony from the dolphins. They seemed to ask her to be their ambassador to the world bringing their wisdom and beautiful energy of love to all. She and her partner, visionary artist Jean-Luc Bozzoli, left the lives they knew, packed a few suitcases and began a journey around the world bringing the dolphin message to all. Not knowing where the next flight would lead, or where they would get the money to pay for it, they lived on pure faith and were totally taken care of. Joan ended up in Kona, Hawaii, living on the ocean and swimming with the dolphins every day, learning their immense wisdom and sharing it with the world through books and dolphin seminars.

We were in awe as we viewed Joan's extraordinary video and listened to mind-expanding information about the dolphins and their multidimensional consciousness. Their energy drew us into their magical spell and we looked at each other and said, "We have to go and swim with the dolphins!" Two months later we found ourselves in the ocean with these magnificent beings. The experience blew open our hearts and brought us into a state of being I can only describe as ecstatic - the adventure of our lives!

We spent four glorious days swimming with the dolphins with Joan. That first day, we spent hours in giddy play. The dolphins graced us with their playful presence and opened our hearts to a deeper level than we had ever felt before. They stayed with us until we were spent with joy, slipping away to the end of the bay to leave us breathless and in awe. I knew that my life had changed profoundly within those few hours. Little did I know, though, that it would change so dramatically so soon. The seed of joy was planted in my heart and I knew that we were being immersed in the deep profound joy of Spirit which we would share with the world some day.

To be met one on one by these creatures, both joyous and otherworldly, was astonishing in its intimacy and in its awesome connection. We felt that they came to us with the desire to communicate and share their magical world with us, in this third dimension and in higher dimensions also. When we were with them, all concerns or feelings of limitation disappeared. We were brought into the present moment in a way that had never been experienced before. It was pure bliss. We could see what Joan was talking about - the dolphins assist us to touch the higher aspects of ourselves and to seek joy through an expansion of consciousness. We knew we would never be the same.

Before leaving for home, Joan said, "Why don't you move to Hawaii and help me with this work?!" She said that there would be more and more people drawn to be with the dolphins in their ocean home and that there needed to be people to help them have that experience. Since I had attended some spiritual training seminars with her in the past, and Doug and I had made the commitment to do our spiritual work, whatever that was, we felt that Joan must have been guided to ask us about this. Even so, we were not prepared to say yes to this fantastic suggestion. We said to her, "We can't do that - we have our lives in California!"

Upon returning to California, to his surprise Doug realized that we didn't have lives! His experience was that what he had been doing no longer had that spark of aliveness or spirit behind it! For several years Doug had been feeling that he was supposed to leave behind his career as CEO of the energy conservation company he had founded, however had not found anything that he would rather do. Upon meditating on it, the only thing that had that spark of aliveness, or spirit, behind it was selling everything and moving to Hawaii to work with the dolphins! However, he refrained from telling me right away, knowing that the perfect moment would come in the next few days.

My experience was a bit different. On the following Wednesday, after returning from Hawaii, I was driving over the San Mateo bridge on my way home from work. While thinking about the dolphins and Joan's invitation, I suddenly had an incredible experience. A "lightning bolt" of white light shot right through my body and I heard the words, "Go do this work." It was as clear as day and I knew this was a powerful message from the universe, the dolphins, and my Higher Self.

When I told Doug about my experience with the lightning bolt, he reacted with assurance that we were on the right track. He said, "Well, we made the commitment to follow Spirit and it looks like we are both being called and are being tested." Happily we both knew that this was the direction we should go and though it meant leaving behind security, we agreed to "jump off the cliff" and follow our guidance.

We sold everything, packed up our books and some kitchenware, and left for Hawaii the following February of 1994. It wasn't easy leaving our children, friends and families on the mainland. Though my daughter and son were adults and on their own, and Doug's two teenage daughters were living with their mother and step father, our hearts tugged at us to stay close by. We made a pact with the universe that we would see them at least four times per year in whatever way we could.

When we moved to Hawaii, we began working very closely with Joan, who became our mentor and inspiration. She told us in the beginning that she could not support us completely financially, but would pay us to assist her in her dolphin seminars and help her with her work. She also encouraged us to create our own dolphin seminars so as to manifest a source of livelihood.

We founded and co-created Dolphin\Spirit of Hawaii and began our adventurous life as facilitators of monthly seminars including dolphin swims and spiritual transformation. While our seminars began slowly at first, we found that facilitating them was the most joyous, stimulating and fulfilling work we could imagine. Subsequently, we facilitated whale-swim retreats in the Kingdom of Tonga as well. Our life had completely changed and began to bring to us magical adventures, interesting and wonderful people from all over the world, and deep satisfaction in the knowledge that we were contributing to the spiritual awakening of the people we served.

Trish - How our experience of being with the dolphins and whales has changed our lives

Working with the dolphins for over nineteen years now has completely changed my life and Doug's too in so many ways.

For me, fear has always been my greatest challenge. Or I might say it another way ... trust in the universe has been my nemesis. Because of my childhood issues, I realized that I had fear about everything, especially financial security. I can say now that with all my years of swimming with the dolphins and whales, I have managed to come into complete trust ... no fear.

In that first year I would awaken at two or three in the morning with gut wrenching fear and pain in my stomach. I would think, how can we pay a mortgage with little income? I would stumble into the living room so as not to awaken Doug, and I would try all of my spiritual practices to allay the pain. Nothing worked. My saving grace was that in the morning, when we would go on our daily swim with the dolphins, the pain and fear would magically disappear in the presence of their loving energy. I kept hearing the message from the dolphins, "Keep on going. You are totally supported." This would save me for another day until gradually, as the fear subsided, the abundance came forth.

I also was one of those people you might call a "control freak" ... people who are perfectionists and if things don't go their way, they resist, hold back and generally are not happy.

Because I grew up in a dysfunctional family and there was at times emotional chaos around me, I felt I had to control situations in order to feel comfortable. Before moving to Hawaii to be with the dolphins, I had experienced many years of therapy and spiritual healing to transmute those feelings; even so, however, I still could see that tendency within. I was much better about it all, but if put into a corner, I could fall back into that pattern.

Swimming with the dolphins every day began to loosen my grip on that perfectionism. Not only was their energy so uplifting, but just by gliding along with them in their beautiful graceful way here and there, I learned what it was like to live in the flow. I would be mesmerized by the ease of their movements and slip happily into the bliss of the moment. That is one of the most beautiful qualities of being with the dolphins in their home ... they teach us how to live in the present like nothing else I have ever experienced. Nothing else matters except that divine eternal moment of oneness with all that is.

I had a direct experience, years ago, in which a dolphin completely facilitated my letting go of a dysfunctional pattern. I was keenly aware that whenever I would hear some sort of news, I would immediately focus on the most dire possible outcome of that news. It was a distinct negative pattern of thinking that was difficult for me to change. It was as if I would constantly look at the glass half empty instead of half full.

I was so ready to let go of that destructive pattern. So one morning, when Doug and I went to swim with the dolphins together, as we slowly swam out toward the dolphins, I telepathically begged them to help me release that pattern.

All of a sudden one large male spinner came right up next to me and looked directly into my eye. Then he proceeded to send his sonar into my body in a fashion I had never experienced before or since. I could feel and hear the vibrating sound coming into me like a jackknife, pounding on and off at breakneck speed and so loudly that Doug could hear it from above the water!

The dolphin continued to stay so close to me I could have touched him. He continued the barrage of sonar for about forty five minutes! It was amazing. When he left my side, I could feel a lightness I had never felt before. I knew that negative pattern was cleared and from that day forward have very rarely had it return.

The whales have also facilitated a great leap in consciousness and letting go of fear for me. During my first whale swim with Joan Ocean in the Dominican Republic in 2000, I was guided by the whales to avoid going in with them for several times during the week and to stay on the boat in complete silence. I was awed by this directive but took it to heart. They taught me how to go within and listen in a way that I had never been able to do before, being an Aries, Type A, achievement-oriented type of being.

That experience and the deep silence of the whales taught me to make time to allow myself to cherish that space of depth so that I could commune with my soul, which eventually lead to my writing my book series, Essential Joy: Finding It, Keeping It, Sharing It.

I believe the most astounding experience I have had over 12 years of swimming with whales occurred during one of our Whales of Tonga Retreats in the beautiful Kingdom of Tonga where I experienced the closest encounter ever with a huge female humpback.

On our first day out in the boat, we had traveled some hours before coming upon five large adult whales. I held the hand of one of our participants who needed just a little bit of support on this first swim with the enormous beings of the sea.

As we gazed down into the blue we could see these friendly whales swimming below about thirty feet or so with one or two gliding up to the surface to swim very close and look into our eyes. At one point, as we were keeping our eyes on one huge female humpback (about fifty feet long!) who was about thirty feet below and maybe fifty feet ahead of us, we saw that she began to head up through the water directly toward us.

This was so exciting as we knew she was heading right for us and thought it was wonderful that she was so clearly in contact with us two as we floated on the surface together. When this female got to about ten

50

feet away from our faces, I thought to myself, "Surely she will turn or dive under so as not to hit us!"

Alas, she just kept coming! I could not believe my eyes when her rostrum (nose) was now looming just about two to three feet from our noses! At that point I admit I panicked a bit thinking, "She is going to really hit us!" Conscious of my responsibility to protect my participant clutching my hand, I instinctively started to push the participant to the side to avoid the collision, when suddenly, quietly and gently, the whale slipped down beneath us ... not a touch or bump! It was as if we were being kissed by the whale! We could have reached out and touched her jaw, which looked as if it was a wall about four feet high!

When the experience was over, my partner in this experience and I let out a breath of awe and felt frozen in disbelief for some moments. She told me that she, in fact, knew the female would not hit us and was in total trust. She said, "I 'might' have done the same as you – but not really sure – I had such trust – I felt like I was just completely present with the whale, I didn't feel separation – I was entirely in the moment. I do think it is natural and instinctive to want to protect."

The whale gave me a telepathic message just then that said, "You must TRUST." This was such a profound lesson for me to trust the universe. She showed me that even when life seems to be coming at me at times like a freight train and things may look scary or frightful, I must go inside and find the place of deep trust. It also showed me how fully aware and conscious the whales are in their perceptions of space as this large female knew exactly where we were in proximity to her.

The whale told me that we can always trust our souls, our guidance, the universe and all the powers that be that all is in PERFECT DIVINE ORDER.

All in all, the dolphins and whales have changed my life so completely that I love to tell people that I truly believe that if we had not followed our spiritual calling to jump off the cliff and move to Hawaii to work with the dolphins, I think it would have taken me two more lifetimes to be where I am spiritually, emotionally and physically. I know they have changed me profoundly and am forever grateful.

Doug - What we do now with our dolphin and whale work

Since my wife, Trish Regan, and I founded Dolphin\Spirit of Hawaii in 1994, we have been conducting spiritually based dolphin retreats in

Hawaii and also whale swim retreats in the Kingdom of Tonga (since 2004).

For the most part, our dolphin retreats in Hawaii are conducted in our beautiful home/sanctuary in South Kona. We like small intimate groups of about eight participants and find the family atmosphere lends itself to deep transformation, not only with the energy of the dolphins in the wild, but also within our own "pod."

These week-long retreats begin with orientation and snorkel practice on the first day in order to teach beginner snorkelers how to snorkel and have people try their gear, but also to have everyone clear the energy to create a clean and pristine energy for the group. Then we learn all about each other and about the dolphins after a delicious meal.

During the week, then, we swim with the dolphins from boats for four mornings. We like the boat experience because we can find the dolphins usually about 98% of the time. We also create much alone time for participants to rest, relax, integrate the high intensity energy of the dolphins, and spend time within themselves. We find that is so important when working with dolphins. Their high frequency opens us to depths of ourselves that perhaps we have not experienced before and it takes quiet to allow this exploration.

We take our groups to sacred sites to experience the power of aloha here in Hawaii and to have time to really be immersed in nature. The beauty of Hawaii is so deep and the spirit of the land and of the Goddess Pele facilitates profound letting go of that which is not of our essence.

We also play and have such fun on the water and in our sharing time. Deep emotional clearings can occur as well as much laughter, which is healing in itself. We always follow Spirit and the dolphins as they guide the content of the retreats. We know what meditations and processes to do according to each individual group.

We find that each group comes to us for a different spiritual reason. It has fascinated us over the years because no two groups have the same theme. Before the retreat starts, Trish and I go into meditation and channel what this particular group is coming for, be it to learn more joy, to clear old baggage, to expand to the next level spiritually ... or whatever is appropriate. It is amazing and fun to tell the group the theme and to watch them nod knowingly.

There have been times that we have offered larger groups for special occasions, such as 12/21/12 or 11/11/11, but for the most part, our retreats are small, intimate weeks. We love the work and are so honored and grateful to have the opportunity.

Since the dolphins and whales are multidimensional beings, who would be better to teach us how to live in harmony, peace and love but these ambassadors of joy? Over the many years facilitating our dolphin and whale retreats, we have had the joy and fulfillment of witnessing people from all over the world coming into the deep awareness of who they really are. We see those who come here filled with stress or confused about their life's direction. At the end of a week with the dolphins or whales, and enfolded in a bubble of love with our group, they look completely different with shining faces, full hearts and deeply in touch with their truth and their future path of life. The dolphins spark within us a cellular awareness of who we are as spiritual beings in human bodies.

There are too many stories of transformation to add here so I will share just a few. Trish and I love to tell the story of a friend who was sent here to be with the dolphins by her spiritual teacher. Her beloved son had committed suicide at a very young age and she was so distraught that ending her own life seemed like a solution to end her pain. Upon the urging of her teacher, she made her way to us.

Since she was a beginner snorkeler, I gallantly took her hand as I do with people who have fear of the ocean, and led her out to the dolphins. Many dolphins came right to her and surrounding her, holding her in a cocoon of gentle love and protection. I knew they knew her pain and were generously giving her their healing energy for what seemed like hours.

When we returned home and had a short nap, she was sitting on the front steps when I decided to sit with her and talk about the experience. She told me that back home, people thought she was alive but that she really was dead inside. Her grief being so deep, she could no longer work and had no interest in living at all. After the swim, she said that now she felt more alive than she had ever felt before. Her face was gleaming with an inner glow of joy and she ended up staying for two weeks. Upon her arrival home, she went back to work and subsequently found the man of her dreams. The dolphins had ignited within her the spark of life and she was able to fully engage in its myriad of experience once again.

One year, we had a wonderful teen counselor in attendance during our dolphin seminar. He had the challenging job of helping troubled teens find their way back to a healthy and productive life. We had wonderful experiences with the dolphins during our week here and he returned home full of joy and with a new lease on life.

Within the next year our counselor friend called to tell us this story. He and several other colleagues were having a challenging time calming a young girl who was hysterical. She became so agitated that she began to kick and scratch and violently tried to escape the restraints of the counselors. He and the others were trying to calm her down and at the point that they had her on the floor in an effort to keep her from hurting herself and others, our friend remembered the dolphins and their loving energy. He suddenly "saw" a blue light begin to ascend upon the girl. It surrounded her and our friend knew it was the dolphin love. Just as suddenly, the girl began to let go. She slipped into a soft mood of surrender and allowed the counselors to gently lift her up and sit her down in the chair. Our friend could not believe his eyes. The dolphin energy of unconditional love simply worked its magic and this troubled teen received help.

Here are some testimonials from people who have experienced a week with dolphins and whales with us:

- "I am in a place of really knowing that all is well being and it is happening right now on this planet in 'the space and the time' that is all that is. I do understand what the whales are saying and am soooooooooooooooo grateful to be in a place of pure love and joy. Words cannot express the awesomeness of all that is. Every day is awesome and full of infinite possibilities indeed and the spirit and oneness of all is amazing. Words do not do justice to it all so I will close now with much love and joy and laughter in my heart." Dene H.

- "The workshop was absolutely transformational for me. It assisted me in integrating various aspects of myself, as though placing the center piece in a puzzle that connects all the rest. Bless you for facilitating this experience." Helen R.

- "The spirit of the dolphins has taught me: exuberance, connecting to pure joy, expressing pure joy, being and expressing the essence of who we truly are, being in the present, letting go and flowing freely, being in harmony with one's environment with one's self and with others, beauty, grace and lightness, to feel the passion of living, being playful, to opening one's heart, connecting to spirit and what is natural, that are all one." Nancy R.

- "This has been a very fulfilling and enlightening experience, touching on many levels. It has been an awakening of the spirit; the breaking down of old and outdated barriers; allowing joy and love to envelop the "Who I am." This has been a fantastic journey." Carolyn C.
- "The love and vibrational intention are extremely profound - emotionally, physically and spiritually. I am truly blessed to be with everyone for this sacred time." Tim B.
- "This was the most beautiful experience I have ever had in my life. I feel I am alive again, more evolved. My spiritual experience was so healing. I know I experienced my soul. I'm in the moment in a bubble of loving peace." Joyce H.
- "I have seen and felt more grace, beauty, joy and love this week than in my whole lifetime. Beyond words. I will never be the same." Elizabeth B.

The beautiful dolphins and whales change lives in dramatic and profound ways. Hope you all can come to be with them in their natural home.

Doug Hackett & Trish Regan - Co-founders Dolphin\Spirit of Hawaii

DOUG & TRISH have been married in spiritual partnership since 1992. They founded Dolphin\Spirit of Hawaii in 1994 when they experienced a dramatic spiritual calling to "jump off the cliff," leave their professional lives behind and come to Hawaii to work with the wild dolphins. Since that time, they have conducted spiritually transformative dolphin-swim seminars/retreats in Kona.

They also facilitate whale swim retreats in the magical waters of Tonga and Mastery Retreats in Mt. Shasta, California. In addition, for seven years they worked very closely with world renowned dolphin researcher and author, Joan Ocean.

Trish, Visionary Writer and Intuitive Soul Reader, is author of the book series: *Essential Joy: Finding It, Keeping It, Sharing It.* She has been spiritually aware for all her life and has been on a dedicated path of Light and spiritual expansion since 1983. Doug's balanced masculine/feminine energies and spiritual insight, enhanced by over three decade's study and practice of meditation, helps create the magical environment for these life changing retreats and seminars.

Trish's blog includes fascinating stories of her experiences with dolphins and whales, amazing photographic phenomena, stories of inspiration and deep wisdom. www.dolphinspiritofhawaii.com www.trishregan.com

Chapter 5: *Whalespeak*

By Grandma Chandra

Introduction by Cat Parenti Hammad

"Grandma" Chandra is my daughter. She was born severely physically disabled, non-verbal but a savant (a knower).When she was 9 years old, she got a communication system that she used with everyone but me. When I asked why she replied that I had to become telepathic with her to "do the work". I laughed and told her to train me. And, she did, in my dream state. Chandra and I along with another 300 people on the Planet are very telepathic and I am honored that she has chosen me as one of her channels/translators. She is a young unique, telepathic multi-dimensional being; a living miracle who provides a safe place to go for answers. As a Being of the Whale Dolphin energy, she translates the messages of Dolphins and Whales. G'ma says, "I have been communicating with Dolphins and Whales since I was in the womb because there is a connection between the Whales from the Planet Sirius B and my home, the White Star Planet. They both vibrate to 100 million megahertz or the Quantum Light Field." "Grandma" is a title given to her by Native Americans for her wisdom. When asked to choose a Native American name she chose, "Screaming Eagle". When Chief Golden Light Eagle asked why she chose that name, she replied, "When the eagle screams, it tells the Truth."

Chandra now shares the rest of her story.

"I AM a 12th dimensional being who has come here to guide and teach those whose internal codes I activate with my readings, oils and MP3s.

"Up until I was six months old, I talked with a series of clicks and sounds like the dolphins and whales, but my mom didn't understand me. I felt deeply connected to whales and dolphins, but realized that the planet hadn't caught up with these intelligent beings yet. The whales are the repositories or libraries of planetary knowledge.

"The grandson of Jacques Cousteau contacted us and asked what he could do for me. I said I wanted a tape of the Whales at 35,000 feet deep so I could translate their messages to humanity. He replied that the ocean is only 25,000 feet deep. I said no and he said you must be talking about a trench and I replied yes, in the South Pacific. I received a CD of the Whales at 35,000 feet deep and translated the message of the Whales to us in my MP3, 'WHALESPEAK'.

"A scalar wave is a term used by geologists, quantum physicists and those using hydrodynamics. It is a non-linear wave of the 5th Dimension that is not bound by 3rd dimensional laws and relative time and space. The scalar wave can pass through solid matter, is shaped like the body's DNA strands and has the ability to imprint itself on the DNA. The human body systems are also non-linear in nature and have an electromagnetic field due to the crystalline structures in all of its cells. Entering a scalar wave causes an increase in our connection to the limitless universal energy of Source/Creator and our ability to manifest whatever we wish. I translated the whales' messages to humanity through my mom. I inserted the Blue, Gold, and Violet rays to activate the 10th, 11th and 12th Planetary DNA strand. I am now working on the 33rd dimension with the 33rd Planetary DNA strand. There are 111 Planetary DNA strands. Whales and Dolphins work on the 44th Planetary DNA strand.

"When I was 18 years old, mom asked what I wanted for my birthday and I said that I wanted to go to Hawaii to swim with the whales and begin my healing. I went into another dimension and picked out a male whale to work with. Mom wondered how we would manifest that. We got a call from James Twyman who was putting a Psychic Indigo Children's Conference together on Kona, Hawaii and invited me to be a presenter. Someone said I would meet the oldest living Kahuna (Hawaiian Shaman/Healer) on the planet there. Mom started putting out feelers but the doors were closed, 'Sorry, too busy. Out of town etc'. Mom felt that if it was that difficult, it was not meant to be and let go of it immediately.

"We had a wonderful time in Hawaii at the conference and met many incredible, conscious people, like Joan Ocean, Trish Regan, Doug Hackett, Laurie Reyon Anderson, Ellen van der Molen, Saleena Ki and many more. Saleena organized a whale boat. The morning of the adventure, I had a dream that mom left me. Mom said, 'Chandra, I would never do such a thing!'

"Off we went on the boat with Captain Veto who has been doing whale watches for fifteen years. The sea was very choppy with huge waves and the boat jumped up and down in the water. Then I looked at mom, she was very seasick and she telepathed to me, 'I am sorry, Chandra, but I have to leave my body now.' There was my dream. But I was busy communicating with a huge male whale that along with 30 other whales kept circling the boat. Captain Veto said he had never seen this many whales at once in all his years of whale watching. I knew these whales were here for me. These words were telepathed to me, 'And now you will receive a healing from the oldest living Kahuna on the island.' The oldest living Kahuna on the island was the male whale I was communicating with! He dove right under the boat where I was sitting. Doug and Trish put an underwater camera down the side of the boat and later sent me the picture. It was the whale with 5 golden beams coming up to the surface from his heart giving me information.

"I created my MP3 'Whalespeak' for deep relaxation, to align our subtle bodies and relieve stress. It is especially good for pregnant women because the fetus understands the language of the whales.

"At the end of the whale boat trip, mom came back into her body and asked people if she had turned green. Saleena replied, 'No, your face was the same color as when you were a Japanese geisha in another lifetime.'

"The messages the Whales gave me that began my healing were: 'The Codes of the Ark of the Covenant are being revealed to us on the solstices, equinoxes and have been known to all ancient cultures since time immemorial. The Codes have begun to be revealed to those conscious enough to receive this information.'

"I AM a Stargate Opener. I opened the Stargate in Kona with James Twyman's group. It lies between two volcanoes and is the portal to ancient Lemuria. Codes of the Ark of the Covenant give us the ability to help ourselves and the planet producing a scalar wave at the 13th dimensional level with the Cosmic Christ who comes through this portal. The second coming of the Cosmic Christ will take us into Ascension. These Codes are in Chief Golden Light Eagle's and my template of 13 and 12 dimensions respectively and we can travel through all dimensions to activate these codes.

"The whales also said, 'When the Ark of the Covenant Codes are activated, they allow beings to enter the 13th dimension where they can materialize and dematerialize while keeping the physical body intact repairing any problems in the Universal Grid or Auric Field. Distortions in this field cause war, pole shifts and floods. The Codes reconnect all life with Creator/Source.'

"These Codes should only be activated when we need to preserve ourselves. Because of so many Lightworkers awakening to their Planetary Missions through the discovery and use of their Master Numbers, we have successfully diffused many Planetary catastrophes.

"My current Mission on Earth is to awaken all souls who have contracted to be here at this time to help with Ascension, to connect to their Missions through their birth dates and the Master Numbers that are within these dates."

NOTE: In the ten years that Grandma has officially been doing this work, we have not encountered anyone who does not have Master Numbers in their birth dates.

Grandma continues, "What are Master Numbers? They are doubles: 11, 22, 33, 44, 55, 66, 77, 88 and 99. These are the harmonic numbers that comprise the universe. Each number has a special meaning. Those with Master Numbers in their birth dates are in my group whom I called to this Planet to help with Ascension. I contact them through their meditations, dreams and visions guiding them to connect with me by email.

- 11 shows the connection between all that was, is or will be, as brothers and sisters. Gifts of #11 are protection, right use of will and harmony.
- 22 is the builder, the square, the realization of the God Self in All. Gifts: rewards and blessings.
- 33 is the ability to manifest. Gifts are gentleness and purity.
- 44 is evolution and revolution of self on All levels. Gifts are sovereignty over the self, elevation and right use of power.
- 55 is the ability to gain knowledge easily. Gifts are marriage, happiness and the connection to the Star Beings.
- 66 is the implementation of the Divine in personal existence and application of organization to life. Gifts are attainment of your highest vision and completion of your Life Path.
- 77 is the completion of everything in All Dimensions. Gifts are relaxation and freedom on your Path.
- 88 is infinity and unlimited understanding coupled with compassion and mercy. Gifts are protection and the highest consciousness.
- 99 is seeing the true Path through the simultaneous enfoldment of the past, present and future. Gifts are joy and rest.

"I have had many experiences appearing as a whale or a dolphin or other animals in this life. I appear like this so people will know it is time to use the spiritual meaning of these totem animals for themselves and mankind.

"Several years ago in a presentation with Laurie Reyon Anderson and Judith Moore, I brought in the Cosmic White Whale who keeps the planet protected in his sheer liquid light magenta cloak. The Cosmic 9 White Whales come through the Star nations with messages of peace that will be revealed on the equinoxes, solstices, sun dances and vision quests.

"Judith saw the Light ships I brought in and channeled the following message for me, 'They dropped balls of Light into the ocean into the Whales and Dolphins. Through their sonar, they were able to receive the DNA codes of the Ark of the Covenant to open the Ark's energies to benefit the Planet.

'And our intention is to bring in the White Whale, and this is from all aspects of Enoch that Chandra represents, a presence of Divine Light. The presence of the Whale Masters in one configuration of Light is possible through the Divine timing of the Cosmic Doorways of Light that amplify the Whale Tones through the heart of every whale on the planet. This opportunity for humanity has never been experienced from the Master Plan on the Earth and was indeed not possible until the Cosmic Codes from the Great Ark Systems and the Enochian Temples of Light opened the Galactic Systems of the Masters of the frequencies of the Ark of Creation. The Master formula now may be amplified through the Cosmic Heart. Each tone and overtone of the master's presence at this configuration of Light is a direct harmonic light and sound frequency that is now introduced in Creation and was not able to manifest in the Universe prior to the opening of the Creation Codes of Light and the initiation of the new Galactic Time Spell.

'I AM the White Enoch. We are present here now to bring unity to all whale systems, and I speak of now the Whales of Creation. I speak of the Whales of Harmonic Universal Oneness. I speak of the Cosmic formulas for the opening of the heart source energies through the heart of Cosmic Oneness. Present here upon the Earth are Masters from many dimensions, and we have gathered here now to present the crystal formulas of Light that amplify the crystal heart grid of the planet through the Whale Tones and the dolphin frequencies by the power of the Eye of Enoch. This is the Master System. ("I'm getting flashing lights everywhere in my eye," says Judith) This is the Master System. We of the Cosmic Christ prepare now the ascending formulas for the 131313 White Whale DNA. I am bringing in the 131313 White Whale DNA Codes and will activate the formulas of light for the new crystalline strands for the Earth. This is the ultimate quantum genetics of the Cosmic Christ. I AM Master Enoch. I am present in all dimensions in the simultaneous reality. I'm present in the 8:10 light that illuminates the light and sound harmonics in the crystalline grid of the planet. All light has been illuminated by the light of Creation and given the crystalline 131313 DNA activation for the Codes of Light of the new Lemuria.

'I am Chandra. I speak from my 131313 vibration. I am able now to communicate this passage of light in preparation for the great gathering of souls upon this Earth.' (End of Judith's transmission.)

Grandma continues, "Sometimes I like to play jokes, to let people know that I am there with them. My friend Celeste Eaton took some people on a whale watch. She said she saw this huge mother whale very close to her. She looked into her eye and the whale's eye began to rotate and became a bulls' eye like on a target! When I saw her she wanted me to tell her what it meant. I said that it was me saying 'Hi!'

"Carey Maccarthy who was on one of my Hawaiian adventures received the following messages from me, 'Whale Codes are energetic patterns, signs or pictures similar but different from hieroglyphics used by Egyptians, Mayans, Japanese, Chinese and other cultures that tell of past, present and future Planetary History as well as messages for humanity. These Codes are sent by the Whales to those like Chief Golden Light Eagle, others, and me because they're able to receive them. Whales are very intelligent mammals. Many Whale Codes have entered the Earth plane and hundreds more are constantly arriving. Since I am a Whale, I telepath with other Whales and can receive their messages. When you see or receive a Whale Code, meditate upon the Code and you too will receive messages of enlightenment through your senses of seeing, hearing, knowing and/or feeling.'

"On a July boat trip with Laurie Reyon and Floyd Streigel, I decided to join them by appearing as a dolphin and was spinning and jumping out of the water for close to an hour. They both knew it was me and heard me when I cried out, 'Here I am!'

(No wonder, G'ma slept for two days after that adventure!)

"Another time I appeared to them as a Whale. Floyd recognized me immediately and asked me to wave at him, so I did with my tail. Then he asked me to smile and I came out of the water with my mouth in a smile. I love joining in on whale and dolphin fun! "

Love to all of you and hopefully you will see me in my Dolphin or Whale forms.

Grandma Chandra is a young, non-verbal, unique multi-dimensional being; a living miracle in a severely physically challenged body who is an experienced, creative and trusted advisor and works telepathically support clients with their physical, emotional and spiritual well-being. When you meet with Grandma Chandra you will experience heart openings, images, sounds, words and cleansing tears as blockages are released. Grandma works with all her clients, Angels, Benevolent Extraterrestrials, Guides and Ascended Masters on all dimensions simultaneously. She has the ability to access information from other dimensions, this reality and the cosmos. She communicates telepathically and, at times, through a translator with humans, Angels, Benevolent Extraterrestrials and other Sentient Beings, such as Dolphins and Whales.

Grandma is an international speaker and travels to Europe and the Middle East taking people on telepathic spiritual journeys raising their conscious vibration for Ascension. Whole Light Beings appear at some of her presentations like Mother Mary and an ET from her home planet, the White Star Planet. During her life, she has formed sacred Sanskrit signs with her fingers called "mudras", i.e. the "mudras" for Universal Intelligence and OM and performed spontaneous past-life readings with everyone she came into contact. Not bound by the body, Chandra has unbroken past-life recall. Chandra was given the title "Grandmother" by Native American Chief Golden Light Eagle who recognized her as an original pipe carrier or wisdom bearer of his race.

It was discovered that Chandra "reads" through her fingertips by spinning papers, closed books, magazines etc. She does this with various spiritual/sacred texts when she performs readings for people. After spinning, she then recounts a page in the material and how it pertains to you or someone else in the room.

See www.grandmachandra.com for more information.

Chapter 6: *My Sacred Moments With the Dolphins & Whales*

By Celeste Eaton

"A generous heart, kind speech & a life of service & compassion are the things which renew humanity."
– Buddha

Greetings Fellow Cetacean Spirits!

Please joyfully join me as we journey through the sacred spaces where I live each day, as an ascending being of love and light. I would like to share my experiences from the mysterious, Blue Liquid playground of the Dolphins and Whales, and from the luminous opalescent realms of the Angelic Beings. I am immersed in these two sacred spaces daily, whether swimming with my cetacean friends or vibrationally communicating with Higher Light Beings. I have learned much about myself from the time of my birth to this present moment, spending special moments within both worlds.

The Realm of Dolphins and Whales: The Blue Eyed Dolphin

I experienced a huge leap in my life towards becoming more of "Who I Am" on my trip to San Diego. Walking along the beach one day, I noticed five or six bottlenose dolphins riding in the waves. It was like seeing them though a clear liquid waveform. I was amazed; it was as if no one else saw them. It felt like they were following me on my walk as they rode the wave. I reached the end of the beach and turned around to head back. To my surprise they did the same thing! They followed me all the way back to my starting point!

I was thrilled! The next day I spent hours at the aquatic park sitting with the whales and the dolphins. I returned for three days in a row, realizing how easily I was communicating with my new friends. On the last day, I was down at the viewing window when this very large dolphin with a BLUE EYE looked at me. I knew what she was saying! I got so excited! For a moment I questioned her blue eye, thinking "dolphins don't have blue eyes, do they?" I asked the attendant about it and he said, "NO, they don't have blue eyes!" Well, this one did. She came around many times looking into my eyes, and her eye was sky blue. I later asked why the blue-eyed dolphin had appeared to me and the answer was "I am here with you my sweet daughter, one day you will love and work with the dolphins!" Remember I said before my passing, "I will always be with you, I will never leave you!" My dad had made his transition only months earlier, and those were the words he said to me. I felt this was my dad's way of saying he is OK, he loves me and wants me to be happy. This moment changed my life; my work was to be with the dolphins to help others to heal their challenges, as well as to enjoy spending time with dolphins in pure Joy! Oh, and by the way my dad had clear ski-blue eyes. Interestingly, I also had sky blue eyes until a major shift occurred in my life at the age of 3 years. After several days of running a high fever, my eye color changed from blue to hazel-brown. Some people call this 'soul braiding'.

As I was leaving the aquatic park I said to the dolphins, "I have to do more than just touch you, I have to swim with you!"

Upon arriving home, there was a message from my friend asking if I wanted to go to Hawaii to swim with the dolphins? Oh my God, this was

Divine intervention! A week later I found myself in Hawaii in a dolphin seminar with Doug Hackett and Trish Regan, who became my very best friends. I was one of 3 participants in their very first seminar. Before leaving, my friend who is a 12th dimensional physic reader said, "A dolphin is going to take you through all 12 dimensions of time!" I responded just as quickly, "Oh, yes I know!" How did I know this?

The real excitement was just beginning! I had never snorkeled or swam in the ocean before. It was the first or second day out in the water, when one dolphin left the pod and swam over to me. I knew this was the Master Dolphin who was to be my teacher; I knew I would be taken through all 12 dimensions of time. All was going as planned. This beautiful, amazing dolphin and I swam for who knows how long, eye to eye, embracing each other with so much love.

I experienced a connection of peace, serenity, pure joy of heart like I had never felt before! I remember many different sensations taking place within my body, mind, and spirit. What I wasn't aware of was that I had become invisible to my swim partner Lisa! I knew I was shifting from one sensation to another, not realizing I had become invisible! How would I know this? I could see the other swimmers the entire time.

The most serene and familiar sensation that registered as I went through all 12 dimensions was within the realm where Big Foot, my 6th dimensional group of guides, had taken me to several times during our encounters. It is an environment of total peace and quietude, a suspended dimension of "no time, no space" that continues today as I swim with my beloved dolphins weaving in and out of "no time/no space", disappearing within our intimate connections, when it is only us!

During my dolphin-induced initiation to the 12 dimensions of time, neither Lisa nor the other swimmers were able to see me. My energy signature was raised so high that I disappeared! I didn't realize that my friends couldn't see me, since I could clearly see them. Lisa panicked, wondering where I had gone. She searched for me thinking she would be able to easily see me in my hot pink bathing suit, snorkel, mask and fins. Why couldn't I be seen? Eventually the dolphins told me to go to shore. I walked out of the water, looked right at Lisa and said, "Hey Lisa, What's up?" Her eyes became as big as saucers. She asked how I had gotten out of the water. I replied, "I walked out!" she asked again, and I could see she wasn't kidding. I quickly got the message from the dolphins that until

I spoke, I had been completely invisible to her. Wow, that was very interesting!

The next day Trish asked me to let her know if the same dolphin appeared to me. And guess what, he did! I motioned Trish over, we locked arms, and he approached the same way as the previous day. The other swimmers were watching to see what would happen. This time, we both became invisible! Not bad for my first swim with the dolphins ... a first time snorkeler!

The dolphins asked me to be a steward for them, a way-shower, to bring people to learn, share, heal, play, and enjoy themselves in their Presence. The dolphins love us as much as we love them; it is a mutual sharing of love and light that is exchanged when we swim together.

What a healing we all shared! We learned how the dolphins can assist us in elevating our frequencies to shift our cells to embody love, light and joy. I decided that this was my life's work. Then, after 5 years of speaking about the dolphins and bringing people to Hawaii to swim and share in their Essence, I was given the opportunity to move to the island. I am so appreciative to Hank, my former husband, who supported me that first year as I spent every day swimming with the dolphins and journaling my experiences without having to worry about anything else.

Trusty... Healing of the Baby Dolphin... My Way of Giving Back to the Dolphins

In June 2001, while assisting a participant and sending out my signature tones to the dolphins, I noticed a baby dolphin approaching me. Instead of stopping he very gently tapped my mask with his rostrum (nose). He swam past me, turned around and came back and bumped my shoulder, then moved directly in front of me and came to a complete stop. I saw that he had fishing line wrapped around his fluke which was cutting deeply into his skin.

I felt that this little guy was not going to make it! I swam to his side and asked permission to place my hand under his heart. The moment I asked, he fell directly into my arms. It was as if I was holding a human baby. His heart was beating was so fast and he was so scared.

I began transmitting healing energy to the baby and at the same time another facilitator attempted to undo the fishing line. Unfortunately the line was embedded so deeply that it would have to be cut away from his tail. We called out for someone to bring us a knife.

I asked the facilitator to take care of my snorkeling companion, and before I knew it I was swimming with the baby dolphin in my arms, listening to my internal guidance. I swam with him not knowing where we were heading. After awhile his heartbeat returned to normal and he started wiggling in my arms. I asked him if he wanted to go, giving him the choice, hoping he would stay in my arms until we could get some help to cut the line.

I saw his mom coming over to us and I knew he wanted to go to her. I released the baby and he swam to her. Then to my surprise three adult dolphins spiraled out of the water around me and landed right next to me. It was amazing! They knew I had assisted the baby and was helping him to swim. They were saying thank you!

I had never intentionally touched a dolphin. We ask swimmers to refrain from touching them out of respect. As it is, dolphins swim so close to me that we are practically skin-to-skin; we swim heart to heart, intimately sharing our time in the water. Our vibrations blend in a soul-to-soul connection, a much higher frequency experience. You can imagine how profoundly honored I felt when the injured baby trusted me to hold him gently in my arms. As I embraced this beloved baby dolphin, I named Trusty, for his complete faith and trust in coming to me for help. It was a Divine moment for both of us. We received a healing and a multitude of blessings as the Golden Master Dolphin of Love and Light flowed through my body to this precious one!

I returned to my snorkeling companion whose life had been changed after witnessing this unusual experience. We swam back to the same area where I first encountered the baby and I was surprised to see the entire pod coming towards me with mom and baby! They swam so close and very slowly approached my friend, showing us that the baby was OK. Oh, I was so happy!! I called to the snorkeler who had gotten a knife to let him know the pod was nearby. He swam over and was able to cut and remove a portion of line that was dragging, thank goodness. I just prayed that this little one would survive when the pod went out to feed for the night.

Once I was back on shore I started to cry and cry. I felt like I finally gave back to the dolphins after their giving so much to me for all these years! The word got out quickly in our dolphin community: carry a knife!

My friend Lisa was on a boat a few days later and saw the baby. She was able to cut more line off of his fluke. I cried again with joy and relief, so very happy to know that he had lived and was still doing well!

The most wonderful part of this story is that Trusty would come to find me at any of the bays I might be swimming in, even when I traveled on the boats. We would say 'hi' to each other, feeling so grateful to find one another and sharing our Essence in remembering that most incredible, amazing, heart to heart experience... with my hand literally placed on his little heart! Today we still communicate with each other; I send him pictures and thoughts of that special day we shared, he receives them and sends his images and feelings back to me. It's like sharing with my most precious best friend, my beloved dolphin I named Trusty. Thank you Trusty for trusting in me.

Whales of Tonga 2005, My First Trip

Our very first contact with the magnificent humpbacks of Tonga was with two large whales we named 'The Lovers' because of their deep affection for one other. The first words out of my mouth were "You look just like 'my' whales!" Later that night, our guide and the owner of the resort said they had never seen these particular whales before, and that they looked like the Pacific Humpback Whales who migrate to Hawaii to mate and give birth. A little shiver went up my spine, as this was truly what I had also thought. However, since we hadn't seen the South Pacific Whales yet, I just shrugged it off. 'The Lovers' were a darker color with no white on their stomachs, which is an identifying feature of the South Pacific Whales. It is my belief as well as others that somehow this beautiful Hawaiian whale-couple had made their way down to Tonga to see us, and I have DVD footage to prove it! How they got there no one knows, maybe they were transported by an ET ship? Did these two giant manifestations of highly advanced Beings travel beyond space and time right in front of our eyes? We were in awe having been allowed to witness this miracle, to have enjoyed watching their amazing dance performance as they entwined and spiraled together, holding their pectoral fins in a loving, nurturing embrace just as you see in paintings. They flowed together to form a dynamic Double Helix formation over and over again. Before we arrived in Tonga the whales had told me that they were going to activate all twelve strands of our DNA and RNA. I believe this is what they were symbolizing as they danced and spiraled to the surface to meet

70

our glances of amazement... eye-to-eye, human and whale, spirit-to-spirit, reminding us of our True Beingness.

At one point while I was watching a whale in front of me, I suddenly felt an immense energy resonating from below me. I looked down to see the other whale's rostrum heading straight towards my mask! All I could do was float motionless in the water above him. Just before the whale surfaced he moved subtly to the side so he would not hurt me with his tail. It was unbelievable that he was able to surface from right below and yet miss me! And this was not the first time I've had whales swim so close when surfacing, yet they never touch me. They are like the dolphins, they know exactly where they are at all times and will never hit or hurt you. The last thing they want is to scare us; they trust us completely with an open heart. They have proven this time and time again. I know we never have to be afraid of these giant, yet gentle beings, they are purely loving and nurturing vessels who are here to teach us to become as they are, constantly modeling behavior to us. What a blessing to have 'my' Humpback Whales come to visit us. Interestingly, they hadn't been seen before or since. This gives us a lot to think about!

Later in the trip we found a mom and baby and spent 3.5 hours with these blessed ones. During one precious moment the baby dove to mom and she put out her pectoral fins, as a mother would do to accept a baby into her arms. It was so nurturing and serene to behold this loving embrace. As the baby became more familiar with us she began to play and interact with us. Meanwhile mom just rested peacefully below, totally trusting us to babysit her calf.

My friend Karen tried an experiment with the mother. She started putting her arms in front of her then to the side, 3 or 4 times. We watched as the mother copied her movements. I was thinking, 'Oh, the movement Karen is making is so wonderful', while at the same time the mother was moving loving energies towards us with her pec fins. She nurtured our Souls as a new mother would do to her baby. We were like her babies too, absorbing her love and nurturance for three and a half hours! We were all positively impacted and shifted at the cellular level by this exchange of maternal love.

Tonga Trip to Whales 2010

I decided to take a Goddess Group to the Haipai Islands in Tonga for two weeks. My friend had purchased property there and we stayed at her newly created eco-resort. Unfortunately the weather conditions were challenging for us Goddesses! My captain said he was going to cancel our outings for three days in anticipation of the bad weather, and that he would make up for the lost days after the storm.

That night after dinner I conducted a ceremony to activate our 'Light Bodies'. A very, very large mother whale came into the meditation, and I thought 'this is a really large mother'! She seemed so real, yet she was very different... she was in her 'Light Body', which may explain why she was so big! The next morning was sunny and beautiful, and we wondered if perhaps it was the calm before the storm? After eating breakfast we asked a Haipai captain named Cecie if he would take us out to look for whales. He agreed but cautioned us to keep watch for the high winds that were headed our way. We packed a lunch and set off on our adventure in his tiny wooden boat that barely held the eight of us. It was actually quite fun to be only a few feet from the water as we traveled around the islands. Cecie said he knew of a place where the whales 'hung out' in a lagoon. We headed that way and saw a few whales here and there, but we wanted to get to the lagoon, knowing that our time on the water was limited.

We had almost reached the lagoon when the winds began to kick up. Cecie suggested that we turn back, as it would take awhile to get back to our island if we were going against the wind and waves. We would be a tiny floating vessel being tossed around on a great big ocean! We all agreed to head back, feeling a little disappointed that we would not meet the whales in the lagoon.

We could see our island in the distance, but in the opposite direction a whale suddenly began to breach repeatedly. We had to quickly decide what we wanted to do. Return to our island or head for the whale? We unanimously voted to go to the whale. So we quickly motored towards the whale as she was still breaching. It was so exciting! We stopped our boat at a safe distance, though we were still very, very close. As she continued to breach, the pounding of her tail on the water was so loud and hard it shook our bodies. Remember, we were in a very small boat and were close to the whale... so having her perform for us was incredible to say the least. The way she would slap her tail made me wonder if she was giving birth, and just as I had this thought, her baby surfaced and she was not a newborn! Momma began to tail slap and the baby started breaching over and over again.

This was truly the largest mother (or any whale!) I had ever seen in all my years swimming with the whales. She was enormous! She moved a second time with her baby and a male escort surfaced next to her, blowing his long-held breath. We were with a mom, baby, and escort! We followed them for a short distance and watched as they dove and disappeared. Cecie stopped the boat and I told my friends to BE READY. I wasn't sure why, but I knew if we were going to get in with them it would be quick. My friend Susan who is a whale sister and I were hanging with our feet in the water barely holding on, when the mother appeared to lunge towards our boat. She was not in direct alignment with the boat but she was heading our way. When I saw her back cresting out of the water I thought, 'Oh my Goddess, she is really, really huge!' The next thing I knew it was as if she had pulled me into the water, as though she was a giant magnet! In I went with Susan right behind me. As for the rest of my story, everything that occurred from this point forward happened within a matter of seconds.

My arm went up to show whoever had a chance to get in the water that I saw the whale. She was a little to the right, maybe 15 feet or so underneath us with her baby slip-streaming on top of her back. My hand was still in the air as she sped towards me, looking me right in the eye. For a frozen moment we were eye-to-eye, just a few feet apart. As she was passing, her eye was moving rapidly, as if it was gyrating. She opened her eye so wide at times that I could see the sclera (white part) of her eye all around the iris (pigmented portion). I didn't know that whales could do this! Through her rapid eye movements I sensed that she was quickly and deliberately transferring 'Soul Information' to me, 3rd eye to 3rd eye. She then turned her enormous body towards me so that we were heart-to-heart, as her throat pleats bellowed in and out. I had one panicked thought as this was happening so quickly, 'Where is her tail?!'. She was so close and near that I was momentarily concerned I'd be swatted by her giant tail! Suddenly there were bubbles all around me and I looked just ahead to see her tail eight to ten feet in front of me. With small flick of her fluke she and her baby were gone! We never saw them again. Afterwards, we all wondered how she swam to me so fast and yet did not hit me?

I then realized that this was the whale who was in our meditation the previous night. We were meant to communicate with her, and she called us to her. It was no wonder we made the choice to go to her instead of heading back to our island. We made it safely back; it was as if she had calmed the waters for our return. Wow, what an experience!!!

The interesting part was that after this exchange I became so sick I could hardly make it to my Falie. For three days I was unable to get out of bed except to use the bathroom, and I survived on a diet of coconut water. My illness coincided with the 3-day cancellation of our boat outings. On the fourth day when the boat picked us up, I felt great... like nothing had happened! What a big shift!

Indeed, a lot did happen. I learned from my inner guidance as well as other readings that this mother whale and I had an agreement to meet and exchange our frequencies, eye-to-eye, heart-to-heart! She gave me the patterns of her Whale Essence, as I gave her my Human/Spirit Essence patterns. It was a complete and equal exchange. My life from that day forward shifted dramatically in every way, as did the lives of the other Goddess participants.

More Transformative Shifts

In March 2011 in Kona, some of my dear friends and I facilitated a conference called "Birthing the Golden Lemuria." A group of us traveled around the island for the purpose of activating Portals. Grandma Chandra asked me to bring in the 'Divine Crystalline Whale Codes for Humanity'. Naturally, I said "Yes!!". During one ceremony, we were sharing stories when a mother whale just offshore began to breach and continuously slap her tail. We all got up and ran to the shoreline, watching her tail slap over and over; it so reminded me of the mother whale in Tonga who gifted me the blessings of her frequency patterns.

My friend Judith looked at me and asked, "Is it time?" I said, "Yes!" then the next moment my hand went up, and a bolt of Light shot into my arm. I spontaneously began sounding the message from the mother whale. It was unusual for me to deliver a message through sound; she wanted me to share the information in this form to the group while anchoring the crystalline codes into Gaia, Mother Earth. When the sounding stopped, I reached my hand up towards the heavens and saw us all in the Galaxy, intermingled among the stars. It was indescribably beautiful, magical, and mystical. I felt the Galaxy within me, instructing us all to bring the heavens, all of the stars... into our bodies. I then placed my hand on the ground and pushed hard into the earth to anchor the "Divine Crystalline Whale Codes" for humanity into the 144,000 crystalline grids of our Beloved Mother Earth, into her soul, Gaia. Wow, what an amazing blessing from this the beautiful Mother Whale who acted as the spokesperson for All the Whales.

Since the Haipai adventure, I have continued to undergo significant transformative shifts here in Hawaii and also while leading groups to Tonga. In September 2011 I hosted thirteen whale-swimmers for two weeks in Tonga. The whales had communicated to me that we were to create a 'Portal' at the 19.5 area of Tonga, where we all swim together. As instructed, I was asked to transfer the Crystalline Whale Codes to my family-pod of human's to consciously create a 'Portal' through which we transferred the Crystalline Whale Codes into the 144,000 crystalline grid of Gaia/Mother Earth. We also conducted crystal ceremonies to activate whale frequencies to be used to evolve humanity. All of the participants who were in attendance were required to create this Portal, and we all remain very close friends having shared this incredible experience.

Now here we are in 2013, continuing to experience the frequency shifts associated with Equinoxes and Solstices with a Super Full Moon so powerful that the process of 'evolving' has become the norm for many of us living on the island of Kona. Our Lemuria is so sacred, intense, and amazingly joyful! I am profoundly blessed as I spend nearly every day with the dolphins and are able to see the humpback whales when they gift us with their presence.

Another amazingly huge shift took place within my emotional, mental and physical bodies on June 23rd, 2013. During Grandma Chandra's teleconference, we opened a Portal to the Universal Sun of the Suns and rebalanced the Earth's Energy Grids!

The Dolphins and Whales Help Us All

I feel that everyone who I have ever introduced to the dolphins and whales has been shifted in many ways, whether they have had serious illnesses or have simply chosen to swim, play, and enjoy themselves in the cetaceans' aquatic environment.

One beautiful example is when I took a woman who was in a wheel chair out to be with dolphins. I had to pull her along with the assistance of a 'boogie-board'; she was paralyzed from the waist down. After our first trip I noticed that she could use her walker better. After the second trip she said she could walk around her hotel room unassisted. At the completion of our 3rd day out with the dolphins she walked from her room to the lobby, which was quite a distance. She came back the next year and experienced additional healing with the dolphins. Her life was forever changed!

Another precious example is a woman who journeyed with me on my first whale trip. She had lymphatic cancer and her medical team had advised her to have surgery. She chose to join my trip even though she was very weak. After spending time in the water enjoying intimate and close encounters with the whales, her energy and her immune system improved and she was able to live a better life.

We are all experiencing more and more changes, individually and collectively on the Earth plane. Let us bless and embrace these changes and know that no matter what we see in our Third Dimensional reality, it is all in Divine Order in the other dimensions. We have collectively asked for change, for a new era, and for a better world... and we are in process!"

I am so grateful to have the life I live, waking up every day in Hawaii, Lemuria, my Paradise! I transmit Love and Gratitude to you All from the center of my Heart! Be and Swim Free! Live in love, light, harmony, and joy... always! Celeste

Aloha and welcome to Celeste's World of Remembering Lemuria. Celeste brings forth the inspiration and teachings from the Beloved ET's, the Whales & Dolphins, the Angelic and Fairy Realms, Big Foot Guides, the Ascended Masters, Star Beings, and her Sacred Doggie Friends. She carries the blessings and wisdom of the Lemurians, Beings of Love and Light who are part of her spiritual heritage and who have been with her from the Beginning of Time.

Please join Celeste as we venture within her mysterious and joyful Blue Liquid playground of the Dolphins, Whales and other Ocean Beings, along with the merged Essences of the Heavenly Beings of Light from the luminous, opalescent realms of the Angels and Fairies. She resides within these two sacred spaces every day, whether swimming with her ocean friends or vibrationally communicating with Higher Light Beings. She has been in communion with Etherial Beings and has learned much about herself from the time of her birth to this present moment.

Even as a young child growing up, Celeste felt that she was living in two worlds at the same time. She was simultaneously aware of herself as a Physical Being in a physical reality while also remaining connected to a mystical, magical world where she had full recognition of past timelines. She has spent her life remembering, playing within, and weaving the mysteries of the unknown and known, realizing that she has always been involved in a much greater Inner Knowing of who her 'other' Self is, even while embracing her current human existence. Her unique capacity to dance seamlessly between worlds makes Celeste a treasure to all humanity.

Celeste is a Healer of the Soul, Heart, Mind, and Body who brings each person into their perfected Balance and Radiance. Through her Soul embodiment of Ke Waine Ka Kalima, she acts as the "Protectress of the Oceans and Seas and all that live within these waters". She facilitates swimming with dolphins in Kona, Hawaii, and with humpback whales in the Kingdom of Tonga. Her Essence resides in All Nature with the Nature Spirits.

www.celestialsonics.com   celeste@celestialsonics.com

Chapter 7: *The Profound Messages of the Dolphins & Whales*

By Joan Ocean, M.S.

> *"....the dolphins have a manifestation of their higher selves*
> *right on your own planet. It is called the Whales.*
> *The idea of the whale is that it is representative of the*
> *over-soul, of many dolphin souls combined into one."*
> *- Bashar channeled through Darryl Anka*

Have you ever thought that your life is being choreographed by forces unseen by you? Have you had a sense of something else, like fate, directing your movements, your contacts and your intelligence gathering? This is the story of how my life with dolphins and whales began; at least it is one beginning. Who can really know when or where it all began? How long ago, in which timeline, on what cosmic wave of existence?

People often ask me how I came to do the work I do. Of course, many people enlightened my path, but I can identify three people who initially inspired me in my cetacean communication work and play. The meetings were all mysterious, synchronistic events. Coming out of the blue, the encounters were seemingly unrelated to my life at the time, and yet the wisdom they brought took over my life. Because it was meaningful and purposeful, I did not hesitate to follow this guidance. The people are psychologist Dr. Carl Rogers, scientist Dr. John C. Lilly and visionary artist Jean-Luc Bozzoli.

In the year 1975, I was employed as the Administrative Assistant for Mental Health Systems in San Diego. I had received my Master of Science degree in Counseling Psychology and moved to Southern California to enjoy the sun and my new volunteer working relationship with Dr. Carl Rogers[1], founder of the Center for Studies of the Person in La Jolla, California. Dr. Rogers was a world-renowned psychologist and pioneer in the counseling tradition of client-centered/person-centered therapy. He was convening encounter groups every weekend during the summer at the University of California, San Diego.

It was a time of great expansion and excitement for me. Dr. Rogers, an experienced professional in the field, who genuinely loved people, inspired me greatly in my work assisting clients to gently examine their deeply-ingrained, limiting belief systems, thereby enabling them to express their true nature in their lives and the larger world. Our role in this expansive process was to be the supportive friend and counselor who would hold a safe space for people while they found their inspired paths. We were leading what became known as Encounter Groups. These compassionate, soul-searching group therapies and ways-of-life that I learned from Dr. Rogers became the foundation for my later work and play in loving communication with the dolphins and whales, a process

---

[1] Carl Ransom Rogers (January 8, 1902 – February 4, 1987) was an influential American psychologist and among the founders of the humanistic approach (or client-centered approach) to psychology. The person-centered approach, his own unique approach to understanding personality and human relationships, found wide application in various domains such as psychotherapy and counseling (client-centered therapy), education (student-centered learning), organizations, and other group settings. For his professional work he was bestowed the Award for Distinguished Professional Contributions to Psychology by the APA and was nominated for the Nobel Peace Prize for his work with national intergroup conflict in South Africa and Northern Ireland.

that the dolphins would define as "Tel-Empathy." Tel-Empathy means telepathy and empathy. It combines the metaphysical ability of telepathy with a genuine feeling of caring for my clients. It was a natural feeling that surfaced while counseling my clients and also while communicating with cetaceans.

In 1975, I had not yet heard of Dr. John Lilly[2], but a friend of mine, Tysen, had. With his own background as a physicist and as a spiritual seeker, Tysen was interested in the research of this renowned scientist who understood the complex functions of the human brain and also the cyber-brain of the new computers.

One Saturday morning, Tysen and I visited Earth Song Bookstore[3] in Del Mar, California. Tysen was interested in the scientific progression of altered states of consciousness, the higher potentials of the human brain and the available soft technologies that could experientially get us there, such as the Samadhi tank. This had led him to books by Dr. Lilly who had introduced the concept of personal flotation tanks for meditation,

---

[2] John Cunningham Lilly (January 6, 1915 – September 30, 2001) was an American physician, neuroscientist, psychoanalyst, psychonaut, philosopher and writer. He researched the nature of consciousness involving isolation tanks, dolphin communication and psychedelics. He made contributions in the fields of biophysics, neurophysiology, electronics, computer science, and neuroanatomy. During the late 1950s he established a facility devoted to fostering human-dolphin communication: the Communication Research Institute on St. Thomas in the Virgin Islands. Lilly was interested in the Search for Extra-Terrestrial Intelligence (SETI) project. In 1961 a group of scientists including Lilly gathered at the Green Bank Observatory in West Virginia to discuss the possibility of using the techniques of radio astronomy to detect evidence of intelligent life outside our solar system. They called themselves The Order of the Dolphin after Lilly's work with dolphins. They discussed the Drake equation, used to estimate the number of communicative extraterrestrial civilizations in our galaxy. Lilly published 19 books in all, including Man and Dolphin and The Mind of the Dolphin which describe his work with dolphins. He designed a futuristic "communications laboratory" that would be a floating living room where humans and dolphins could live together and develop a common language, to chat as equals. He envisioned a time when all killing of whales and dolphins would cease, "not from a law being passed, but from each human understanding innately that these are ancient, sentient earth residents, with tremendous intelligence and enormous life force. Not someone to kill, but someone to learn from." In the 1990s Lilly moved to Hawaii, where he lived most of the remainder of his life.

[3] Earth Song Bookstore was founded in 1969. It went on to become one of the most treasured businesses and bookstores in Del Mar, California. It closed on November 13, 2011.

visualization, rejuvenation, self-observation, creativity, time travel, prayer, solitude, rest and relaxation.

As we browsed in the peaceful setting of this welcoming bookstore, Tysen found a shelf with books by Dr. Lilly. Fascinated by what he was reading, he passed one of the books to me. I looked at it briefly, but the book appeared too technical for me. I set it aside. This is where and when everything became strange.

After placing the Lilly book back on the shelf, I continued to peruse books on topics such as, contacts with advanced civilizations on other planets. When Tysen asked for the Lilly book back, it had disappeared! Feeling responsible for finding it, I asked the individuals standing near me if they had taken that book from the shelf, but no one had. I even asked the store owner to locate the book, since Tysen wanted to buy it, but it was missing and could no longer be found anywhere in the store. There was no rational explanation for its disappearance. We had held it in our hands, we had read excerpts from it, and now it was gone!

We finally left the store without it, frustrated and mystified. Perhaps by repeating the name "John Lilly" over and over again while searching for his book in the store, I may have imprinted his name on my brain!

Returning to my apartment, I opened my mailbox to check the mail. Inside, addressed to me was a large, colorful flyer from ... Dr. John C. Lilly. A printed, mass-marketed brochure, it announced a workshop he was planning at Feather Pipe Ranch in Montana.

The brochure probably mentioned his dedicated interest in developing communication technologies for human-dolphin interactions, but I didn't notice that part. I only focused on the sentence that said he would share his experiences with off-planet beings. In the 70s, this was still a relatively new idea among the masses, and rarely did information like that arrive in one's mailbox.

Now I was interested!

Tysen and I promptly enrolled in the workshop with John and his wife, Toni. We were amazed that this man whose name had been on our lips all morning was now coming into our lives in a very physical and meaningful way.

At the opening meeting in Montana, Dr. Lilly asked what had brought each of the 30 people there to attend his workshop. When I shared my experience, he casually mentioned that things like that happened often around his workshops, and gave credit to the intervention of E.C.C.O. - Earth's Coincidence Control Office, a Galactic substation that provides protocols to John and any other human willing to follow their rules of engagement[4].

John did share his experiences of out-of-body meetings with off-planet beings during that workshop, but mostly he talked about the dolphins he had met, and he played their sounds. Over the hills of Montana, day and night, recordings of dolphin whistles and calls could be heard. Although my last name is Ocean, I had not yet been in the ocean. I didn't know it at the time, but the dolphins were talking to me right then and there in Montana.

In 1984, Jean-Luc Bozzoli, was traveling in California with his visionary art presentation, having come to the United States from Australia to participate in a gathering of shamans in Ojai. He was invited to present his unique and soul-inspiring art images to the Shamans. Someone gave him my name as a person to contact who would most certainly love his luminous, colorful images, and his accomplished geometrical sigils and art forms. Jean-Luc soon arrived at my front door.

His multi-media presentation in my home for my weekly meditation group was well-received; however I was unprepared for my own personal reaction to his art. Upon seeing the pure, vibrant colors and the pyramidal, geometric shapes beneath the ocean in the presence of dolphins and whales, I burst into tears and couldn't stop sobbing. I was emotionally overwhelmed with the beauty and the sacred noetic codes revealed in his simple and elegant forms. They awakened memories of a familiar world where great love and peacefulness once filled my soul. The images pierced my mind, came directly into my heart and touched the deepest core of my being. What was going on? It was a transitional moment for me.

Subsequently Jean-Luc and I traveled throughout the United States and then the world to bring his beautiful, heart-opening films to thousands of people. It was a journey of love and the dolphins and whales

---

[4] E.C.C.O. -- Excerpt from *The Dyadic Cyclone* by John C. Lilly, PhD: "In one's life there can be peculiarly appropriate chains of related events that lead to consequences that are strongly desired. After such experiences, one wonders how such a series of events developed; sometimes there is a strong feeling that some intelligence (greater than ours) directed the course along certain lines which It/He/She was/is programming. There exists a Cosmic Control Center (C.C.C.)

were a big part of it. Visiting many wonderful countries, we met the people, and we met the dolphins and whales who lived there. Spiritual enlightenment through beauty, joy and the cetaceans was (and is) the absolute focus of our lives.

And as we travelled, I realized more and more how intelligent and advanced the cetaceans are. This foundation of meeting these three significant people prepared me for the loving interactions that were soon to come into my life from the free-swimming, oceanic dolphin societies.

Cetacean Behaviors, Physiology, and Advanced Abilities

Now, in 2014, I have been swimming among dolphins and whales for 30 years. John Lilly was absolutely right! They are even more intelligent than we have ever imagined. Living with them on the Big Island, I have witnessed many of their advanced qualities and abilities. With all the attributes and behaviors they demonstrate, they make clear that equivalent potentials are available within us, the human race, and we will achieve many of these abilities ourselves in the months and years ahead.

Dolphins and whales can read the minds of humans, and they respond according to vibrational frequencies they perceive emanating from us. They are able to heal people, the ocean and each other, and they use their sonar, sounds and vibrations to do this. Sending acoustic, holographic images to each other and to us, they interact with the intelligence in the cells of our bodies. They spiral in the air, activating their energy chakras and stimulating synchronization between the lobes of their brain. They are conscious breathers, choosing every breath they breathe. They never sleep as we do; they live on less sleep, taking naps by shutting down and resting one area of their brain and lowering their metabolism as they play and swim continuously. They dive deeply but do not get decompression sickness, because of the inherent physiology of their internal organs. They demonstrate compassion and kindness, taking care of each other and honoring their family members. They are altruistic and cooperative, competing in play but not for gain. They love their environment and express joy within it. They eat when hungry, working cooperatively to find food, never hoarding or over-consuming it. They understand the power of eye-to-eye contact, and they intimately share the depths of their love through the light of their unblinking eyes with swimmers whom they know and trust.

They have control of their emotions and use them positively. When electrodes to the brain, administered by researchers, triggered false aggression responses in captive dolphins, they did not attack anyone, but they floated in the tank, shaking their bodies until the anger was dissipated. They remain athletic and active until they die. They make love often. They spend quality time with their young, teaching them about life and the world. They understand the value of being happy, expressing joy. They have a sense of humor. They understand the spiritual value of playing games with us, using leaves and bubbles, telepathic messages and acoustic images to engage us. They treat all humans with love while "reading" our emotional history and feelings. They are fearless. They do not attack people who capture them and put them in captive facilities or who kill their babies. Although they grieve and feel deep sadness, they continue to express unconditional love. They have integrity. They are not materialistic; they live simply and do no harm. They have evolved beyond the limiting social structure of duality and have instead embraced complementarity.

They know they are more than their physical bodies. They can shape shift and alter their molecular structure. They are telepathic. They have a unity consciousness, and they are multi-dimensional. They intentionally heal people as appropriate. They can die by choice at will, by shutting down their blowhole. They know they never "die" in the way we think of death. They remain in contact with each other, even after death. They send beacons of directed sound into the waters of the earth, creating sound patterns that balance and improve the beleaguered oceans. They are activating dormant potentials in our DNA[5] and thereby assisting us to evolve into Love.

These are some of their qualities and abilities that I have come to know over the past 30 years living among them.

Becoming a Time Traveler

One of the messages I have perceived clearly while swimming among dolphins and whales is that everything they do and communicate

---

[5] Deoxyribonucleic acid (DNA), a substance that carries genetic information in the cells of plants and animals... any of various nucleic acids that are usually the molecular basis of heredity. A complex organic compound found in all living cells. It is the chemical substance of genes.

to me has significance. They communicate with acoustic images and empathy. Their holographic, multi-dimensional transmissions reveal the universal wisdom of love.

While swimming alone with them for many hours, day after day, I began to realize I was experiencing a peaceful, trance-like field of energy within and around my body. Eventually I realized I was often out-of- body having an experience of floating above the water and observing the cetaceans swimming below. I also began to access other timelines.

Swimming with the dolphin pods an average of twenty mornings a month, from 6:30 am until mid-afternoon, year after year, led to my visiting places, astrally, that were unfamiliar to me and yet quite fascinating. Always wanting to be more and more like my dolphin friends, I was determined to merge with their behavior patterns and do the things they did. Hearing their messages encouraged me to spend more of my free time experiencing quantum traveling by entering a peaceful state of higher consciousness.

When swimming with the whales, I received their messages of cosmic and practical intelligence: "You talk about inner-space and time/space travel. These are good words to describe how we whales spend our time and energy, and the dolphins do as well. Like whales, the dolphins have also become specialists of consciousness. They have an amazing intelligence and a great depth of wisdom."

The dolphins have shown me scenes from the past and future of this timeline. Initially I felt confused because I saw many different versions of the future during different swims with them, some that I liked and some that I didn't. I wondered, which was the real one? As I communicated this question to the dolphins via tel-empathy, they clearly sent back the information that all of the places I visited were the future. They then asked, "Which one would I choose to make my own?" At first this seemed nonsensical to me, until I suddenly understood that we have a choice. I could choose now, at this point in my present timeline, which future I preferred. The way we live our individual, personal lives in the present, the way we think and behave, is the way we create our future. For me, it was a very empowering realization.

After exploring these multiple realities for a number of years, in 1995 I realized my next cetacean-related role was to teach the process of time travel to other people. I was guided to find the best procedure to use: the most loving and acceptable to the human race, to help people overcome their disbelief in the extraordinary process of time travel, once relegated to science fiction. I was especially interested in those people who were in closest contact with the wise, inter-dimensional dolphins themselves, the people living here in the Kealakekua community in Hawaii, who had chosen to live here because of their love for the dolphins. These people were overcoming the belief that time travel is impossible and realizing that believing in their ability to time travel was the key to success. If you did not believe that you could enter other realities, then most likely you never would. Fortunately the human-dolphin swimmers, who live on the Big Island, also know that we can consciously travel to multi-dimensional places. It is part of our dolphin-human play together. As the dolphins often remind us: imagination creates reality. As part of our spiritual growth, we acknowledge our multi-dimensional abilities and enter many other realms of endless beauty and inspiration, and we do this intentionally, by choice, beyond fleeting dreamtime memories or sudden déjà vu experiences. As we enter the Alpha state and set the intention to time travel into a parallel positive reality, we quickly access this natural but previously latent skill. It is an enjoyable and educational experience.

As part of the curriculum in my classes I share the documented experiences of people who have already accessed multiple timelines, such as people from the Monroe Institute in Faber, Virginia, and others working within classified projects of the U.S. Department of Defense. They are time travelers and "chrononauts," accessing a vortal tunnel and traveling to the past, the future and parallel timelines, often going forward and backward in time, reliving parts of their lives. They do this clandestinely while continuing to live in their everyday three-dimensional reality. Being the first space/time travelers is a fascinating and positive event for these pioneers.[6] It is fun and it is enlightening. And for me, it all began while swimming with the highly-intelligent Hawaiian spinner dolphins and the humpback whales. Many people are drawn to have contact with these cetaceans without fully grasping the significance of it. All they know is they love them, and they are following the joy in

---

[6] For additional information about some of the time/space pioneers, research the Internet for: Al Bielek, Duncan Cameron, Andrew D. Basiago, Bernard J. Mendez, Michael Relfe, Joseph McMoneagle, Henry Deacon (aka Arthur Neumann), Dan Burisch, Ingo Swan, Pat Price and Courtney Brown.

their hearts. The dolphins and whales have called them. That's all that matters.

Meanwhile the world of quantum physics [7] has been evolving with scientific, peer-reviewed studies backing the theories of multiple dimensions and parallel worlds, validating my continuing interest and research in the interactive, holographic science of the cetaceans.

The Humpback Whales Speak of Unity Consciousness

The humpback whales have clearly explained multi-dimensional living, referring to it as "multiplex consciousness."

According to the whales:

> *"Within multiplex consciousness is all the accumulated wisdom and knowledge of every life form that has contributed to it. And yet within this unification, the choice of individuality and detachment is still honored and respected. It is your choice to live within unity consciousness or separation.*
>
> *Unity consciousness is also known by you as Love. It is a link-up that is more than telepathy. It is telepathy that includes resonance and empathy. As someone who serves as a counselor you know the experience of empathy to be feeling the feelings of another and resonating with their energy field.*
>
> *We whales understand that our physical bodies are composed of energy or light, formed by Mind. There is no significant difference between energy and physical matter. What is matter? It is coalesced light. Your physicists are now beginning to accept, that we are much more than our physical bodies, we are bodies of light and that light is one with the totality of all that is.*
>
> *As we perceive your future along your evolutionary timeline, we see you fully realizing and manifesting bodies that are photomorphic, i.e. light bodies.*
>
> *"The resonance and expression of Love is the active power that catapults you into higher and higher realms of light. Love is the frequency propelling evolution."*

---

[7] Many physicists believe that we live in a multi-verse that exists simultaneously with our present identified reality. We are vibrating waves, and these waves vibrate and then split apart with time. In quantum physics, there are parallel universes surrounding us. To enter them we need to vibrate in unison with them.

We Are Light

The whales speak about physics. Physics is known as the study of matter and its motion through space and time, along with related concepts such as energy and force and how they behave in the universe.

The whales have a more advanced understanding of an expanded physics that is inter-dimensional. It is available to you, once you go beyond the parameters of linear, earth-based science, biology, technology, mathematics, time and space. It is sometimes identified as "hyper-dimensional physics."

The whales have communicated this:

> *"Your scientists are now beginning to evaluate and quantify your mind energy. It relates to the most recent scientific studies which recognize the influence of consciousness. It is consciousness that holds sub-atomic particles together. The researchers are learning to precisely move and direct particles via the Mind creating new atomic structures. This new science is what we whales call Molecular Geometry. Within this science we understand the composition of atoms in relation to higher dimensional physics."*

The Science of Molecular Geometry follows advanced laws of physics with different mathematics, substances, measurements and consequences. Some of this new physics has been shared with the human race from benevolent civilizations that live light years away. As this information trickles down to us, some of it is being released into the minds and hearts of scientists endorsing humanitarian goals with integrity and cosmic knowledge.

The whales have named it Molecular Geometry, while German Physicist Fritz-Albert Popp, PhD[8] has named it Molecular Biology.

---

[8] Dr. Fritz-Albert Popp was born in 1938 in Frankfurt. His first diploma was in Experimental Physics (1966, University Würzburg), followed by the Röntgen-Prize of the University Würzburg, PH.D. in Theoretical Physics (1969, University Mainz). Prof. Popp rediscovered and made the first extensive physical analysis of "Biophotons" founding the company "Biophotonics." Popp is the founder of the International Institute of Biophysics in Neuss, Germany, an international network of 19 research groups from 13 countries involved in biophoton research and coherence systems in biology. Prof. Popp has been an Honorary Professor at Universities in Germany, China, USA and India. Popp has published over 150

Recently he learned in his studies of living cells that our cellular structure is composed of light. Physicist Popp found that these cells store and release photons.[9] He has been quoted as saying: "We now know, today, that man is essentially a being of light." Dr. Popp coined the term "Biophotons" to differentiate the astounding implications of ordinary light versus Biophotonic Light or what others call "higher dimensional light." Living DNA communicates with other DNA in the body via these biophotons, which have the capability of communicating to other bodies, and even other life forms. In fact Dr. Popp has determined that DNA can send out a wide range of frequencies in all directions. It seems that DNA is the "master tuning fork of the whole body."

Using the Light of Love to Assist the Earth

I wondered, what does this mean about our potential to use our living DNA, the "light of love," to assist the earth and humanity, and civilizations beyond our own?

The dolphins told me in 1991 that there were at least five types of readily-available resources that the human race was not using yet. These five natural energies and higher-consciousness realities would be of great benefit for the earth: hydrogen as used by the Sun with the waste product being water; anti-gravity researched with a revision to our current laws of gravity; cold fusion; bubbles, as in "bubble universes;" and pod mind or group mind. They told me the greatest power on the earth was that of group mind, the power of people to come together and use their minds with empathic love and common intention to effect positive changes on earth, creating beneficent societies.

I believe we are now witnessing the evolution of humanitarian intentions, as people worldwide choose to befriend those who were once thought to be our adversaries. Many people around the globe are

---

research papers on questions of theoretical physics and biology, complementary medicine and biophotons.

[9] A photon is an elementary particle, the quantum of light and all other forms of electromagnetic radiation, and the force carrier for the electromagnetic force, even when static via virtual photons. The effects of this force are easily observable at both the microscopic and macroscopic level, because the photon has zero rest mass; this allows long distance interactions. Like all elementary particles, photons are currently best explained by quantum mechanics and exhibit wave–particle duality, exhibiting properties of both waves and particles.

acknowledging our commonality and our relatedness to other humans. One of the new scientists in the field, reflecting the reality of this process, is Russian biophysicist and molecular biologist Dr. Pjotr Garjajev.[10] He believes that human DNA operates as if it is a biological internet, superior to our familiar, artificial Internet. "Researchers think that if humans with full individuality would regain group consciousness, they would have godlike power to create, alter and shape things on Earth," says Dr. Garjajev.

Once we, as a planet, come into our integrity as a loving and kind people, we will be resonating with the innate frequency of love. Resonating positive attitudes, thoughts and behaviors draws to us a reality in kind, that reflects and sends out that same balanced, compassionate frequency to the world. Within this mind-set of global empathy, war will be impossible.

This is what the dolphins are telling us, and this is what scientists and physicists are now learning as well. We already have within us the capability of being godlike: kind, compassionate, wise, loving, all-knowing and multi-dimensional.

As the whales explained it to me:

"There is only One Mind, working for us. The dolphins are very, very much in tune with that mind. They are, and you will also be. They know that it is very hard for you to say that there are creatures on your planet

---

[10] Russian biophysicist and molecular biologist Pjotr Garjajev and his colleagues have been carrying out cutting-edge research regarding the more esoteric nature of DNA. They simply do not believe that 90% of our DNA is "junk DNA" that is discarded. From the German book, *Vernetzte Intelligenz*, by Grazyna Fosar and Franz Bludorf (summarized and translated by Baerbel): "The latest research explains phenomena such as clairvoyance, intuition, spontaneous and remote acts of healing, self healing, affirmation techniques, unusual light-auras around people (namely spiritual masters), mind's influence on weather-patterns and much more. The Russian scientists also found that our DNA can cause disturbing patterns in the vacuum, thus producing magnetized stargates! These are Wormholes that are tunnel connections between entirely different areas in the universe through which information can be transmitted outside of space and time. The DNA attracts these bits of information and passes them on to our consciousness. *What we are seeing here is 'Hyper-communication', where information is passed inter-dimensionally. It is as though the DNA acts as a 'Stargate' between this dimension and others.*" In the book there are several stories of how this information is downloaded via DNA.

that you may view as higher forms of life. We do not see it that way, because we see all life as inseparable. That would be hard for your people to accept. Nevertheless, the dolphins have progressed beyond you in their specialty. You have clearly progressed beyond them, in your technologies.

"The dolphins are explorers. It could be said that they spend all their time in unification, deep meditation, or what you would call dreaming, or imagination, or visualization.

"They do all of this and much more, because mind does not end with the body. Mind does not end at the perimeter called species, or even at the family levels, or even at a planetary level. You must think without limitation, when you think of mind.

"Your species is finally coming to know that our little sisters and brothers, the dolphins, are intelligent and wise. As you begin to understand this, they will begin to increase their communications with you. Your languages are familiar to our minds. We have only one language, but its complexity is at such a level that your civilization is not able to decipher it, at present.

"In time, you will develop the wisdom and technology needed to decipher this language. Then you will understand what we are saying. This is our song; this is also our way, our communication with our community. We are not separate. The dolphins are a part of us, as much as you consider your fingers or ears, to be a part of you. Or perhaps, more correctly to say, they are a part of our body. They provide us with playfulness and joy.

"The dolphins are the very incarnation of purity, innocence, joy, and love. But they are also encapsulated temporarily, as we all are, in physical bodies. This is the way we function. This is the way we grow, by creating a distinction between self and others; however much of that distinction is illusion. We use it to work out what we are and finally, upon discovering who we are, we are willing to let go of who we are.

"It takes a long time for this evolutionary process from psyche and soul, to full identification with Spirit. First, we believe in separation. Then, we believe in unification. And then, we give up the idea of self altogether; we then realize that all draw from the common pool. Here, there is no fear and there is no credit; but there is also no blame. Here, there is no death, but only the continuity of life. This is a life that is deathless because it is not physical.

"The dolphins have developed a circuit, or circle, of light-mind, that is specific to them alone. It is their frequency, and when they attune to it, they leave the physical planet as the ultimate reality, whenever they choose to. They leave the world in the same way that mystics, of all species throughout the universe, leave behind their personal world, in order to embrace the greater universe, the cosmos as a whole.

"We do not leave the world because of problems. We seek to solve them. We would not be doing this work today, at this moment, if there were no hope for all our species to join together in unity, joy, and wholeness. We must begin with words. It is, however, a primitive way of sharing.

"Your words rarely express the essence, but words can lead you to where the essence lies in your heart. When you know that, words will be optional; they will no longer matter.

"We whales are living ideas coming forth from deep levels within the unconscious. It may be strange for you to think of living ideas, because you believe that ideas come forth in the brain of a person. But ideas can have a life of their own. They can be living entities. When ideas coalesce within a matrix of love, honor, honesty, truth, integrity, peace and joy, those ideas are a reflection of the Source. When this occurs, this is really not called 'channeling'. It can better be described as an opening of universal vision, a transparency of your mind that allows the higher mind to shine through. At that point, there is no desire to manipulate or forcefully change outcomes. Instead there is a flow, a release, and a letting go. There is no desire to control, and in fact, all the desires disappear except for the desire of love. Everything in your life becomes a way to glorify the One; because you realize that you don't need to do anything; the Spirit of Love does all things."

The Spirit of Love is what inspired the profoundly dedicated lives of the three people I honor in the beginning of this chapter; Carl R. Rogers, John C. Lilly and Jean-Luc Bozzoli. Their passion and humanistic goals have helped educate and uplift the world. They have each produced deeply inspiring work, but their greatest gift to humanity, conveyed through their enthusiasm and expressed through their spirit, has been their ability to share universal visions. This is what we can do as well when we mirror the qualities of the cetaceans in their natural habitat and shine unconditional love from our hearts, out to the world. We are privileged to have the dolphins and whales in our lives and present on our planet during this extraordinary time of positive transformation; as our earth spirals into higher, refined dimensions with all of us aboard.

93

These messages and many more freely given by the whales are excerpts from a book soon to be published by Joan Ocean.

Joan Ocean is one of the nation's leading researchers in the field of dolphin and whale behavior and communication. She is co-founder with Jean-Luc Bozzoli of Dolphin Connection International, based in Hawaii since 1984.

An author and video producer, Ms Ocean's internationally acclaimed books have been published in ten languages. With a Master of Science degree in Counseling Psychology, Ms Ocean is a scientist and a psychologist who creates safe environments for human-cetacean contacts. For the past thirty years she has traveled to oceans and rivers in the world swimming among 28 different species of dolphins and whales. Ms Ocean is the originator of international human-cetacean Ocean Swim Programs, providing safe passage, educational seminars and deep communication between humans, dolphins and whales. Studying cetaceans through respectful interactions with them in their natural habitat, Joan has been welcomed into their pods. She experiences their sonar and sound frequencies as acoustic images and reverberating tones, which are directed to swimmers; releasing blocked energy, correcting imbalances and enhancing human potentials. In addition she has recorded the multiplex sounds of the cetaceans that create a field of harmony in the water and impart a sense of well-being and joy among swimmers and conceivably all sea life.

In 1988 she initiated her present on-going relationship with more than 200 highly intelligent Spinner dolphins in Hawaii and subsequently, with the Humpback whales of the Caribbean, She understands that the cetaceans have profound wisdom to share with the human race.

Ms Ocean is the mother of three children, and has seven grandchildren who enjoy swimming among the dolphins and visiting the horses and donkeys at their grandmother's ranch on the Big Island of Hawaii.

Joan Ocean can be contacted through the Dolphin Connection website: www.joanocean.com

Dolphin Connection - P.O. Box 102 - Captain Cook, Hawaii 96704

Phone: (808) 323-8000 - Email: joan@joanocean.com

Chapter 8: *The Golden Dolphin Avatars – You Swimming in the Air*

By Nina Brown

"There is a need for sensitive humans
to interact with the cetaceans and bring
(ancient memories and advanced technical knowledge)
to the populace in a manner that will ensure acceptance."
Cetaceans through Joan Ocean

Who are the Golden Dolphin Avatars, ambassadors of the cetacean nation?

We are.

We are golden dolphins who have come back to planet earth to create, anchor, nourish and grow the Golden Age of Divine Love. Whether you consciously "know" it or not, you are this energy, and we are even more. We are sovereign beings expressing as golden dolphins, as divine humans and as individuated consciousness. There is an aspect of you that is a golden dolphin wishing to be fully integrated into your wholeness to assist you and all star seeds who returned from the stars to anchor the next golden age, the new ways to be on earth. The golden ages of Atlantis and Egypt were not anchored, only created—and then they vanished. They were created and seeded, but it was not time for the roots to take hold into the earth...so those seed pods floated around and floated around until now—the time of planting. We have collectively returned to complete the mission, but this time to recreate, anchor, root, nourish and grow the Golden Age of Divine Love. We will do this successfully with the assistance of the Golden Dolphin Avatars—an aspect of you and me.

How did this awareness come to be?

The full return of the golden dolphin energy occurred June 6, 2012, but the story begins way before that with tales from the Dogon tribe in Africa and more recently by the *Legend of the Golden Dolphin* received by Peter Shenstone, in 1976.[11]

Dolphin Legends and Lore with Clues of Truth

The stories connecting humans to cetaceans span many cultures and continents from the Mirning people, an aboriginal tribe of South Australia, to the Dogon, who currently live in sub-Saharan Africa in the nation of Mali. This information from the Dogon tribe was presented in 1976 through Robert Temple's extraordinary book *The Sirius Mystery,* which has been both believed and discredited.

"The Dogon tell of star beings in the shape of whales, who came to earth to swim in the sea. They came in tall starships with flames on the bottom. Named the Nommo, or Nommo Dié, these star whales created children to live on the land to be their family. Called Ogo, these children began to forget their origins. In time, Ogo became Ogo Anagonno, 'the one who introduces disorder to the Universe,' 'the one who forgets.' "[12]

On a different continent, in a more current time period, the cetaceans Nommo and Ogo appeared again in the writings of Peter

---

[11] The original story of the legend has been described by Scott Taylor and can be seen at http://dolphintale.com/Legendbackground.html (From the article "Our Father...who art in water?," *Simply Living*, issue number 12, 1980, Avalon NSW, Australia).

[12] *Souls in The Sea, Dolphins, Whales, and Human Destiny*, Scott Taylor, Frog, Ltd. Berkeley, California, 2003, p. 46.

Shenstone. In 1976 while living in Sydney, Australia, Peter wrote: "I watched half in awe, half in horror as my hand picked up a pencil lying nearby and began to write at a furious pace. The writing kept going until dawn, and continued every night for almost two weeks, pouring out an incredible fantasy/story about the impending tribulation and concurrent transformation of human consciousness, the role which the cetaceans will play in those events, and my specific job as their messenger. I was told this would form the seed of a new global tribe of dolphin dreamers, a tribal gathering that will transcend the old barriers of race, creed, colour, ego, fear and alienation to become the new leaderless Aquarian network of free beings..."

"We have to begun (sic) to live a legend, the legend of the golden dolphin, which simply represents the spirit of freedom, our guide through the reefs of time. Every being who enters into the dolphin tribal adventure brings their own unique contribution, and thus the legend grows, and grows....and the dream of a perfect family, a perfect brother— and sisterhood, a perfect life in harmony with each other and the world, a perfect human-dolphin tribe draws near. Our only job on the planet now is to spread the word about dolphin dreaming and as that dream grips the human imagination, the world will turn."

Here are brief selections from the legend as received by Peter Shenstone and transcribed by Scott Taylor.[13]

It is the Time of the End of the System of Things,
the Great Tribulation... the cusp of AQUARIUS!
The beautiful blue-water world of Oceania is
dominated by the two space races:
The NOMMO, "Master-of-the-Waters,"
And OGO, Man who subjugates the islands
which dot a quarter of the planet's surface.
OGO has discovered the god-energy
of destruction... and seems intent
upon destroying the water-world
he arrogantly calls Earth!
The amphibious NOMMO came to
Oceania from the star system SIRIUS

---

[13] *Souls in the Sea: Dolphins, Whales, and Human Destiny*, Frog, Ltd., Berkeley, CA, 2003, pp. 256 - 258.

many millions of years ago.
They then evolved fingers and feet into
flippers and flukes the better to appreciate
their new watery paradise...
OGO, arch-killer, has unleashed a
merciless attack on the NOMMO,
driving them towards extinction!
Now they have only their minds and their music,
the power of their Dreaming, with which to combat
OGO's terminal threat to the planet's existence.
But their Dream-plan is daringly simple:
To reCreate Heaven on Earth
before OGO vaporizes Her!
And build a new New World
under the new Aquarian heaven.
Mankind is an unbalanced, spiritually
immature race dominated by its brute,
killer nature. The only way NOMMO
can save themselves and their beautiful
blue-water world (and indeed Mankind itself!)
is to tap Man's loving feminine potential,
and liberate the human Spirit.
Time and time again for thousands of years, the
    NOMMO
connected with OGO planting the seed of civilization,
a process intended to "conquer the beast in OGO-
    Man."
In India and Sumeria, the so-called Cradle of
    Civilization,
contact was made, and was repeated throughout the
    lands
bordering the Great Sea.
Each time the NOMMO simply offered themselves in
    loving
friendship, leaving behind nothing but an image of
    goodness in
the myths and legends of OGO-Man.
And the promise of things to come!

"WE ARE NOMMO
WE COME IN PEACE TO SPEAK TRUTH.
AND DECLARE IMAGE WAR ON OGO, Animal
  Man."
Scattered among the OGO's
  are the resurrected souls of
  an invasion force of NOMMO
  Image Warriors, sacrificed in the
  holocaust OGO wrought upon
  the planet in his quest for power
  and possessions... reincarnated now
  in OGO-form to infiltrate and
  guide the barbarous OGO masses
  into the Oceanic future...
The Time draws near for the
  gathering of these Freedom-loving
  NOMMO-souls..., in preparation
  for the final battle of the Image War
  between NOMMO's Dream and OGO's Nightmare.
Australia... Island of Dreamers and Dreams,
  Green—and Gold jewel, never quite what it seems.
  Set in the midst of an ocean of Space,
  Aquarian Ark for the whole human race.
On the Boomerang tip ancient Mount Warning
  Is first to reflect the light of the dawning
  Outback in the Centre, Uluru, Ayer's Rock of Ages,
  The hub of the world is calling the sages.
Australia... an Isle where The Spirit can roam
  Free as The Wind to the wild dolphins' home.
  To the Monkey Mia at The End of the Earth,
  Where the promised Family will find its rebirth.
Here in Australia at The Time of the End
  Awaits welcome reunion with a long-lost friend.
  For the Great ancient Whales are NOMMO of old,
  and Freedom lies in a Dolphin of Gold.
 - Peter Shenstone, *Legend of the Golden Dolphin*

101

Scott Taylor adds a few additional comments to "The Legend of the Golden Dolphin:"

"I have added the name Uluru to the legend in recognition of the Aboriginal connection to this sacred site, a name not in common use in 1976. I wish also to briefly elaborate on the Nommo and Ogo. These terms can be confusing to anyone who has not heard some of the Legend directly, or read my book or studied the Dogon materials. The Nommo include both the Whales and the Dolphins, and Ogo is of two types: Ogo as typical human, still unbalanced, overtaken by the dark half of human nature (Ogo Anagonno), and Ogo reborn (Ogo Titiyayne, the Rainbow People at the end of time). Ogo Titiyayne, in the Dogon mythology, describe the reincarnated souls of Nommo, sacrificed by humans over the centuries, who now embody the Delphic Wave, bringers of Peace and Freedom (the Ambassadors of the Cetacean Nation)."

Once I was well on the path of being a messenger for the Golden Dolphin Avatars, I found that information served to verify what I had intuitively known.

The Messages: Swim in the Air

The term golden dolphin was introduced to me in 2007 by James F. Jereb, Ph.D, who told me they swim in the air at Stardreaming (www.stardreaming.org). I have come to understand what James was sharing with me. I, as a golden dolphin, would swim with ease and grace through life's experiences knowing myself to be a sovereign being. That, however, was all I knew at the time until I became a messenger for the golden dolphins on October 10, 2010 (10/10/10) at a conference of Earth-Keepers (www.earth-keeper.com) in Arkansas. Before I could share the channels that were to come through me on a regular basis, I had to embrace and declare my human divinity, which I have come to know as the principle message of the Golden Dolphin Avatars.

The path to that expression was difficult and taxed my physical, emotional and spiritual bodies. My ego personality struggled to maintain the status quo while my divine aspects called to me to expand beyond all that I had known and experienced. Agony was meeting ecstasy, the ultimate experience of duality. As the root of my fears, anxieties and doubts surfaced, I questioned if this path was the right choice for me. Many healers came to soothe me, wipe away my tears or to encourage me. One wise friend said that if I said, "No" the universe had a "plan B," and someone else would be chosen by the multi-dimensional field. An internal force, an innate knowing, was driving me forward. It was not the desire to be courageous but a deep knowing that this was the path to choose. So I said, "Yes" and allowed the flow of events to teach me how to swim in the air and into an expanded expression of me as a divine human.

On October 10, 2010, with all the inner strength that I could muster, I stood in front of four hundred plus people, most of whom were strangers from all parts of the globe, and declared my divinity—aloud. I then said that I knew who those in the audience were as well—divine humans. As I stood taller and more firmly in my new skin, the first message from the Golden Dolphin Avatars came through.

> *"Welcome, dear one, to a new adventure, which will express your pure consciousness in a way that will serve humanity during these months of shifting. There will be fear and anxiety. You will bring calm and an answer to many for the question, 'Why?' You know the answers, and we will speak clearly through you in your language so that all will understand on a subconscious level. You already have clear ideas of how you wish these upcoming numerous channels to be transmitted and the definition of humanity's message. We heard you, we are you, you see. It is the highest vibration of your higher self, the one that you can actually hear that is coming forth now presenting itself in a new format. The you that is a golden dolphin is the highest frequency that you manifest, that of purity, of crystalline clarity. This is about what you will speak. This is what others will wish to emulate. You will be speaking from your highest vibration of mastery. You will be writing from your highest level of mastery. This is the time, now that the stretching of Mother Earth is so prominent. There are many who need your calm, your wisdom to give them balance, to reassure them that they are the creators of this global change. The heavens rejoice that you have said, 'Yes' to the call. This is a call not only from Archangel Metatron but of Melchizedek, of Sanat Kumara, of the entire Cosmic Council of Light, of the Galactic Federation, of the Syrian-Pleiadian Alliance, of all of your lifetimes. Do you comprehend the vital nature of you?*
>
> *With our deep love,*
>
> *The Golden Dolphin Avatars"*

The messages were consistent and simple:

"It is no longer necessary to look outside of one's own self. Truly all the answers are contained in you, for you are divinity expressing in human form. Many talk about this concept, but the time is now for thought, love and action to fully express the concept, no longer existing as a concept, but being expressed as a knowing. That is the difference. We will continue to share these insights with you often repeating the same message, for there have been thousands of years of forgetting and the remembering will take repetition and practice.

The ancient wisdom will always be about the divinity that you are. There have been so many who have told you otherwise, but we are here now to share our truth with you, for we have been with you since the beginning of time. We tell you that the gold vibration that we are is you. The pure gold vibration of your divinity is who you are here on planet earth. We ask you to remember that frequency that has been long cloaked."

As the messages were beginning to come through me regularly, I got a call from James Tyberonn (Tyb), messenger for Archangel Metatron. He said, "I have been nudged by Archangel Metatron all week to call you, but I am not sure why."

He knew that he was to encourage me to write for *Sedona Journal of Emergence*, to do webinars and write a newsletter, but there was more.

"What would I write about?" was my question.

Then I told Tyb that I had been planning to initiate something that would be called a "Gathering of Golden Dolphins." I had identified a location, The Bishop's Lodge Ranch Resort and Spa in Santa Fe, New Mexico. I told him that the first gathering was scheduled for Sunday, June 5, 2011 from 1:00 to 4:00 p.m.

"That's it." said Tyb.

He immediately began channeling over the phone. Through Tyb, I was told by Archangel Metatron that my work was to present and anchor the golden dolphin energy on the planet and that my message would take off like wildfire. What was so curious was that Tyb only knew the framework. The messages from the Golden Dolphin Avatars that had been flowing through me were what fit in the frame.

I felt a sense of enormity about the upcoming gathering, so I got to work creating a website, a newsletter and arranged for live-streaming for the first Gathering of Golden Dolphins. My ego personality expected that maybe twenty people would show up, however the magic began. Tyb received a message from Archangel Metatron, and it was broadcast to thousands and thousands of people around the globe the day before the gathering at Bishop's Lodge.

Archangel Metatron stated that the cetaceans were on the earth before humanity and even before duality. Golden dolphins are avatar dolphins who have an enormous auric field of pure golden crystalline light, that of pure unconditional love. They have been anchoring the light in the waters of the oceans, which carries a message of joy, freedom, play and unconditional love. This golden dolphin energy is within each one of us. The golden dolphins are reminding humankind to remember our inner divinity, who we truly are. They are highly evolved beings whose energy is returning to the planet from their ancient and timeless lineage. Metatron shared that the golden dolphins are returning, the golden dolphin is YOU! I was learning to master swimming in the air...or naturally flowing with great ease from experience to experience.

Perhaps for the first time, thousands of planetary golden dolphins around the planet heard this message and at the same time learned that the first Gathering of Golden Dolphins was to occur the next day in Santa Fe. The magic of the universe was definitely manifesting.

Bishop's Lodge had been instructed to arrange the large "Thunderbird Room" with a circle of thirty chairs. It never occurred to me that we would need many more chairs! What transpired was that sixty people showed up in the physical, three hundred connected via live-stream, and 1,500 people accessed my website that Sunday afternoon. Why? People around the planet are hungry to come together in a safe space to declare their human divinity.

The message of the Golden Dolphin Avatars expanded, as we met the first Sunday of each month to "create pods around the planet." And so it came to be. Pods formed across the United States and in many countries such as the Netherlands and South Africa. As I traveled with the Earth-Keepers, we had gatherings on the Giza Plateau in Egypt and even Jerusalem, Israel, on the roof of the Church of the Holy Sepulcher. The basic message was always the same, "Know thyself as divine, have self-love, live in the *now* and live by the Expanded Golden Rule (Do unto all creation what you would have all of creation do unto you)."

Golden Dolphins Messages to Activate the Golden Matrix of Human Divinity

On November, 11, 2011 (11/11/11), again in Arkansas, I presented a new message from the Golden Dolphin Avatars.

"Gold is a frequency that will be important to the pods going forward, for it has been upshifted and no longer carries the lower vibration of duality. It will be imaged in our likeness and will carry with it the sounds as well as the light that we are. Know that as these new upshifted gold, golden dolphin images move throughout the expanding pods, that they will be more than ornaments, more than jewelry. They will be the carriers, the transmitters of the Christ consciousness, pure love and light vibration that will be the physical carrier of our frequency."

The message spoke about a gold matrix that had been created in the multi-dimensional field as a super conductive communication system to connect the coherent intention of all of those present. Periapts of Golden Dolphins were inspired by the Golden Dolphin Avatars and created by their chosen goldsmith to be generator and transmitter points in an etheric gold matrix that was set in place on November 11, 2011. A select group of individuals around the planet became the custodians of the twenty-two carat gold images and thousands of others received the same image in the etheric. This gold matrix was put in place to assist us in coming together to dream the new earth into reality.

"The images, by means of harmonic oscillation, will affect the frequency of those to whom they come in contact. They will be directly connected to us. We will be transmitting through these images our sonar sounds that will have an undetectable pulse that will resonate with the carrier. That sonar sound, joined with the intention of the carrier, will be a transmitter for our messages. We can communicate by means of the metal gold, which has universal communication properties."

Another pivotal event occurred at that gathering in Arkansas. I merged with my golden dolphin aspect becoming a more expanded consciousness than the two separate parts. The union occurred when I was in a private session with the ancient crystal skull, MAX. The gold

Periapt of Golden Dolphin was around my neck. I felt an energy exchange between me and MAX and a knowing overcame me. I had accepted and been accepted by my golden dolphin aspect and in that coming together I had an expanded awareness of my sovereignty. I was forever changed.

With the gold matrix in place, human divinity being accepted and expressed and the merging of each one present with their golden dolphin aspect, all was in place for the full expression of the golden dolphin energy to return and anchor on planet earth. Archangel Metatron, through James Tyberonn, transmitted the message that this event would occur almost exactly one year to the day that the first Gathering of Golden Dolphins occurred in Santa Fe, New Mexico.

June 6, 2012, was a day of great significance. It was the day after the Venus Transit and the exact day when the golden dolphin energy was to be fully anchored on the planet. A global broadcast was arranged at which time, I read a section of the *Legend of the Golden Dolphin*. Another amazing thing that transpired was the emergence of ambassadors of the golden dolphin energy. No longer was I to be the predominant messenger, now the thousands of people across the planet who had embraced their golden dolphin aspect were being encouraged to not only create pods but to speak the messages of the Golden Dolphins Avatars.

> *"In only one year, you are at a point where we wish to grant you our full energy removing the veils, giving you the power, the courage to stand boldly in place and say, 'I accept this mission.' We say to you, 'Do not do it alone.' Swim in a pod in the bio-plasma that surrounds you. Swim in a pod so that courageously you can hold each other's hands. Use the gold matrix that has been created as a web to connect each one of you to the other telepathically and each one of you to us. Reach out for support. Be the ambassador of the dolphin golden consciousness."*

Each message that followed, that was transferred through me, reinforced the shift that was being requested. I was to step back and allow others to join me in an intimate relationship with the Golden Dolphin Avatars. My last submission from the Golden Dolphins to *Sedona Journal of Emergence* was December, 2012. My last channel was on December 21, 2012. All of the messages are currently archived in a new website, (ninabrown33.com). I had completed my tasks. I AM swimming in the air! I swam into a new form quite gracefully. With the messages from the golden dolphins, I opened the gate, greeted everyone, explained a few key concepts and then stepped back to allow others to flow where they were guided. This is a new style of leadership. I do not wish to or want to control. We are each sovereign beings. We each have the universal hologram of full knowing. I now wish to empower the remembering and to receive sparks of remembering from other sovereign beings. This is the new paradigm, the new earth.

"In this state of being, which can only exist in the moment of now, the events and the experiences that you have chosen for your path begin to realign and your identity shifts from the ego state, living in the past and the future, to your wholeness being present in the moment. This is to be a sovereign being, beloveds. The planet is moving into a new energy, into new dimensions, and the old way of being no longer serves you. You have moved beyond the limitations of ego self, into divine human and now you are expanding into that of a sovereign being.

As a sovereign being totally self-realized, you shift your relationship with others and the planet. Love becomes the relationship with all of creation. Then it is with ease and grace that you will greet your neighbors, for the knowing is deep within that all of your neighbors are sovereign as are you, an individual aspect of All That Is. This message comes to you today on the full moon, for the fullness of the moon is the metaphor for the full understanding and knowing now of who you are.

As you step across the threshold from the end of one cycle into the beginning of a new cycle, we ask that you do so wearing the golden mantle of your sovereignty. At that moment you will walk into an expanded universe of the divine Creator's eternal creation. You will see the smallest particle as you. You will see the stranger, who appears to be expressing foreign characteristics, as you. And then, ambassador, you will be in right relationship not only with self and your planetary neighbors, but you will be poised to greet your galactic neighbors as you as well. This is the next evolution of awareness, and it begins as the threshold is crossed.

The universe and the universes await you. They await planet earth, but arms are outstretched only to receive love. To accomplish this, ambassadors you must know who you are. You must love yourself, and you must live in the eternal now. This is the beginning of the new earth, the Golden Age of Divine Love."

Final Message: Our Remembered Wisdom

In the new paradigm, the new 26,000-year cycle, much is unfolding as we dream the new earth. For me, the new is that I have accepted my sovereignty, as was originally requested by the Golden Dolphin Avatars. As a sovereign being, the words that I express are from my wholeness, my human divinity. Inspired by the Golden Dolphin Avatars, I refer to this as S.T.A.R.[14] Wisdom. My intention is that what flows through me is no longer the occasional message, but the remembered wisdom of the universe that is who I am. The Golden Dolphin Avatars gifted me with this knowing and empowered me with the remembering that we are ALL divine humans, and now we are safe to proclaim our sovereignty. Each day I find evidence that more and more people are awakening to this remembered wisdom.

---

[14] Acronym for surrender, trust, allow & receive.

Nina Brown, a *cum laude* graduate of Bryn Mawr College, is retired from a successful career as President of a company she formed to assist women in establishing business enterprises.

From there, Nina acted as a consultant and leader in the field of alternative medicine, collaborating to form a company to bring neurosensory diagnostic tools to injured veterans who suffered brain impairment in the Gulf and Vietnam.

Nina has been acknowledged for her pioneer work. In 1995, she was appointed by President William Clinton to represent him at the White House Conference on Small Business. The next year, she was chosen as a Charter Member of Pennsylvania's Best 50 Women in Business.

Between 1990 and 1996, she was published in the *Philadelphia Tribune Magazine, Women Lawyers Journal* as well as being featured in *U.S. News & World Report, Money Magazine, Inc. Magazine, Business Week, Venture Capital Journal* and was on the cover of *Business Philadelphia.*

Speaking engagements include US House of Representatives Field Hearings, Pennsylvania Department of Commerce, the League of Cities Women's Caucus, Wharton Executive MBA Reunion, and keynote speaker for the Entrepreneurial Women's Expo.

Nina Brown has been published in *Kindred Spirit, Inner Tapestry* and *Sedona Journal of Emergence.* She is the award-winning author of *Return of Love to Planet Earth: Memoir of a Reluctant Visionary* (Cauda Pavonis, 2010, 2011) Upon publication, Nina began attending to being a messenger for the Golden Golden Avatars and the birth of Golden Dolphin pods all over the world to spread the message "Know thyself as divine."

Brown then focused on the creation and expansion of the S.T.A.R. clinic. a multi-dimensional tool to assist others in awakening to their human divinity, based on the principles of surrender, trust, allow and receive. She currently lectures and consults on her newest book, *S.T.A.R. Philosophy* and is co-authoring with Kristy Sweetland its facilitator's guide, *S.T.A.R. Philosophy Fascinated Observer's Guide* (gatherinsight.com). Contact: nina@ninabrown33.com / www.ninabrown33.com / www.facebook.com/ninabrownSTAR/

Chapter 9: *Awakening the Dolphin Within*

By Debbie Takara Shelor

"Well I was born in the sign of water
And it's there that I feel my best
The albatross and the whales
They are my brothers"
~ From Cool Change by Glenn Barrie Shorrock

Twenty years ago I experienced a spiritual awakening. Like most people, it occurred amidst severe emotional trauma.

The pharmaceutical company I worked for had gone through a radical lay off and restructuring. Many of my closest friends in management had been let go. Those of us who remained were reassigned to positions we may or may not like. Personally, I hated my new assignment as front-line supervisor in liquids manufacturing.

I had observed front-line supervisors for several years and the situations they dealt with every day on the job. I watched as petty complaints, bickering, and back-stabbing occurred within and between work teams. I likened the position to babysitting, another activity I never cared for. I had no desire to work with adults who often acted like children. Yet, that is where I found myself.

Soon the company decided to implement a plant-wide software program to track production, inventories, shipments, and other things. With my engineering background and my new knowledge of "the floor," I was made part of the core implementation team. It was a train wreck waiting to happen.

The stress involved was simply more than I could handle. When the system went live, my name was paged over the intercom about once every five minutes. I ran from one data entry disaster to another all day long. There would sometimes be three or four people standing in line waiting to ask me questions. Every decision I made affected the company's bottom line for the day. One day an employee pulled me aside and asked if I was OK. He said I looked like I had aged 10 years in the past year. Sadly, when I looked in the mirror that evening, I had to agree.

Eventually I cracked.

I woke up one morning not feeling well and called in sick. Next thing I knew, I was on the floor in the fetal position remembering being raped. The images were so vivid; it was as if it were still happening. I could see and feel his body and even smell his breath. I found it exceedingly repulsive. I was nauseous and could barely move. I was 33 years old and had never shed even one tear over the horrific experience I had the summer after graduating from high school. Fifteen years of denial is a bloody long time!

Soon I was seeing a psychiatrist and got a much-needed paid leave of absence from work. In talking through the situation, it was determined that the work restructuring had put me into a deep depression. Top that off with a position I hated and the severe stress of being in charge of the plant-wide computer program going live on the production floor, and I had the perfect stress-inducing cocktail for my suppressed rape memories to come flooding to the fore. The psychiatrist introduced me to journaling, which later lead to my career as a best-selling author.

Something quite wonderful happened as I journaled my way through the mountain of tears and anger I had been stuffing about the rape and every other emotional trauma I had ever experienced. It was as if a switch had been flipped inside and suddenly I had easy access to intuition. I began to simply "know" to go places and do things. The first intuitive "hit" I had was to visit a New Age bookstore and find something on "clearing." I was very uneasy about the first and had no idea what the second even meant.

I grew up in a very religious household. It was within that framework that I experienced my first Divine encounter. At the age of fourteen, I was literally engulfed in a powerful wave of divine energy (Shekinah). It wasn't imagined or some sort of hallucination since everyone present at the teen event saw the same Dove of Light descend from above and rest just above the alter in the sanctuary at the church I attended. The energy that came in felt like a tsunami that literally knocked people over, knocking them off their feet and rendering them speechless. Several minutes passed before we all came back to our senses. We were filled with great joy, and there was singing, dancing, and much laughter. I began speaking the powerful Language of Light for the very first time.

Suddenly I saw with new eyes and heard with new ears. I knew I had to leave the church because my direct experience of the Divine Presence was vastly different than what the church taught about who and what God is. I wandered around in metaphorical darkness for the next 15 years.

Even though I am primarily a spiritual creature, the comment from the Bible about "beware the soothsayers" had prevented me from learning much about other religions and definitely kept me away from new age spirituality, shamanism, and the like. There was a giant hole where the Divine was supposed to be in my life.

When I "woke up" by remembering the rape and felt prompted to visit a new age bookstore, I trusted that intuition. I was quite nervous and had no idea what I might find there. I picked out a couple of books and an audio called *Ocean Dreams* with beautiful music and real dolphin sounds. I found nothing on clearing. When I got to the counter to pay, there was a sign that read "energy clearing." I almost laughed out loud. I made an appointment and headed home to listen to my audio and journal some more.

At my appointment that evening, before the energy healing portion of the session began, the healing practitioner sat me down and asked me several questions. I realized as we were talking that in just 15 minutes this woman had asked me things that had me experiencing realizations that were vastly more relevant to who I am, what I needed, and the situation I was facing than I had experienced in five visits to the psychiatrist.

She had about 50 audiotapes (it was before the time of CDs) in an organizer hanging on the wall. She reached over, grabbed one, and put it in the player. When the music started, I was awestruck. It was the Ocean Dreams music by Dean Evenson that I had been listening to at home all day. She cleared my energy field using a beautiful fan of large bird feathers. She did all sorts of things around my body, sweeping the fan through my field and throwing out the icky energetic stuff that only she could see. I spent most of the session wondering how on earth she picked that music.

When the session was over, I asked her why she chose that particular cassette. She simply said, "It's the one I felt you needed." Even now that makes me cry.

This woman, this moment in time, was my doorway into a whole new world of information, philosophy, healing modalities, and people who operated by intuitive knowing, that I knew absolutely nothing about. And that world seemed significantly more relevant and helpful than the "normal" way that I had been lead to follow, believe, and trust my whole life.

Not long after that I saw an ad for the Body Mind Center in Reading, PA. The owners, Karen and Greg Schweitzer, had worked closely with Deepak Chopra at the Maharishi Center in Boston.

I soon became Karen's client and she introduced me to the exciting world of energy healing, past life regression, meditation, and much more. She became not only my first spiritual teacher, but also a very dear friend. She encouraged me to attend a nine-month Women's Wisdom training near Philly. She taught me the energy healing modality called Reiki. Her husband Greg became my first meditation teacher. Together she and I explored essential oils by attending classes for holistic nurse practitioners taught by world renowned aromatherapy expert, Dr. Jane Buckle. I didn't know it at the time, but all this training would become significant in the dolphin-related healing work I would be doing later on.

Another inner prompting I soon had was to explore Native American spirituality. I picked up a book about medicine wheels and built one in my extra bedroom. The first time I sat inside the wheel and meditated by "walking the wheel" in my mind, something truly extraordinary happened.

As I was communing with the energy of the South direction, I could see and sense, even feel the presence of Coyote, the trickster - keeper of the South in some traditions. The coyote in my meditation began running around in circles as if it was chasing its tail. I found myself laughing at his antics. Then he began to transform. I suddenly realized the coyote had morphed into a dolphin swimming in circles.

I cannot even begin to put into words the joy I felt, the tears I cried, or the changes that began taking place within me on every level because of this virtual dolphin experience. I felt that same wave of Divine energy surrounding and engulfing me as it had when I saw the dove in the sanctuary all those years before. It was nothing short of miraculous. After that first encounter, the floodgates opened and each time I closed my eyes in meditation, the dolphins would magically appear.

At first I just saw them in the distance. Later I could see and sense them much closer and even touch them in my imagination. Pretty soon I found myself bell-to-belly with a spinner dolphin, and the sensation was that of being torpedoed through the water spinning all the while. The spinning movement, coupled with the divine energetic presence I always felt engulfed by whenever I saw and sensed the dolphins, helped me let go of years of unshed tears and emotional pain.

I was a pretty wounded soul after experiencing rape, severe bullying in high school, numerous rejections by guys I'd fallen in love with, parents who always seemed to expect more than I could deliver, betrayal by someone I considered a dear friend, and the job restructuring that felt like a demotion. With Karen's continued support, guidance and healing methods, my practice of daily meditation and silent time in nature, as well as these full-sensory virtual "dolphin encounters," I was able to make giant strides in becoming happy and whole again. Whenever I felt the divine dolphin presence, it was as if the emotional wounds were being magically erased, and I was being put back in tune and alignment even at the deepest levels. It also became a doorway to higher wisdom and consciousness.

Intuition led me to Stuart Wilde's teachings and I attended his eight-day Warriors in the Mist training in the Sangre de Christo Mountains of New Mexico. It was an amazing experience, and I enjoyed several truly profound moments and breakthroughs while there. Anjou, one of the women in my group, was also very dolphin-connected. We developed a friendship, and she shared with me the story of Lolita, an orca from the northwest that had been captured and separated from her family when she was six years old, and enslaved by the dolphinarium entertainment industry. She was now at SeaAquarium Miami doing shows for tourists.

Something about Lolita's story grabbed me and just would not let go. I found myself thinking of her often, telling people her story, and writing articles about her in the health and nutrition newsletter I published monthly.

Eventually Anjou invited me to join her in the project to help Lolita. She was creating a compilation CD with tracks from famous musicians like Olivia Newton-John. After all the stress I had experienced at work and my new-found interest in Lolita, dolphins, and energy healing, the idea held great appeal. I left the security of my high-paying career in pharmaceuticals to move to San Juan Island to be near Lolita's family and co-found a non-profit for dolphins and whales.

I quickly developed the ability to "feel" when the orcas were near. I would be going about my day and suddenly simply "know." Jumping in the car and speeding across the island, I would quickly park and sprint to the top of my favorite hill. Within minutes I would be viewing an entire pod swimming past. Communing with them in this way, I began to understand who they are energetically. Orca energy is "bigger." There is a power, intensity, and vastness to it that their smaller dolphin kin do not possess.

Part of our adventure took us to Florida to meet Lolita. While others filed in to take their seats prior to her performance, we stood next to her tank. She swam over to where we stood and simply stopped. We gazed at one another for a very long time. I felt completely enveloped by such an immense sense of love. She felt like a long lost sister I never knew I had.

Periodically she would dip her head under the water, then come right back up and stare some more. Even though we couldn't communicate through words, a great deal was being communicated nonetheless. I promised her that I would be an Ambassador for the dolphins and whales, that I would share her story with the world, and encourage humanity to free cetaceans from captivity and themselves from their own self-inflicted prisons.

She never left that spot, continuing to stare, dip her head under, then stare some more, until the show began. She must have been behaving differently during the show, because her trainers kept saying things to one another as they looked and pointed in our direction.

Despite efforts by many organizations, Lolita remained captive. Anjou headed off to Hawaii. I moved to sunny southern California where I spent hours at the beach walking, meditating, watching the sea gulls and the occasional dolphin swimming past.

I soon met my future husband, and we moved to a home on Palomar Mountain in California. We lived in a very secluded location in the middle of the forest. Every day I sat out in my nature sanctuary surrounded by a circle of trees while listening to the birds, enjoying the wild flowers, and writing for hours. I lived in absolute bliss. I had a dear friend who lived a block from the beach in Carlsbad. Once a week, I spent the night at her home and enjoyed getting up early to commune with the ocean all day the next day. It was a truly glorious existence.

Even years later, whenever I visited the Southern California coast, even if I had been driving for days in order to get there, the dolphins would show up to greet me at whatever beach I was visiting within five minutes of my arrival.

We were about to leave Southern California to move to Toronto and I was inspired to take a weekend workshop in Santa Barbara with Star Riparetti of Star Flower Essences. I naively thought I was taking the class to then share the Andean Orchid Essences with my clients and customers.

David Jonas, a wonderfully gifted healer and flower essence aficionado, was also in attendance. The final day of the workshop we had the opportunity to make an essence. David was asked to hold the bowl since he had already made several essences in his travels across the globe studying flower essences. We were to meditate with the plant and then ask which bloom wanted to be cut to make the essence. As soon as I looked at the plant, I saw a flower blossom literally glowing. I couldn't believe that when it was their turn, none of the other participants chose the bloom that was obviously "The Bloom."

Finally it was my turn. I had David hold the bowl under the glowing bloom, and he said that the instant my bloom hit the water a rush of energy blasted through the bowl into his hands. He had never experienced anything like it. The essence was "made" as soon as the bloom hit the water. It typically takes several hours in the sun. David and I have remained dear friends ever since.

While living on Palomar Mountain, I walked a mile to the only store on the mountain and back again every day communing with all the flowers I came across along the way. Within days of returning from the flower essence workshop, I began being jolted awake at precisely 4 a.m. with an image of a particular flower in my head. By 6 a.m. I was out clipping glowing blooms. This went on for several days. These fabulous flower essences from Palomar Mountain became the first in my Dancing Dolphin Energy Healing Oil & Mist product line.

As has become quite typical, as soon as I learn something, I am given ways to enhance it, to take it to a significantly higher level vibrationally, and to expand its use. The flower essences were no exception. I was inspired with a way to add sound and anchor dolphin healing and other high frequencies into the product. I had already learned a great deal about energy healing. But sound was something else entirely.

I did an Internet search for sound healing and came across Jonathan Goldman's website. Of all the things I read about sound healing, I felt the strongest resonance with his information. We developed a friendship by email and eventually, while on the phone with him one day, I simply blurted out what I'd been given as a method to infuse sound into the product. He "tuned in," communing with Archangel Shamael whom he channels, and came back with "Yes, that absolutely does work."

Soon after that I met Jonathan and his fabulous wife, Andi, at the International New Age Trade Show in Denver. We have been dear friends ever since. Jonathan and I created an entire line of products together, infusing his sacred sounds into my energy healing oils. We call them *The Essence of Sound*.

My friend, Karen, of the Body Mind Center, had introduced me to Dr. Marsha Greene of Ocean Mammal Institute just before I left Pennsylvania to move to the San Juans. Marsha shared with me what she knew about the military's use of LFAS (Low Frequency Active Sonar) and how devastating it was to cetaceans. I found the information quite disturbing. The more I learned about it, the more upset I became and wanted to do something that could make a difference. I was contemplating LFAS as I fell asleep one night in 1998. The next morning I was jolted awake at precisely 4 a.m. with the words to the Golden Water Dolphin Meditation for Planetary Healing burning in my brain.

My inner wisdom indicated that I should let as many people as possible know about the meditation. As I searched the web for people and organizations, I came across Barbara Wolfe and her Global Meditation announcement list. I sent her an email explaining about the meditation. She responded by saying that I needed to get in touch with David J. Adams from Australia. She didn't tell me why.

I sent him an email. It turns out that he had channeled a meditation from Master Germain in 1992 with a similar focus. We decided to send each other our meditations. When I read his, tears began streaming down my face. It was almost identical to the words I had received. Obviously it was an important message if two people on opposite sides of the world had received it six years apart. I put up a web page, and we combined our efforts. The meditation has been shared by people all across the globe every Spring and Fall Equinox since then. Using the words and visualizations I received, people send healing energy to water and then pour it into waterways everywhere. Imperial topaz and quartz crystals have been placed in many locations globally, and these stones are used to anchor the energy whenever the meditations are performed.

It wasn't until 10 years after my initial virtual dolphin experience that I actually got to swim with live dolphins. It was while co-leading a wild dolphin experience in Bimini.

After practicing snorkeling in the morning, our boat headed out to deeper water to find dolphins. We found them right away. The captain and other swim guides on board encouraged us to leave our underwater cameras and just get used to being in the water with the dolphins. Later, we regretted taking that suggestion.

It was an extraordinary encounter. We were surrounded in every direction imaginable with dolphins. Unlike stories I've heard about pods in other locations, these dolphins were spinners and they like to interact by spinning with you. For many of us, it was our first time swimming in open ocean and it was certainly the first time we had held our breath spinning and diving as deep as possible with every breath. It was completely exhilarating and exhausting at the same time. It was a physical manifestation of the spinners who had visited me in meditation all those years ago.

There was a moment when I hung there at the bottom of my dive, with a dolphin that did the same. I stayed there transfixed as time seemed to come to a complete halt. A great deal of energy and information passed between us. It felt glorious and surreal. It is a moment forever etched within my heart. For a brief moment in time, we were as one.

Once all the participants got in the water that afternoon, the encounter lasted for about 45 minutes. Our swim guides said it was much longer than normal. Sadly, it was our only sighting of dolphins the rest of the time we were there. The water was so rough that a couple of days we didn't even attempt to take the boat out. My underwater camera remained empty until many years later when I lived aboard a yacht in the South Pacific.

The more time I spend in the divine dolphin frequency, in meditation, in nature, in communion and conversation with other spiritual teachers and healers, the higher and more expanded my consciousness becomes. My energetic sensitivity is now extremely highly refined. I have the ability to access and "bring in" higher wisdom and energetics, healing methods, technologies, and meditations to assist others as well as myself.

Because of the Warriors in the Mist training with Stuart Wilde, I fell in love with the canyon south of Taos, NM where the program was held. Eventually I moved just north of Santa Fe and visited the canyon on numerous occasions. It is where Stuart wrote his Taos Quintet, and the energy there is what he wrote about in his book, *The Quickening*.

I, too, was inspired to go there to write. I spent several days sitting by a stream in a trance-state all day long while "bringing in" a whole series of transformational dolphin healing technologies. They are a series of guided meditations, visualizations, and actions that literally heal emotional wounding at the root cause, release cellular memory and emotional pain, and reweave joy back into a person's body, energy field, and life. They, along with many other dolphin energy healing tools, are included in my program called *The Dancing Dolphin Way of Healing and Enlightenment*.

Meditating daily and using the Dancing Dolphin products, transformational technologies and information I have received over the years to heal emotional wounds from the past and let go of fears, limiting beliefs, judgments, and expectations, has allowed me to live in such a state of flow that I often simply "know" exactly where to be, what to do, and what to say. This ability led to the friendship and business deal with Jonathan Goldman that I described earlier, the glorious experience of living on a million dollar yacht in Fiji and the South Pacific, a divorce that only took one hour and 15 minutes, and my first book in print easily becoming a bestseller.

I'm far from perfect, and I sometimes have bad days. But most of the time I live in joy, routinely experiencing awe-inspiring moments, synchronicity, and flow. Friends who observe how I handle the occasional unexpected or unpleasant situation often remark at the level of grace with which I navigate life. I definitely learned that from observing and communing with dolphins and their consciousness.

I absolutely love my life. I feel an enormous level of wholeness and inner peace. I would not be who I am today had I not experienced the total emotional melt-down followed by the powerful virtual dolphin encounter I had all those years ago. The worst moment of my life turned out to be the absolute best thing that ever happened.

Many people are drawn to dolphins, and miraculous things can happen when they are near. People who are afraid of water suddenly feel completely safe even when swimming in the open sea. Studies show that people who swim with them develop brainwave patterns of long-term meditators. Sometimes non-verbal autistic children actually begin to speak.

As dolphin and whale experts, communicators, and healers go, I tend to hang out in the deeper end of the pool, focusing primarily on spirituality, emotional healing, developing and maintaining a pristinely clear divine connection, enhancing intuition, achieving wholeness of body, mind, and soul, and attaining enlightenment. I find that when someone focuses on their own divinity and spiritual journey, the other areas of life all seem to magically fall into place. They learn to flow with the Universe, and that is the stuff of both miracles and legend.

Dolphins live in a particular band of consciousness that is significantly higher than most humans are normally able to access. Connecting with that frequency can accelerate your personal evolution and healing as well as raise your consciousness and awareness. They drew me into their world, and now I hold the door open so others can easily access it as well.

It is said that when an Avatar (Jesus, Buddha, etc.) walked through a village, the consciousness of the entire village was raised. Being in the presence of dolphins, including the energetic ones that I assist people to connect with, has a similar effect.

I have been given the rare gift of being able to hold their frequency, their energetic presence in my body and energy field, infusing it into objects like the Dancing Dolphin products I offer and projecting it to others through my presence, voice, and long distance energy healing sessions.

Everything in life happens for a reason. Because I experienced so much hardship, emotional pain, feelings of unworthiness, betrayal, lack of confidence, stress, rape, I "know" what those feel like and can, therefore, alchemically create the exact frequencies necessary to help others heal from those experiences.

When I do sessions with private clients, sending them the various finely-tuned healing frequencies at my disposal, they often remark that they have never felt anything even remotely like that before, and they feel like a huge weight has been lifted. They are finally able to feel happy, free, centered and balanced sometimes for the first time they can remember.

I lost count long ago of the number of emails I have received over the years from people who say finding my website was literally like "coming home." It is a great honor to be blessed by the divine presence of cetaceans and to share their consciousness and healing energy with the world.

One of my primary focuses is helping individuals and organizations achieve magnificence by developing confidence, clarity, and connection with divine wisdom. Employees learn harmony and cooperation in order to achieve common goals. Individuals attain magnificence and regain their joy by become healthy, happy, and whole, body, mind, and soul.

Another project near and dear to my heart is the development of healing systems, techniques, and technologies that allow humans to experience the brainwave and healing effects of being in the presence of dolphins without dolphins actually needing to be present.

As odd as it sounds, cetaceans completely changed my life, and it began years before I got to be with them in the water. That's how I know it's not only possible to experience dolphin healing without needing their physical presence; it's what I'm here to share. My greatest desire is for others to find the level of joy, wholeness, grace, divine flow, and sense of freedom that I have found.

Debbie Takara Shelor is a bestselling transformational author, award-winning speaker, gifted story teller, engineer, and private consultant. She left the comfort and security of a high-paying career in pharmaceutical engineering to pursue enlightenment. Twenty years ago she moved to an island, co-founded a non-profit for dolphins and whales, and began traveling the globe following Divine inspiration wherever it led. People the world over affectionately refer to her as "Takara" ~ a Japanese word meaning treasure & blessing.

Marrying left-brained engineering know-how with laser-targeted intuition and spiritual finesse, she assists clients in developing profound levels of clarity, confidence, and connection resulting in the achievement of greater health, happiness, and success as they define it. She helps individuals who are tired of feeling stuck and are ready to catapult themselves into high gear both personally and professionally. She is a catalyst of radical positive change for both individuals and organizations. The focus is on greater levels of fulfillment, more meaningful relationships, improved confidence and self worth, the courage to go after your dreams, and the tools and support necessary to remove all obstacles in your way, regardless of their origin.

She is the bestselling author of *Peering Through the Veil: The Step by Step Guide to Meditation and Inner Peace*, as well as several other books. She is the creator of the *Mastering Your Magnificence System* and *The Dancing Dolphin* Way with *Dancing Dolphin Energy Healing* oils, mists, and other tools. Part of the Dancing Dolphin product line is the *Essence of Sound*, co-created with sound healing expert, Jonathan Goldman. Each Spring and Fall Equinox she leads the *Golden Water Dolphin Meditation for Planetary Healing*. Her newsletter, *Here's to Your Magnificence*, is enjoyed by thousands of readers from over 100 countries across the globe. She is President of the New River Valley Chapter of the National Association of Professional Women and is a homeschool mom.

Visit http://www.MagnificentU.com to join her mailing list and receive a complimentary copy of her ebook, *7 Secrets to Dancing Through Life EmPOWERed, EnRICHed, and EnJOY!*. She has numerous websites and blogs. She is very active on Facebook and many other social media platforms.

www.AbsoluteJoyNow.com   www.DebbieShelor.com

Chapter 10: *The Animal School of Life*

By Anne Gordon de Barrigón

"We welcome you and invite you to dive deep within yourself
to reconnect to your soul and higher self
through the messages and wisdom
we will be sharing through this medium."
-message from the Humpback whales of Panama (to Anne Gordon de
Barrigón)

Animals of all kinds have always been a huge part of my life. In fact, my first spoken word was "doggie." As a child and young adult, I always felt most comfortable in the presence of animals and had a fear and mistrust of humans. When I was 11 years old, we moved to a beach-front home near Olympia, Washington. My father loved the ocean and boating. Every summer we spent our family vacations on my dad's boat in the San

Juan Islands of Washington State where I grew up. My favorite memories as a kid were playing on the beach or sitting with my dad as we cruised the Puget Sound waters. We often saw orcas on our boat trips, and every time we did, it was incredibly thrilling. I could never get enough of seeing them. I would stare after them until they were tiny black dots on the horizon. I also remember a few summers when we took the boat up to Victoria, BC. We stayed at a marina that was in the same bay as a small aquarium called Sealand. Each day while we were there, I would go by myself and hang out for hours, watching the orcas, harbor seals and fish until closing time. I would sleep outside on the deck of our boat so I could fall asleep and wake up to the rhythmic sounds of the orcas' powerful exhalations. I would spend much of my time at the beach in front of our home. I vividly remember doing my homework on our beach one warm spring day and watching orcas swim past our beach.

The orcas figured prominently in my childhood. To me they were like good friends who always brought me joy when I saw them. I never knew when I would see them, but simply knowing they were there and could show up at anytime, brought me much comfort and joy. I, like many people, grew up in a typical middle-class dysfunctional family. I had many struggles with self esteem, feelings of not being loved or wanted in my own human family. Knowing the orcas were always around was very soothing to me. They never failed to help me feel complete joy whenever I saw or even thought of them.

It was an obvious choice for me to study biology and animal behavior in university. After graduation I got a job as a zookeeper at Woodland Park Zoo in Seattle. I loved being surrounded by all the animals and found the zookeeping staff to be extremely dedicated and loving to the animals in their care. I was even the first woman zookeeper to be assigned to the carnivore unit taking care of Kodiak and polar bears, wolves, tigers, lions and snow leopards. I loved the work, the animals and was thrilled and honored to be there.

After three years working at the zoo, I realized I was getting bored, not because of the animals, but because of the very nature of the work. A zookeeper's job can become very routine and repetitive, which is important and comforting for the animals. I have an active mind that thrives on a mental challenge and does not do well in a repetitive environment. I left the zoo to work as head keeper at the Wild Animal Training Center in Riverside, California. The WATC was a school that taught people how to train wild animals. At this center, I was allowed to help train the animals and have one-on-one contact with them, like I never had at the zoo. The zoo had a mostly hands-off style of management, and the WATC had a very hands-on approach. This style allowed for some really amazing bonds and relationships with lions, tigers, chimpanzees, raccoons, etc. It was great fun, and I learned a lot about and from the animals during my time there.

Since WATC was a new company, I made an agreement with the owner that I would get paid after a few months when money was coming in. After eight months of living off savings, I was running low on money. I also realized the owner was spending any income on drugs, not our salaries, so I decided it was time to leave. I learned a lot and have no regrets about the time I spent there.

I returned to the Seattle area and started my own business with a raccoon that I had a particularly close relationship with (it was given to me as "severance pay" from the WATC). My raccoon, Arrow, and I would go out to schools to teach children about wildlife. Our message was about education, conservation and respect for nature. I acquired a number of other animals, such as a tiger, lion, cougar, wolf, reindeer, deer, fox, etc., to share with the students in my programs.

All of the animals I acquired were bred in captivity or were rescues that were hand-raised and trained as ambassadors for their species. It was an amazing and thrilling feeling to have a 350-pound tiger or lion look up to you as "Mom"! Developing a close and personal relationship with the big cats, wolves, and all the animals I was blessed to have in my care was such a gift and has taught me so very much. (I have written an entire book on the subject called, *Listening with your Heart*.)

About five years into running my outreach programs, I was introduced to some people working in the local TV and film industry in Seattle. I realized that nobody was providing animals for movies and television in the Pacific Northwest. So I started spreading the word and quickly added training both my wild animals and some domestic dogs and house cats for TV commercials, commercial photo shoots, and even some local film projects.

I loved the film work, and at the same time, I was again becoming bored with the educational wildlife programs. (Do you sense a pattern here?) I felt really wonderful about the message and animals that I was sharing with over 30,000 school children each year, but it was starting to feel very repetitive giving the same speeches over and over again each day. The film work was completely different and always kept my mind challenged. No matter how much information I was given prior to shooting the commercial or film project, there was always some change or crucial bit of information that I had not been told about until I arrived on set. So I had to think quickly and come up with a workable solution to pull off the shot as the director wished. Sometimes it did not work out so well, but most often it worked out even better than I had hoped for.

At about the same time as I was transitioning from the educational programs to doing more film work, something very shocking happened. I was working with my Bengal tiger, Sultan, that I had raised from 10 days old for a TV commercial for the Boeing Company. We were shooting in the back field of tall grass behind my house and animal compound. I had several people assisting me, including a woman horse trainer who had been volunteering with me to care for the animals. I gave this woman the task of holding one end of a section of fencing to help keep the tiger corralled in the unfenced field. For some unknown reason, while the tiger was loose, she let go of her section of fence, turned her back to the tiger and tripped and fell down. There are two rules you never break when you work with big cats. Never turn your back on them and never fall down. She did both. Sultan bounced over like a kitten after a ball of yarn, and then his predatory instincts took over. He grabbed her by the back of the neck with his powerful jaws and started carrying her away. The other three of us trainers, jumped into action and were able to get Sultan off of her and back to his enclosure. She was rushed to the hospital, where she came within two minutes of dying because her carotid artery had severed. This experience was the worst moment of my life. Thankfully, she made a complete recovery.

For me, this very intense event with the tiger was not only emotionally devastating, as I was the person in charge, but it was also a huge wake-up call. I learned that I clearly needed to completely re-evaluate my life. I had been on a no-win path for a long time, always needing to spend more money to maintain the animals in a manner they deserved and never having enough for them and even less for me to buy food or pay rent. After my intense emotions started returning to normal, I realized it was time to start looking at myself for the first time in my life, as I was the only person in charge of my life and something had to change, fast.

I attended some self-help seminars, saw a counselor and was given a life-changing book, *Conversations With God,* by Neale Donald Walsch. As I started exploring myself, I had a very profound and funny realization. I was terrified of people and the human world. So what did I do to prove to the world that I was not afraid? I trained lions and tigers to prove how I was not afraid of anything! Because of this incredibly difficult event in my life, I was opening up to myself, learning, healing and awakening spiritually. I hated that I was so stubborn that it took something of this magnitude to open my eyes to a much healthier path for me.

While I was on my path of self discovery, I stopped doing the school outreach programs and concentrated completely on training animals for film and TV. This allowed me to learn, in a fun and exciting way, how to be more comfortable with people, because in the film industry you meet and work closely with many interesting and varied people, including directors and actors with very big egos. I learned and even enjoyed the art of coaxing the directors and producers into choosing my ideas for how to best succeed in working with the animals and thinking they were actually their ideas.

The film work was great fun and always kept me on my toes. You never knew what the next phone call would be. I received calls like: "Can you take a raccoon to New York tomorrow?" "Can you come to Alberta, Canada and work for four months on a movie with Brad Pitt?" "Do you have deer fawns for a remake of 'The Yearling'?" "Can you provide spiders to put in Whoopie Goldberg's hair?" "Can you find a moose, armadillo, and a fruit bat, we have called everyone else and nobody can help us?" and "Can you train a dog to bump Tom Cruise in the crotch with his nose?" I received all of these calls and was able to say "Yes" to them all.

I worked in the film industry with my own animal training company for 18 years. I loved it, and the unpredictable nature of the flow of income could be stressful. Raising and training animals requires a 24-7 commitment, without a day off, ever. I was feeling tired and ready for a change.

At the same time, around 1999, I started feeling a strong call from the dolphins. I often found myself dreaming, both at night and during the day, about dolphins and orcas. For my birthday in late September, 1999, I booked an orca watching day trip in the San Juan Islands and sent out an open invitation to any of my friends and family who wanted to join me. I found a tour company called 'Whale Spirit Adventures' that was captained by a man who played his flute to the whales to thank them for showing up. He had a dog named Spirit, who loved to announce the presence of the orcas before they were sighted. To seal the deal, the make of the boat was the same as the one my father had when I was a kid, which is a very rare boat now, because the factory burned down in 1962 and was never rebuilt. We went out and soon found a Super Pod, which is when all three resident pods of orcas get together for socialization. It is not a common event. We were with over 100 orcas for two hours and saw every behavior possible: swimming very near the boat, very young calves, fantastic breaches, and more. It was an incredible day that re-established my connection with the dolphins and whales.

After that magical day with the orcas, my new path became clearer. I needed to shift my career in a way that allowed me more time for myself and to further develop my relationship to Spirit.

In the beginning of 2000, I sold my film animal business to a former employee and moved to Southern California. I intended to become a freelance film animal trainer while in the L.A. area. Although I sold my business, many of the film producers and directors who I had worked with previously sought me out and hired me as a freelance film animal coordinator and head trainer. Funny thing, when I had my own film animal training company, my big goal was to be hired as the animal coordinator on a big animal movie, where the animal was the star of the movie, and it never happened. When I moved to California and completely let go of that goal, I landed the job as the head trainer of the new "Benji" movie. I was also hired as animal coordinator for "Air Bud: Spikes Back", "Air Buddies" and several other animal movies.

More importantly, after I moved to California, for the first time in over 18 years I was not consumed with work. I could sit and read a book in the middle of the day, take a yoga class, go hiking or take my few pet dogs to the beach. I would drive out to Henry's Beach just north of Santa Barbara where I loved to spend the day alone with my dogs walking the beach. I saw dolphins just past the surf line on every trip to the beach. I noticed that they often paralleled my walking. Even when I turned to go the other way, they turned with me. They often also matched my speed. It was great fun. Sometimes, I even saw whales in the distance too.

While I lived in California, I enjoyed reading spiritual books and meditating. I often had amazing dolphin dreams including one that was quite vivid. In the dream, I was out on a boat near Santa Barbara, and we found a huge pod of dolphins. I jumped in the water to swim with them, and the dolphins invited me to come and live with them forever. I came back to shore to say goodbye to my friends and family before I went back to live with the dolphins. It was a powerful dream.

Not long after having this dream, I read Mary J. Getten's book, *Communicating with Orcas*. I loved the book, and it really hit home with me, especially since I grew up watching the J pod of orcas she was writing about. I felt that my life in California was all about self discovery and developing a strong, loving relationship with myself. I also felt a strong presence of the dolphins and orcas now constantly around me. I also knew it was a time of transition, but I had no idea to what.

Before my move to California, I had never been married nor lived with a man. I had dated a bit and had a few boyfriends, but none, not even a date for the previous 13 years. When I lived in Washington State, I had desperately wanted to have a serious romantic relationship. Now, in hindsight, I realize I was afraid to let someone into my heart and trust him not to hurt me or abandon me. During my spiritual expansion and self-appreciation development, I came to a great place of peace about a love relationship. I realized that I loved my life just as it was at that moment and that I no longer felt a need to have that intimate relationship I had so desired before. I was completely satisfied and felt that if I remained single, it would be totally fine.

Not long after that powerful realization, I received a call to work on a film project that was slated to film in the country of Panama. I almost turned the job down, as I was working on a big film project when I received the job offer and wanted some time off afterwards. The producer convinced me to work on his film, and on January 6, 2004, I flew to Panama, and a whole new chapter of my life was about to unfold before my eyes, one that I could never have imagined in my wildest dreams.

The film project in Panama had hired a local indigenous tribe called the Emberá to perform as actions in the film. Most of the Emberá people still live in traditional villages in the rainforests of Panama. I got to hang out with the Emberá on the movie set and found them to be very warm, caring, open and friendly people. I spent many of my weekends out in their villages, which are only accessible by dugout canoe. The Emberá still live in communities of around 100 people with no electricity, no

Internet and not even cell phone signal. I loved being with these happy people who had little money, but have the quality of life the rest of the world seems to be searching for. They were rich in family, friends and most of all love and support for one another. Their lives are literally transparent, as they live in one room huts on stilts with no walls and quite close to one another. You can easily hear a conversation in the huts nearby. The first night I spent in an Emberá village, I woke up with a strong sense of knowing that the Emberá people would be in my life forever. I just did not know how yet.

While working on the film set I met one particular young Emberá man, Otniel, and he and I became friends and then romantically involved. It was very clear to us both that we were soul mates, even despite the obvious cultural, geographical, age and even language differences. When Otniel and I met, he spoke no English, and I had basic, and mostly forgotten, high-school Spanish. Our first few dates were with a Spanish-English dictionary between us. Despite all odds, including my disapproving family, we fell deeply in love. We met in February 2004, and by November of that same year. I had packed up all my belongings and moved to Panama to be together with Otniel.

Once I returned back to the USA after four months working on the film in Panama and with Otniel, a good friend of mine, told me about a wonderful woman, Linda Shay (also a part of this book), he met who was offering a spiritual dolphin school, Dolphin Heart World in Arizona. Yes, dolphins in the desert, well at least the dolphin spirit. I checked out her website, and it looked and felt amazing. I had a phone conversation with Linda about the school, and she explained how the school helps you to incorporate the dolphin living skills such as living in joy, flow, abundance, transparency and love into our every-day human lives. She also commented after hearing my story of meeting and falling in love with Otniel and his Emberá tribe that it seemed that the Emberá community in its true unity-community mind set was the human version of a dolphin pod. I signed up immediately.

Diving into Linda Shay and her husband, David Rosenthal's Dolphin Heart World School at the same time as meeting and developing my relationship with my future husband, Otniel was amazing and very enlightening, as well as a bit frightening to dive so deep within myself. I loved Linda and David's dolphin school. I embraced it completely. Learning how to fully invite the dolphins and whales into my life on a deep spiritual level, gave me strength to face any challenge and to live in complete joy at all times, no matter what is happening. The dolphin school experience was also very healing. One huge healing that I experienced was around a deep unconscious anger I had been carrying inside.

During my time in California, I thought I had handled all my inner issues, but when I moved to Panama and was living with Otniel, this deep-seated anger came out in force when we had disagreements. I was also an animal trainer, who had lived alone my entire adult life up until then, so I was very used to being in control and making all the decisions in my life and for others. Now, I had to completely readjust to sharing my life with someone whom I loved deeply but did not always do what I wanted nor agree with me and my decisions and desires. The anger that came out during some of these times frightened me, and I had no idea how to deal with it. In the second weekend of dolphin school, Linda and David introduced an exercise given to them by the dolphins as a way to identify, locate and gently release an issue. In this exercise, I was able to easily and completely be free of emotion, locate, observe and let go of the anger within me. In a simple twenty minute exercise, the anger was simply gone. I can tell you that now, 10 years later, it has never returned. Sure, I can still get mad, but that uncontrollable scary anger is gone. Thank you Dolphins! Thank you Linda and David! Releasing that deep-seated anger is one of the most significant gifts the dolphins ever gave me.

One of the skills taught in the Dolphin Heart World School was the art of Dolphin Energy Healing. While I was in the school, learning the healing skills was the least interesting part to me. I had no interest in opening a healing practice nor doing healings for other people. Practicing in the school was fun, and after the school I thought I would play around with it for some friends of mine just for fun. I found I enjoyed it, and more importantly, my friends did too. They felt very relaxed and peaceful after the sessions. I decided to pursue getting my Dolphin Energy Healing Practitioner certification, which involved doing a number of sessions for others, both in person and distance healings.

While I was in the process of getting certified, I began to ask the dolphins to send me their healing energy as I lay down to sleep each night. I also gave them permission to adjust my frequencies in any way that was for my highest good. One night, as soon as I had finished these statements to the dolphins, I had a vision of swimming in my "dolphin body" very fast through the waves with other dolphins. It was very joyful and playful. Nothing profound happened during the vision, and I received no major insights. It was simply fun and felt very real. Upon returning from this vision, I felt my body vibrating at a new higher level, so much so I could not sleep at all that night. Nor for the next two nights! It seems the dolphins gave me a major adjustment to my frequencies, and it took my body three days to catch up. Interestingly, after that night, whenever I gave a dolphin energy healing session to someone, I experienced a steady stream of visions and messages during the session for my client. Some of these visions and messages made no sense to me, but when I shared them with my clients, they made perfect sense and often moved them to tears. My friends/clients were also reporting great healings after the session, even for health or emotional issues that they had not shared with me prior to the session. Some clients even reported cancelling doctor's appointments and even a surgery as a result of the healing they received during one of my dolphin energy healing sessions! Now, I have a dolphin energy healing practice, a website and am available to do individual healing sessions in person or distance healings for anyone who feels it is right for them. For me, it is such a great honor and blessing to be able to be the facilitator and channel for the incredible healing energies of the dolphins and whales for others.

Up until now, my focus had mainly been on the dolphins and not as much on the whales. We did learn a bit about the whales during dolphin school but not as much. One day, as I was driving to Northern California along the beautiful coastline, I saw some humpback whales splashing offshore. I stopped to enjoy them as they played. Then back in my car, I began to think about abundance as I drove. I thought about how in nature, animals do not struggle to find their food. They may work hard to get it, but they rarely struggle to find it. For example, a baleen whale simply has to open his mouth and filter out the water and keep all the krill inside. A deer or antelope simply puts its head down to eat the succulent grasses at its feet. A lion lives surrounded by potential prey. A bird has access to limitless supplies of fruits, seeds or insects, and so on. It seemed that having abundance in the life of the animals was a God-given right.

We humans have created a system of money that we use to buy the things we need to survive, like food, housing, clothing, etc. Why was it so easy for the animals that are surrounded by abundance and so difficult for me and so many other humans who were struggling with a lack of money and abundance?

Then an image popped into my head of all the animals being surrounded by all they need to survive, and an invisible brick wall that sat between me and my own natural right to abundance. I saw how our limiting beliefs have created this invisible brick wall, and that most of us have bought into this way of thinking. I also saw that because it is simply a belief system, all we have to do is become aware of how ridiculous this belief is and drop it. All that we need will then flow in easily.

I remembered a news report I had heard a few months before, about several American business men lost in the Amazon jungle for several weeks. When they were finally found, they were near death from starvation. This shocked me. I remember thinking, "How can you starve in the tropical jungle?" There is such a wealth of plant species with fruits, berries, animal & insect life everywhere you look. I could not comprehend how these men were starving when food was everywhere around them.

I realized that this was exactly like the invisible brick wall that we have created between us and the flow of abundance. To these American city dwellers, the jungle was so foreign that nothing appeared edible, or they had a fear of eating the unknown. I realized all we have to do is open our eyes to reality. That abundance is all around us to be had and utilized -- just as the jungle was all around these unfortunate men, whose limited beliefs and lack of knowledge prevented them from partaking in the abundance that surrounded them.

The planet Earth is designed to provide for all who live on her. Everything has its place and should be in perfect balance with all around it. There are enough resources on the earth right now for every species, humans included, to have all their basic needs met, such as housing, food, water, clothing, shelter, etc. It is time for all of us to break down that invisible brick wall and open up to allow the flow of abundance that truly is here for each and every one of us. Abundance is a natural state of being.

After this thought process went through my mind, I remembered something that was taught in the Dolphin Heart World School: Whales represent abundance. Whoa! Could all of this line of thinking have been directed to me from the whales I had just seen? Whales are the very definition of abundance. They are the largest animals on the planet. Their massive bodies are abundance incarnate. Many of them eat some of the smallest animals, krill and plankton. Humpback whales, for example, consume between 4,400-5,500 pounds of krill, plankton and small fish each day! If a whale is not open to the flow of abundance, he will starve. They are truly masters of abundance.

The more I thought about the connection between the whales and abundance, the more I was convinced that, indeed, they did help me understand the limiting barriers we humans have created for ourselves. Whether it came from them directly via telepathic communication or my brain made the connection between the whales representing abundance and how humans are not in the flow of abundance really does not matter. Seeing the whales was the catalyst for me to really think about and see how we as humans are actually preventing the natural flow of abundance from entering our lives. I was truly humbled and grateful, and I sent a telepathic message to the whales of my deep gratitude for helping me make this connection and see how to open myself up to the flow of abundance.

Not long after this realization about abundance from the whales, I came up with the idea to offer our own tours to my husband's Emberá village and put up a website. Within one week I had a request for a tour. Our previous dire financial situation quickly began to turn around as a result of my abundance realization, thanks to the whales.

Soon after I moved to Panama. I started asking everyone I could about what kind of whales and dolphins were found in Panama and where and how could I get out to see them. Nobody could answer my questions. I found it hard to believe that in a country with only 50 miles between the Pacific and Atlantic oceans nobody knew anything about where to see dolphins and whales. I finally found the answer several years later. I took a few days to rest from our now very busy Emberá village tour business on Contadora Island in the Pearl Islands. The Pearl Islands are located 35 miles south of Panama City. While I was on Contadora, the locals all told me that during the months of July to October many humpback whales were there. I hired a local fisherman to take me out to find dolphins. It was not long before we found about 40 pantropical spotted dolphins and four humpback whales! This was in

February, not peak whale season. I have since learned that Panama is one of the very few places in the world where humpback whales come from both the Southern Hemisphere (July-October) and the Northern Hemisphere (December-March) to breed and give birth. I swam with the dolphins, and the whales were nearby too. It was incredible and my first experience to swim and see dolphins all around me in the water. That night in my hotel room, I realized that I had completely released all the tension and stress of working nonstop on our Emberá tours and had an overwhelming feeling that everything would be fine. I knew this feeling of peace and joy had come from my swim with the dolphins.

After finding the dolphins and whales so easily and having such a beautiful encounter with them, I thought about how our Emberá tour business was now thriving and how we could easily add whale and dolphin-watching tours also. So I started Whale Watching Panama, which was the first and still the only dedicated whale watching company in the country of Panama. Now, five years later, we have a 99% success rate in finding the humpback whales during the peak season.

Taking people out to see the whales and dolphins has been such a joy for me. Not only do I get to be out with them almost every day, but I get to share that joy with others, many of whom have never seen whales before. It is so beautiful to see the joy and ear-to-ear smiles of our guests after being on one of our tours. One thing that I have come to realize is that when you are in the presence of the whales and dolphins, it is impossible to think of anything else at that moment. You cannot think about your worries and fears of yesterday or tomorrow. You are in the present moment of NOW when you are with these incredible animals. This is a huge gift to us all and something so very important for our very cluttered and stress-filled human lives to simply BE in joy and right here and now with the dolphins and whales.

I lead five-day Whale and Dolphin Wisdom retreats that are so magical and powerful with deep connections and insights from the whales and dolphins for all who participate. After the first of these spiritual retreats I offered, I came home and found myself in sadness. I could not figure out why I felt so sad, after five delicious days immersed in whale and dolphin energy. Then I realized that the whales take you very deep within and help you to release anything within that no longer serves you in a very gentle way. My sadness was simply emotion being released after my time with the whales.

On one particular five-day Whale and Dolphin Wisdom retreat, I had a woman whose adult son had died unexpectedly in the previous year and a half before she came on this tour. I cannot imagine the deep sadness and guilt of a parent whose child precedes them in death. This woman had been struggling with how to move on with her life after her son's passing and had not found anything that brought joy or purpose to her life since. On the trip, I was very gentle with her and never pushed her to discuss her feelings unless she came to me. I simply took her out with the group to spend time observing the humpback whales and dolphins. Each day she opened up more and more and allowed herself to smile and simply be in the moment, enjoying the cetaceans that showed up to be with us. On the last day, before she said goodbye, she hugged me and thanked me for helping her to smile, laugh and feel at peace for the first time since her son had died.

Over the last five years, I have been blessed with many incredible whale and dolphin encounters and some very powerful and insightful meditations and healing sessions with the cetaceans. Very recently, I found myself surrounded by ugly, unethical and backstabbing competition with my whale watching tours. It affected me both emotionally and financially and had me quite stressed out for many weeks. During these challenging weeks, I thought about how the whales, especially the gray whales, were brought to the brink of extinction by whalers in Baja California. Now the gray whales are the friendliest whales on earth, seeking out humans to touch them in the same bay where they were hunted so ruthlessly within the lifespan of many of these same whales. They even bring their newborn calves to meet and be touched by the humans. The whales are the ultimate example of forgiveness and compassion. I decided the only way to deal with my current challenges was to emulate the whales and simply Be Whale. By being whale and by remembering and relying on my deep spiritual connection with all the dolphins and whales, I have found the strength and positive outlook to continue moving forward and offering my unique, respectful whale and dolphin watching tours.

Looking back at my life, I can easily see how strongly the animals have influenced my life all along. I am grateful to each and every one of them for helping me to become who I am today. It seems to me that the dogs and cats in my early life were my elementary school, the wild animals of my zookeeping and school outreach days were junior high.

My film career with both domestic and wild animals was high school. My spiritual awakening with the dolphins was university and now my time with the whales is graduate school.

I could go on and write an entire book about how the whales and dolphins have influenced my life and through me, others. I will save that for another time. It is hard to quantify in human terms how much they have influenced my life. I will say that I always feel a deep and profound connection with the cetaceans at all times in my life, happy or sad. I cannot tell you how incredibly grateful I am for their loving, compassionate guidance, love, and support while I bumble my way through this human life. In meditation, the whales have given me a new white humpback whale light body and the name of 'Walking Whale.' I am humbled and so deeply honored to be a walking whale in a human body, and I embrace every opportunity to share my love, connection and insights from the cetaceans with others.

I am Whale
I am Love
I am Abundance
I am Wisdom
I am Aware of All That Is

Received from the whales during meditation.

Anne Gordon de Barrigón grew up watching orcas in Washington State boating with her family. The orcas gave her a sense of joy and peace from a very early age. She studied Biology and Animal Behavior in university. She worked as a zoo keeper, trained wild animals for educational outreach programs and trained wild and domestic animals for movies and TV for many years.

Anne graduated Linda Shay's and David Rosenthal's Dolphin Heart World school and is a certified Dolphin Energy Healing practitioner. During her healing sessions she receives profound visions and messages from the dolphins, whales, other animals, angels and spirit guides for her clients. www.DolphinHealing.net

Anne is married to an indigenous man from the Emberá tribe in Panama. The Emberá people still live in traditional villages in the rain forest as they have for centuries, without electricity, internet and cell phone signal. She has been welcomed and accepted as family by the Emberá people. The Emberá people live in true community and complete transparency, putting family first, much like a dolphin pod does. Anne believes the Emberá have the joyful, loving quality of life the rest of the world is searching for. She and her husband, Otniel, run respectful tours to his village. www.EmberaVillageTours.com

Anne runs Humpback whale watching tours and Whale and Dolphin Wisdom retreats in Panama. She is an Ambassador member of the Responsible Whale Watch Partnership, a group of international whale watch operators dedicated to promoting responsible whale watching worldwide. Anne has developed a deep spiritual connection with dolphins and whales through her studies and countless hours observing and swimming with wild dolphins and whales. She has a strong spiritual relationship with the humpback whales she spends so much time with. They have enlisted her in many healing efforts to spread light, love and joy throughout the Pearl islands and all of Panama. Her life's mission is to instill a deep respect for the cetaceans and all of nature and to share the beauty and wisdom of the dolphins and whales with others. www.WhaleWatchingPanama.com

Chapter 11: *Cetacean Nation*

By Roberta Quist Goodman

Long long ago, in a life now forgotten
His ancestors journeyed with the man
Bound by a sacred love the kings of the ocean
Held for the dwellers of the land
And deep within Cetacea there lies a memory
That stirs whenever these sailors come below
They seem to be friendly, speaking in their way
As if maybe even man may know
The Dolphin
- © 1981 David Goodman / BMI

Arriving on a one-way ticket, I landed in Maui carrying a case of wine and $200. At 22 in the late 70's that was enough to make a start in Lahaina, the place of the Relentless Sun. Gayle decided to move from California and I was joining her. Riding in the back of her boyfriend's pickup at sunset, Maui whispered with the scent of plumerias, the sloping strength of Haleakala and the beckoning fingers of the West Maui Mountains. I headed to my destiny, climbing up across the cliffs and wandering along the shores.

At the base of a sugarcane factory, beside the only traffic light in town, sat the Mango Manor, a shady plantation house owned by three generations of lesbians from Alaska. I found work at the Batik Bird and Gayle worked at the Upstart Crow Bookstore.

I was invited onto a 68-foot schooner for occasional sails and overnights. While rolling gently at anchor, we woke to the sharp barks of the Doberman. Lying at the surface alongside the yacht, a whale blew mist across the decks. The humpback rolled sideways, and I looked into a dark eye glistening in the moonlight. Disturbed in her reverie, she dove. I had to catch my heart, stopping my breath, longing she would stay, but she slipped away without a sound. An enormous creature from the deep had been sleeping quietly beside us unnoticed, divided only by a ship's hull. I wanted to know who this immense, mysterious being was. The whale grabbed my soul and took me into the depths of her sea.

At Gayle's bookstore, a cover photo with a white whale peering at a woman captured my attention. *Communication between Man and Dolphin: The possibilities of talking with other species*, by John C. Lilly, M.D. Gayle got it for me.

Bottlenose dolphins evolved large brains 15-30 million years before we did. Dr. Lilly found these social dolphins to be exceptionally communicative and surprisingly telepathic. After years of study, he realized that his research subjects should more appropriately be seen as his friends. In 1967, Dr. Lilly relinquished work with dolphins, intending to set them free, and he turned inward to explore and describe the boundaries of his beliefs.

Reading *Communication Between Man and Dolphin* was the first time I heard that another animal had as big a brain as we do. Everything about them intrigued me. They have a structural capacity for higher level thinking, consciousness and language. Dr. Lilly's chapter, "Rights of Cetaceans under International Law," was completely logical. Large-brained tribes of Cetaceans should be fairly represented in international decision making.

After several years of soul searching for a career, I found my passion ~ to communicate with dolphins. I wanted to live with them as John Lilly had and find out who they were.

Terry

In 1979, after a year on Maui I moved back home to the emerging Silicon Valley south of San Francisco. I read everything I could find on dolphins. Although I knew I wanted to work in research, I had no idea how to begin.

A small article appeared in the newspaper. Dr. John C. Lilly was opening a dolphin communication lab at Marine World/Africa USA in Redwood City, 30 miles north of where I lived! Searching for an inroad to research, I never considered going to a dolphinarium. On a hot summer day, a tiger-crazy girlfriend and I drove up to the park housing a menagerie of animals in a safari-like setting. Down a winding path past rides and restaurants, in the shade of overgrown trees, noisy people crowded around a pool. Inside circled three dolphins. Children squealed, slapping the water. Adults clanged the concrete with rings and keys. How could they be so insensitive to these dolphins who I believed embodied intelligences much wiser than we. Occasionally a dolphin rose to let a person touch her. They broke my heart! The dolphins were reaching out for human touch. Although aching to reach out to one of my idealized dolphins, how could I become part of this chaos? I could not bear to stay.

I believed that cetaceans had abilities which matched and exceeded those of our spiritual gurus. It would be natural for them to have a consciousness extending beyond their bodies, to be aware of and interconnected with energy fields saturating their environment, to have worldly and universal perspectives on their lives, and to be participants in a greater evolutionary process. I wanted to learn from them, have them teach me in person. I wanted to know and understand who dolphins were, truly and deeply. Rather than teaching them English or a symbolic system, I hoped to acquire a sense of Delphinese, their way of understanding and communicating with the world.

I hoped dolphins would become my mentors.

Before returning to Marine World, I stretched out on my bed in meditation. In an ecstatic state, I energetically transported myself to the tanks of Marine World. I called to the dolphins, pleaded to this imagined etheric audience floating in space above their pools and above my head, "I'm coming to you! Please accept me. I want to work with you. Dolphins, accept me and show them that you will work with me. Show them I'm different! Recognize me! I'm coming!"

As I drove to the park, I called to the dolphins in my mind, "I'm coming. Recognize me." Approaching along the walkway from the front gate towards the tiny pools, I yearned for their recognition and acceptance. I wondered if my feelings and thoughts could enter their consciousness and hoped they could read me.

Seven or so people surrounded the pool with their hands in the water. Unobtrusively, I slipped into a space along the wall and dipped my fingertips into the pool. A dolphin circled and rose nonchalantly to my touch. A luxurious stroke thrilled me. Silky, misty grey dolphin skin! The dolphin broke her circle, rose her head to scoot around at the surface eyeing me. Returning, she glided into my arms and lie motionless there, letting me hold the unexpectedly vulnerable gift of her body. She quivered, fluttered loose, circled the tank, and came again. I would later learn that her name was Terry.

My body draped over the short concrete wall. The other two dolphins joined Terry directly underneath me. I felt infinite respect, love, and trust for the dolphins. A window opened with our touch, communicating through their skin. I felt them; I was sure they felt me. I found myself body-to-body and heart-to-heart with these three dolphins!

From that first touch, Terry became my teacher. Playing hours a day throughout that year, we were more intimate than human relationships I had known. I stroked her sides as she slithered through my arms and held her tail while she pulled down into the water. As I steered her limp or flexing body, we danced, plunging and swirling and lifting her body.

Terry relaxed completely as I pulled her tail out of the water, around my neck, and stroked her sides. She taught me to surrender my will while she waited a foot away. I let go of my thoughts and desires even more, hanging loose over the wall, staring into the water. She came into my arms, and I kissed and licked her finely crosshatched skin.

I was deeply in love with a dolphin. I felt connection where I never even knew loneliness and emptiness existed. At night, my fingers frozen, I dallied. Somehow, I imagined, I would take her to the sea.

A graduate student closed the pool to public interaction. When I returned to the park, she described details of her bi-lateral communication project and asked me to join as a volunteer. I promptly accepted. I quit my job and became a full-time research assistant. The protocol of the communication study dictated my new relationships with the dolphins.

I taught Terry to face me perpendicular to the wall, stationing there until I presented a circular wooden block above the water for her to touch, or not touch. She used her jaws, or rostrum, to touch the target, and then I would throw a fish into her open mouth head first. The sequences of station, tap the block, get a fish were repeated twenty times in a session, three times a day. A triangular block was used as the target to touch for balls. An H-shaped block got her strokes for thirty seconds. These protocols and playing with the balls were the only way we could interact with the dolphins during lab hours.

Within this new restrictive paradigm, Terry continued my mentorship. Even within the restraints of protocol, unexpected responses from the dolphins had me ask, "Who was testing whom?"

The dolphins stopped coming to push the button for Human Interaction. Terry and Gordo would instead lie in the far side of the pool. Spray, the primary subject of the research, circled endlessly. Eventually, Gordo stopped eating. Although the staff tried to cajole him, reinstating free time for play with Gordo, he was inconsolable. After 40 days of starvation, the 50-year-old Pacific bottlenose died. Twenty-one year old Terry lived another 20 years.

Joe and Rosie

Prominent marine scientists repudiated Lilly's groundbreaking research as they tried to repeal the Marine Mammal Protection Act. Dr. John Lilly's Human/Dolphin Foundation (HDF) had begun research with Joe and Rosie, two young bottlenose dolphins captured in the Gulf of Mexico with the stated intention of keeping them for only one year before returning them to the wild. My director wanted to distance herself from Dr. Lilly and his reputation as a free-thinker. We were told not to talk with Dr. Lilly's assistants when we met in the fish house, certainly not visit his lab.

In the middle of a hot August day, I sat on a picnic bench with Sonny Allen, Director of Marine Mammals. I longed to get in the water with the dolphins, and while the chances of that happening seemed remote, Sonny was the guy who could give me permission.

"Gosh it's so hot! Sonny, where can I jump in to get wet?"

"B-tank."

"B-tank? ... Bee-tank?"

"Joe and Rosie's tank," he said casually, gesturing towards the back lot across the bridge behind us.

"Are you sure? Do they care?" I dared question his authority.

Sonny shook his head. "Tell Tom I said it's OK if he says anything."

"Thanks Sonny! Thanks!"

At last! An opportunity to swim with dolphins! Sonny nonchalantly told me to swim in the research tanks. Would the HDF staff care? In an entanglement of politics, I had my opportunity to swim with dolphins!

My heart beat quickly as we crossed the bridge and found Tom Fitz.

"Roberta's going to take a swim in B-tank," Sonny explained to Tom.

"Sure," Tom said, as if Sonny sent a regular stream of women to swim with Joe and Rosie. His easygoing response relaxed me, and I dropped concern about the politics. He handed me a mask etched with John Lilly on the metal frame. "Have fun!" he cheered me on.

Sitting on the wall of their tank, I watched the dolphins circle and lift their heads above the water line. Joe or Rosie gazed at me, through one eye, then the other. "Hi," I thought. "I'm coming in. I hope that's OK with you."

I slipped in. No dolphins in sight. They were on the far side of the pool which was 75 feet in diameter and 20 feet deep. The water was cool and refreshing. My boss had joined Sonny along the rim. I sighed and stretched out on my back, closing my eyes, slowing my heart rate, melting into the surface. I was finally in the water with this sentient species. Floating, smiling, I lapsed into quietness, aloof from the personalities and politics around me, ears submersed in salt-water silence. Completely in the moment, I had no expectations for what might happen next.

While my eyes were closed, the crook of my right elbow was nudged by a stiff fin moving across the surface. Outstretching my arm, it was natural to grasp the fin fitting into my hand. While being pulled through the water, I rolled over and to the dolphin's left side. The other dolphin squeezed close on my left. The three of us sped across the pool to the opposite wall. The dolphins dove at the last moment. I released the fin, hurled myself into a flip turn, and rose to the surface laughing at what seemed like the dolphins' attempt to crash me into the wall. Now I heard their whistles. Swiftly they returned to pick me up again. The three of us cavorted, clasped in corkscrews, and swirled around each other. I dove, holding onto fins of the sleek dolphin bodies. "Ride me!" "Ride me!"

146

they seemed to argue. Astonished by their sudden intimacy, I was breathless and filled with joy. They paused at the surface to let me breathe. I turned to stare at the eye of the dolphin close at my side. He looked at me with total acceptance, as a playmate. They were discovering who I was through play! They tested my range of roughhousing skills: agility, grace, breath, buoyancy, spontaneity, and humor. When I left the tank, the dolphins followed me around to where I thanked Tom.

I was blissed. I wanted more. But when I returned to the office, my boss was stern, "That's the last time you will swim over there. We've got to keep totally separate from John Lilly's group. Don't go over there or associate with them again." I had to resign myself, no more swims.

Shiloh

The joyful freedom of interaction with Joe and Rosie contrasted with the stark protocol at the petting pool. I didn't want to train dolphins; I wanted to learn to communicate with them. I longed to enter the water with Terry. Three men climbed into her tank at will, the scuba divers. Cleaning the tanks and hand-feeding sharks was considered a man's job. There was only one dressing room, with three shower stalls, and it was beyond the doors of the men's bathroom. When one diver, Allan Therkelsen, was bit by a shark and had to take some time off, I applied for the opening. To my surprise, head diver Don Reed hired me!

The divers did everything that needed to be done underwater while the occupants were present. On SCUBA, breathing through one hundred foot hookah-hoses, we cleaned tanks housing harbor seals, sea lions, moray eels, sharks, fish, and turtles, as well as bottlenose and Pacific white-sided dolphins, a pilot whale, and orcas.

The research dolphins were always wary when one of us entered to remove discarded fish from the drain each afternoon. So used to intimacy from them, it was disconcerting to jump into their small tank while Terry and Spray kept their distance or Gordo rushed by. My role had changed and so had my relationships with these three.

Don introduced me to the boss of the show tank, Shiloh. This sassy alpha female teased and threatened me at first, but she eventually became my closest dolphin friend. The show dolphins took on my mentorship. Bayou, Schooner, Stormy, and Shiloh played games in which

I had to trust that they weren't going to hurt me. I stuffed my fears and took on an attitude of confidence.

Shiloh and Bayou patrolled the tank, sometimes showing their displeasure at our presence by knocking us on the head with their beaks or tails. My trusting bravado that they would not strike me as they brushed by overhead, despite their proclivity to wanton knocks, was rewarded with solicitous offers of their sleek bodies. My distrust warranted a knock. One day I was hit on the head and watched as every diver was also hit. In a show of adamant force, the dolphins began jaw clapping at us, producing a percussively loud snap. Don gave us the thumbs up, indicating we could quit work and rise to the stage. There we found the dolphins chased us out because an audience had already filled the bleachers and were waiting to watch a show.

The dolphins wielded stern mastery over us during the hours we dared to encroach upon their space. During the four hours we needed to clean every inch of the pool bottom with steel brushes, we were always aware of the dolphins' activities and moods.

It became apparent to me that the dolphins were also very aware of my intentions, feelings and fears, my deep trust and respect for them.

The dolphins invented and perfected games. They enjoyed being shoved backwards and pulled by their tails. We blew bubble rings, imitating each other. When the mood was right, I would be taken on a dreamlike effortless ride between four dolphins, flying around the crystal clear water.

I often worked weekends alone cleaning the behind-the-scenes tanks that held Joe and Rosie. The other divers avoided working these shifts because these two dolphins did not seem to like people. As I swam in circles around their tank walls and floor sweeping off algae with a soft pool brush, the water became a cloud of green. Visibility dropped to two feet. Joe would offer his dorsal fin and carry me around the tank. After a break, I had to return to sweeping. Not knowing where I had dropped my brush, I would think, "Joe, take me to my brush. I have to work now." Joe would immediately bring me to an obscured location and drop me off by tilting his fin. My brush would be right at my fingertips!

Once, lying on the bottom looking skyward, I watched as Rosie swirled past me and launched 20 feet to the surface and into the air. She plunged back into the water directly over my head and plummeted to my forehead. I was frozen in amazement, stunned at what might happen but strangely, not terrified. Just before contact with my head lying on the concrete, she swerved.

That afternoon, holding Joe's fin as we spun around the tank, it was as if we were enclosed in a bubble propelled by unseen forces. There was no effort to swim yet the walls flashed by with no sensation of water movement or resistance. Slipstreaming?

After six months of working together as divers, Allan and I flew to the Grand Canyon with a friend in a rented Cessna. We fell in love while camping on the north edge of a narrow gorge. Back at work Monday morning, we scrubbed the show tank alone. The dolphins nudged my side, pushing me over the floor. Scrubbing new spots as they moved me, I suddenly found myself on top of Allan. We shrugged, separated, and got back to work. Once again I was prodded by dolphins to scoot across the bottom into an awkward position right on Allan. Four dolphins studied us, chattering, pointing their noses at us and zapping us with sonar.

A light went on, and it occurred to us that they knew! We gleamed at each other. Nudge nudge, wink wink! The dolphins somehow knew about our new connection, so we gave them the show they clearly wanted! Longing to embrace, we stroked wet-suited bodies and gazed, blue eyes into blue. We rose while nuzzling, removed our regulators and kissed, to the dolphins' rapt attention. The dolphins had somehow caught on to our new intimacy without any displays of affection. They knew! They know! The dolphins ran off in a chase as we returned to scrubbing with a wink.

In a quest to be with wild dolphins, Allan and I moved to Lahaina. Again I lived on the island of Maui in Hawaii. I brought my windsurfer, my ticket to the whales and dolphins. We had fortuitous opportunities to swim with humpback whales. These first experiences witnessing their gigantic lives underwater will always stay with me. Camping on Lanai, we saw wild dolphins, but encounters on Maui were rare. Dolphins in the ocean can be elusive, and I missed my dolphin friends at Marine World. So, after a year in Maui, Allan and I moved back to California.

Allan got a graveyard job in filtration at Marine World, and I joined him during his shifts at night. On my first visits, the dolphins treated me as if it were only yesterday that I had last seen them. Stretched out on the floating stage, draped over the edge, the show dolphins always took time to come into my arms. The patrolling security gave me leeway to play with my beloved friends in this midnight rendezvous. Lying on the wet stage, wearing a swim suit but never entering their pool, I opened my mind to slip into their world.

I loved kissing the dolphins, murmuring to them. I draped my hair across their foreheads, rubbed my cheek on their silky, airbrushed bodies and wondered that they seemed to return my love. One night, lying still in my arms, Shiloh kissed me back. My face pressed on Shiloh's smooth head, the tongue of her blowhole created a gentle suction as it wiggled on my cheek. Did she need to breathe? I pulled away, but she remained still. I pressed my cheek to her forehead; once again she kissed me as I caressed her with my face. Relaxing into her, I surrendered my face, neck, and shoulders to her delicate kisses. She pulled aside to breathe and returned to my embrace. Shiloh, dear Shiloh. I'm entranced by this exquisite sensation and Shiloh's tenderness. We bridged worlds sharing kisses in the moonlight.

Dolphins are conscious breathers, as we are conscious drivers. We may say they meditated. I often thought that when they dreamed, they must dream in the open sea. One moonlit night, Shiloh and her companions only briefly diverted from swimming in a tight cluster to come over to me. After a time I left the stage, puzzled at what was different. The next morning I watched from the sidelines as the divers netted the show tank, separated a dolphin, and pulled a thrashing body out of the water. It was Shiloh.

Shiloh had prevented the show dolphins from performing. Show dolphins are required to perform the same behaviors up to seven shows a day during their lifetime in captivity. Dolphins have moods and sometimes they don't perform. Shiloh had been distracting the other dolphins from stationing at the stage, biting at their tails and swatting them with her tail. This long streak of non-compliance was not allowed to continue.

After two weeks of upset shows, Shiloh was pulled out and placed in a tank on the back lot. Isolated, she was never allowed to rejoin the others. Dolphins are extremely social. Except for tossing fish in her mouth three times a day, the staff was instructed to ignore Shiloh. Trainers passed by on the way to their office, but they never glanced her way. After all our intense interaction, I was commanded to leave her completely alone.

I imagined a retirement home for dolphins like her, Gordo, and Terry.

In four months Shiloh was dead.

Dr. John Lilly

In 1983, I finally realized my dream of working for Dr. John Lilly with his dolphins, Joe and Rosie, at the Human/Dolphin Foundation lab. Dr. Lilly encouraged volunteers and visitors to spend as much time as possible with Joe and Rosie. Swimming with dolphins was an obscure idea, and I talked only a few friends into joining me. Even as a diver, I had often swam with Joe and Rosie after work for fun. Dr. Lilly's insightful experiment with the Human/Dolphin Foundation introduced hundreds of people to dolphin encounters.

Celebrities came to swim at the lab. Ram Dass, a well-known spiritual leader, credits Rosie as his "greatest teacher of intuition." During Ram Dass' swim, Rosie gently took his arm in her mouth. Having no previous experience to tell him how to behave in such a situation, Ram Dass had to totally trust his intuition for his next move. Rosie brought him to a point of acting on pure intuition in that moment of emptiness.

In 1984, John and Toni Lilly asked me to become Director of Research with Joe and Rosie. Dr. Lilly and I had differing ideas of communication; his vision was to teach the dolphins to speak English with a computer interface. My approach was to learn what I called Delphinese, a primarily nonverbal exchange without technology. Dr. Lilly gave me no guidance and unconditional support. I was free to do as I pleased!

In Dr. Lilly's original design for the JANUS Project, computer-generated frequencies were assigned to each letter of the alphabet. By typing words, a series of pure tones would be produced. But in a modification, the computer was programmed with 40 discrete whistles, each assigned to a behavior, location, or object. For three years, Joe and Rosie were rewarded with a fish each time they demonstrated the appropriate trained behavior when cued by these whistles. They could do this 100% correctly when they felt like it, but were often given time outs for inattention.

Assuming charge, I replaced the tedium of JANUS with a number of experimental opportunities. Standing at a new position for the first trial, I gave them the cue for "wave pec fin." They performed their usual opener, a "bow." Although this was an incorrect response, I tossed them fish and cheered them on. I must say, they had an amused tilt to their heads. From that first trial, they never did anything "right" in these sessions. Rather, they gave 100% incorrect responses to each cue, and yet I rewarded them every time! Joe and Rosie continued experimenting with creative responses to every sonic cue in these sessions throughout the summer. Yet, when I needed them to perform for a television crew, I stood in the original station and began the session with "bow." They went right back to the Janus behaviors, 100% correct again!

As much fun and elucidating as it is, as affectionate as they can be, working with captured dolphins sequestered to live in small concrete tanks is heartbreaking. From my first moments at the side of the petting pool at Marine World, throughout years of communication work as a diver for the park, and as Research Director for Dr. John C. Lilly, my heart and soul cried for the dolphins' freedom. As Director of Project Communion for the Human/Dolphin Foundation, I was Joe and Rosie's un-trainer. I encouraged them to think for themselves, find new meanings, make up behaviors, and discover the fun in novelty. My wide array of experiments demonstrated that the dolphins were capable of higher-order reasoning such as complex thinking, taking on challenging tasks, and creativity.

Cindi Buzzell came to my work/scholar program with a background as an exotic animal trainer. She became my co-conspirator in keeping Joe and Rosie entertained. In the water and out, Cindi and I offered the dolphins authentic communication and deep respect. We made a sincere and enthusiastic effort towards understanding them and evolving our beliefs.

When the three-year-old dolphins were captured at Gulfport, Mississippi, Dr. Lilly expressed his intention to return the dolphins to the sea after a short term with humans. He had pledged one year and four years had passed. The time to honor that promise had come. With the financial assistance of a German family, we were offered the extraordinary opportunity to fly Joe and Rosie back to the sea.

Under a full moon in September 1984, Cindi and I relocated from Redwood City to the Florida Keys with Joe and Rosie. Dolphins Plus, the original swim-with-dolphins facility, let us put a door in the fence between their enclosure and the channel leading to the ocean. I began feeding them from my windsurf board in their pen in preparation for following a boat into the sea. Just as adaptation to captivity from the wild is a gradual process, re-adaptation to the wild is also a progression.

Rick Doblin invited John Lilly and me to Sarasota, Florida, where a passionate community supported our efforts to bring the dolphins closer to home. On a private island, in the dolphins' home waters of the Gulf of Mexico, we proposed the development of a long-term rehabilitation, adaptation, and release center. The nearby Mote Marine Lab stepped up to assist us. Unfortunately, this project came to a halt when we determined that Rosie was pregnant. We did not want to put her through the trauma of a move.

Tanks to Sea

Almost 30 years later, there is no protocol today for successfully releasing captive dolphins back to their natural habitat, the ocean. Tanks to Sea is my proposal to document previously captured dolphins making the shift from human care to the sea and to create a protocol to support them in acquiring behaviors necessary for survival.

Proof of successful adaptation and release protocol is needed for the U.S. government to grant permits for release and thus open the door for more dolphins to return to their native environment. I've searched for the perfect location for such a temporary research facility. Kona's year-round clear, calm waters are perfect for documenting behaviors. There is a healthy population of several subspecies of dolphins, who associate with each other. Here, or somewhere similar, is where I imagine demonstrating a protocol for integration to the sea.

Stage one of this project involves open-water work and documentation, leading to establishing a protocol for future release permits. Although not always feasible, the best case would be to complete the reintegration at a Stage Two location closer to the dolphins' original home.

I invite you to join my efforts to bring appropriate dolphin candidates home to the sea. My project, Tanks to Sea, will provide the possibility for dolphins to return to their natural environment. I'm looking for locations and people of the sea – humans and dolphins -- to participate in this ocean-breaking research.

153

Dolphins in the Wild

The summer of 1985, John Lilly returned to Malibu to be with his wife Toni as she was dying. They assigned the dolphins to another non-profit formed to release them. They were let go into the Atlantic three years later.

I turned my focus to dolphins in the wild. While pregnant, I traveled with my husband, David Goodman, on a magical journey with a household of 13 from Nashville to New Zealand. We stayed at Estelle Myers' Rainbow Dolphin Centre for two months before moving on to Australia. My dream came true when I looked out my window to see dorsal fins rising through the rosy water of Shark Bay at dawn. David and I lived in a campervan on the beach at Monkey Mia where exceptionally friendly bottlenose played with us in the shallows. Well known matriarch, Holy Fin, frequented the beach. Her three-year-old youngster, Holly, swam into my lap as I knelt in the sand, lying belly-to-belly and eye-to-eye with me when I was nine months pregnant! My daughter, Harmony, was born shortly after in Perth, despite efforts to have her there on the beach.

After returning to the States, my husband, David, Harmony and I lived in Key West, Florida. We went out with our housemate, Ron Canning, to swim with the bottlenose he had befriended. Captain Ron took out daily charters to this pod.

Maui called me back for the fourth time. John Lilly sent me a ticket to join him in Paia with a proposal of marriage. To be free, I had to wait for a divorce from David. In 1992, while living with John Lilly at the edge of the sea, we wrote and signed a declaration of the Cetacean Nation. The Cetacean Nation was first presented by Dr. Lilly at the Whales Alive conference the following year. John and I remained close friends for the rest of his life, and again I was his fiancée during the month of his death in September 2001.

David Glickman introduced me to whale research with Dan Salden's Hawaii Whale Research Foundation. David and I shared incredible moments in the midst of the humpbacks' immense presence. I enjoyed two years on a research permit taking underwater video of humpback whales. Our footage was shown at Whales Alive and internationally.

In 1994, I visited friends on the Big Island of Hawaii, swam with the spinner dolphins, and decided to stay. For 12 years I was the only one in my harbor taking a boat out to see dolphins and whales. The fishermen would bet on whether I would return.

The influx of boats now has me concerned that that the pods will be overwhelmed with the demands of tourism. Now with my own boat, I am finding new ways to simply BE with the dolphins, absorbing their presence with minimal disturbance. My guests take new meaning back to their lives at home. People who have been to dolphinariums usually ask me three questions about the wild dolphins: Do you touch them? Do you feed them? Where, or when, will we find them?

In the wild, we do not intentionally touch physically. We meet dolphins who touch people, not with their bodies, but with their uplifting spirits. No one feeds them, and they do not eat dead fish. Each day we never know where the pods will be or how far we must go to be with them.

Dolphins Are From Neptune

To gain a deeper understanding of their psyches and their effects on our lives, I say, "If women are from Venus, and men are from Mars, dolphins are from Neptune.

Applying the symbolic, astrological association of the planet Neptune to dolphins is my way of trying to express a deeper understanding of their psyches and the effects they have upon our human lives. Dolphins clearly expand what we consider possible. Neptune rules our imaginations and dreams, the frontier of today's generations. Those who guide others into the realm of the cetaceans live esoteric lives rich in artistic expression.

Exploring consciousness, we are perched on the brink of a new reality through expanding consciousness. Our wonder and awe are opened wide by dolphin contact, tempting us into altered states and finding the limits of belief.

Dr. John C. Lilly's maxim applies, defining the boundaries of our imaginations: "In the province of the mind, what one believes to be true either is true or becomes true within limits to be found experientially and experimentally. These limits are further beliefs to be transcended. In the province of the mind, there are no limits." After several near death experiences, he later cautioned, "In the province of the body, there are limits."

Dolphins aren't aliens. They show us another way of prioritizing life on Earth. When we visit dolphins in the sea, we have the opportunity to release old concepts and take on new ones. Sociable wild dolphins offer pivotal moments such as Ram Dass experienced with Rosie. I suggest a protocol for these encounters, calling three basic steps the Dolphin Secrets.

First, the more relaxed you are, the more relaxed the dolphins will be around you. Float, breathe, relax, and surrender to the ocean. You are weightless. The second Dolphin Secret is to Go in Grace – be smooth and respectful in your movements. Release expectation and open to the grace of being among dolphins in the sea. The third Dolphin Secret is to be present in the moment as you come into eye-to-eye contact. You may experience timelessness, slow motion with a feeling of being understood.

Relax and breathe. Go in Grace. Be present in eye-to-eye contact.

We learn from dolphins how to restore our harmony, interconnection and resonance -- with ourselves, our relationships, our world, nature and our higher purpose.

Cetacean Nation

In 1992, while living with John Lilly at the edge of the sea, we began Cetacean Nation. Lilly and I wrote and signed a declaration to introduce the Rights of Cetaceans under International Law.

Cetacean Nation

Dr. John C. Lilly announces the formation of Cetacean Nation, representing whales, dolphins, and porpoises from Oceania, covering 70% of our planet.

Dolphins have brains comparable to ours; whales have brains up to six times larger. No matter the differences between species, no matter differences of anatomy, no matter differences between media in which they live, creatures with a brain above a certain size will be considered equal with man.

Human decisions have major repercussions in the oceans and in the lives of Cetaceans. Cetacean Nation assumes human responsibility for protecting the interests of the world's Cetaceans until they can speak for themselves. Learning to communicate with Cetaceans, we are forced to take a much closer look at our own deficiencies of communication, within persons and between persons. For the well-being of each one of us, for the national and international peace of all of us, communication is a paramount and pressing issue.

Cetacean Nation aspires to representation in the decisions of the United Nations. We propose a platform for expressing outlooks from the Cetaceans' point of view.

John Lilly and Roberta Quist, co-founders of Cetacean Nation, ask that you discover more about the lives of the people of Oceania. We invite you to join in harmony with each other and voice a positive difference for both Cetaceans and Homo sapiens.

Dr. John Lilly   Roberta Quist
December 20, 1992   Paia, Maui

Roberta Goodman's career began in 1978 when she read Dr. John Lilly's book, *Communication Between Man and Dolphin.* In 1980 she found nine dolphin mentors and began a five-year relationship under their tutelage. As Research Director for the renowned Dr. Lilly, she initiated the release of the Human/Dolphin Foundation's dolphins, Joe and Rosie. Since 1986, Roberta has spent time with dolphins only in the wild. Her communication studies continue during daily trips to pods in Hawaii.

With stories of both domesticated and wild dolphins, Roberta illustrates the reasoning behind considering Cetaceans as persons with culture, sentience and exceptional intelligence. Roberta co-founded Cetacean Nation with John Lilly in 1993, declaring the rights of whales and dolphins as a People. One day she says we will all understand the wisdom of the dolphins as we now understand the wisdom of indigenous peoples.

Readers find connection and intimacy with dolphins through Roberta's stories, allowing dolphins to enter the reader's consciousness. Roberta escorts those who come to her into the emerging human dolphin culture evolving around the world. Receiving tips, techniques, and guidelines for entering the water with the pods, guests experience an endless stream of natural behaviors and games from breathtaking numbers of dolphins in close proximity. Some guests conquer a fear of deep water for the reward of watching dolphins play right under them as they float calmly on the surface. Other guests go on the swim of a lifetime, keeping a slow pace along the shore within a pod of frolicking dolphins. In every case, lives are altered.

Roberta's vision is to create a center for rehabilitation of domesticated dolphins into their natural ocean environment. *Tanks to Sea* is her ongoing readaptation and documentation project.

www.WildDolphinSwimsHawaii.com

Chapter 12: *Bubbles and Circles With the Dolphins*

By Cyndie Lepori

Let us now dance above the ocean, as we have sung the stars below;
For those who listen from awakened mind,
we herald the path to Home.
Let us now rejoice in transcending our way home into the Sun,
As we have known the moon of our waters,
and allow Love to see us on;
Let us now Love all we are in each other's soul,
For we have been within, where you are, and know we are not alone.
All we are is each other. All we are is Love. So be it. Amen.
- From the upcoming book, Prayers from the Heart of the Sea,
by Lindsey Kelly

I was introduced to the dolphins and whales in a very roundabout way. When I was 24 years old, Spirit told me to go to nursing school. I was already a healer and had been getting messages from Spirit since meeting my first teacher, Charles Thomas, in Ellisville, Mississippi, when I was 18. He informed me that I would surpass everything that he was doing and more. I, of course, did not believe him at all. Then I heard that spirit voice one night that clearly told me to go to University of Southern Mississippi Nursing School and get my Registered Nursing degree.

For the Nursing Degree Program, I had to take a physical education class. Since my journeys had always involved water, and I had friends who were scuba-divers, I chose the hardest program to pass: scuba diving. I was totally enthralled with breathing under water. From the first moment under water, I was very comfortable and excelled in this class. Only 10 of us made it through, and I was the first female to get certified in several years. When we did our first dive in Pensacola, Florida, I had a tiny seahorse wrapped around my little finger and fish all around. It was amazing. I felt more free and easy than I did on land. My love affair with the ocean began. We spotted dolphins on our first trip out, and I had no idea where these adventures would lead with these beautiful beings. I can still feel the amazing joy that I felt on that day.

I graduated my nursing class with honors and then spent every dime I made, and every moment I had, going to Gulf Shores, Alabama, and Playa Del Carmen, Mexico. I spent my time in the clear blue Gulf of Mexico with the dolphins and ocean beings. During this time I became a scuba instructor. My next goal was to relocate from Laurel, Mississippi, to Hawaii to really start my spiritual, diving, and healing adventures. After six months, I landed in Aiea, HI, working at Wahiwa General Hospital as a travel nurse. Nursing was also my passion, plus spirit was still at work.

Aiea, Hawaii and Ocean Adventures

I also had as a second job in Pearl City, Hawaii, teaching Navy Seals to pleasure dive at the Pearl Island Diving Center.

I first met the humpback whales on a trip to see my stepbrother, Tom, who was visiting in Maui. Tom was an avid sailor and scuba diver. During my visit, we went to swim in the ocean with the humpbacks, and I met a whale eye-to-eye as we swam in their frequencies near Maui. Meeting the eye of the humpback whale showed me what wisdom the humpbacks hold, instantly transforming how I saw them forever.

The spinners swam with me, dancing their dolphin dances on many dives that I made from the Big Island to Oahu that year. I was diving every weekend and many times during the week, mostly from the shore. For my 30th birthday, my friends from the hospital invited me to come to a party with them where they called up the whales and dolphins with singing, drums and guitars. I dove in. It was at night, the stars were shining, and I was in a whole pod of dolphins and whales for hours with no gear, just playing with them. At that time, I had no idea who they really were or that I could communicate with them. I did know that these experiences were changing how I experienced the world. I was filled with joy at every encounter with the dolphins and whales. After a year of bliss in Hawaii diving with every creature that I possibly could, it was time to go home. My contract was up, and I could only stay for a year. So on to Orlando, Florida, I went.

I had met Jeff, my husband-to-be, while I was attending nursing school. While I was in Hawaii, he asked me to marry him. My son, Charlie, was living with Jeff and my Mother while I was in Hawaii. We all reunited when I flew to New Orleans. On my way back from Hawaii, Jeff and I married in Gulf Shores, Alabama, with my son and the dolphins in attendance on a boat in the Gulf of Mexico. We all moved together to Orlando, Florida. I had a job at Orlando Regional Medical Center as a level-one trauma nurse which would enable us to live there quite comfortably.

Orlando, Florida and Introduction to Sailing

My stepbrother Tom lived in Ft. Lauderdale, Florida, and owned a sailboat shop. He called right after we moved to Orlando and needed a deck hand for a couple of weeks to go to the Bahamas with him. For me this was not even a question! I got my husband and son settled in Orlando and off I went with their blessings. Dolphins, sailing from island to island, living on the sea. I added sailing to my ocean addictions. Tom and I had a wonderful trip with the dolphins and others of the sea coming to visit every day. We shot our food and lived much as the people of old on this primitive sailboat. Again I was swimming with my friends the dolphins almost on a daily basis.

The next year, I went from the Keys to Jefferson Island, located below Key West, on the same sailboat. Tom remarked about how he had never seen so many dolphins and how they seemed to hunt me out. At one point, when we were trying to hunt for lunch but the dolphins were getting in the way, Tom suggested that I ask my friends to leave so that we could get lunch. This idea was far beyond my comprehension at that time. When I asked them out loud if they could give us a break, they all disappeared at the same time. (I should have asked them to round up the fish for us, but it did not occur to me at the time.)

Laurel, Mississippi

After three years in Orlando, Florida, Jeff, Charlie and I had to return to our home in Mississippi to take care of my stepfather who had cancer. Tearfully we left Orlando to move back home. While in Orlando, I met my next spiritual teacher who did re-birthing in water. His name was Angel.

Like a dolphin jumping forward, I learned Reiki in Mississippi, and how to define what I was doing in my healing/spiritual work with Angel's assistance. I started to carry this information out to people in Mississippi. I worked for Forest General Hospital and taught many nurses therapeutic touch and Reiki energy healing. I ended up doing home and hospice care during the day, and at night, I would carry my Reiki table to clients' homes and work with them until all hours of the night. My husband did not understand what I was doing and his family did not approve. I could not refuse to be a healer and not use my abilities, so we had a parting of the ways after I became desperately sick trying to please everyone.

Angel reappeared to tell me about an organization called Lifesprings in Ft. Lauderdale and how these empowering classes could change my life and take it to the next level. Lifesprings is a class on living skills and how to create a better life. I was absolutely not going. I got very sick. I did not have the money and was too ill to drive. A miracle occurred. Checks arrived in the mail until I had full tuition. I drove straight through to Ft. Lauderdale and took every class that Lifesprings offered. In fact, it did change my life.

Gulf Shores, Alabama

A year later, after I had returned home from Ft. Lauderdale, I received a call from my friend Arlene. She told me that her parents were sick and asked if I could go down and run Pleasure Island Dive Center and be an instructor in her shop in her absence. So, within a month of my return to Mississippi, I moved to Gulf Shores, Alabama, to work at the dive shop. There, I could be with my beloved dolphins and beings of the sea again.

Now I could spend more time underwater than above; sometimes I did four to six dives a day! Even on my days off, we went diving. We saw dolphins on a daily basis, and many people remarked that they seemed to come to me. I just knew I loved dolphins and loved introducing them to my students. I spent many hours organizing and cleaning up the ocean and Gulf. I truly enjoyed teaching people about the ocean and promoting environmental awareness and the importance of every being that lives in the Gulf.

I worked with many different boat captains for the three years that I played in the Gulf. A bond forms with your dive buddies. I formed a bond with Frank. We spent hours talking about our dreams of living on the ocean and what would it be like to dive, sail, and live this dream, not knowing that it would lead to it happening in a very real way. I eventually ran off with my boat captain and permanently moved to Gulf Shores to fulfill our dream of living on a sailboat for the rest of our lives. We sold everything we had and started to manifest our dream of living on a sailboat. We walked every dock in Florida looking for the perfect boat.

In the middle of this adventure, I had a medication reaction and had what I call a "dead as a hammer" experience. (Most people would call it a near death experience.) I stood in the light and watched one part of myself walk into the light and another being came back to continue this life. The doctors still can't figure out how I am walking around, but that is another story.

Frank and I found the sailing vessel *Sanador* on a canal in Ft. Lauderdale, right behind the house where Angel, Karen and I were roommates. I walked with Karen's mother Barbie everyday beside these canals and had seen the boat many years before. (Karen had a beautiful condo where she took care of her mom.) As a retired nurse, I had helped Angel and Karen while I was going to the Lifesprings classes, before moving back to Mississippi. Frank and I were down in Ft. Lauderdale so that he could take the Lifesprings courses while I looked for a boat for us to live on. The dolphins were completing another circle so that I could be with them again!

Frank and I sailed that Thanksgiving on the *Sanador* with our little Chihuahua, Abbigale, off to parts unknown for the great adventure, and sure enough, it was.

In my book, *Bubbles and Billy Sandwalker,* there is a chapter called "The Puppies Speak." In this chapter, I relate how my dog Abbi taught me that she could communicate with me. She was a very exceptional Chihuahua and so very patient with her human in teaching me communication. The story is pretty close to what actually happened in real life. We saw dolphins daily, and when they would come near, Abbi would start barking and howling to get out of the cabin of the boat. She loved the dolphins and loved to play with me on the front of the boat, so the combination was her idea of heaven!

One day when she started to howl to get out and tell me the dolphins were coming to play. I ran and grabbed her up and went to the front of the boat. We were looking at the dolphins coming toward us, and Abbi pointed out to me that there were no babies with them. They came to the bow to wave jump with us, all turning sideways and looking at Abbi and me, as we watched them. I was happy and giggling. Abbi suddenly went still and told me to talk to the dolphins and tell them to go get their babies. Just for a lark, I turned to the dolphins and said out loud, "Abbi would love to meet your babies. Go get them!" Instantly they all disappeared. I was upset. After a few moments, they all reappeared. Lo and behold their babies were in tow! I was so shocked that I had to just sit down. Then I heard Abbi say to the dolphins that I was a little slow, but thanks for teaching her human that she could talk to dolphins too. I had to laugh at that and we played together, Abbi, the dolphins and me the rest of the day. After that amazing breakthrough, it became a common occurrence for the beings of the sea such as turtles, dolphins, and other beings to communicate with me and Abbi. Abbi, Frank, and I sailed and lived on the *Sanador* for three years. It was heaven-on-earth to me.

Mobile, Alabama to Stringer, Mississippi

Spirit led us to start a green oil spill company using peat moss in Mobile, Alabama. That ended with the economic crash of 9/11. I moved back to Mississippi thinking that I was leaving the boat, but again spirit had other plans. I started a Reiki group in Petal, Mississippi, and was teaching one class a week when my soul mate walked in. His name was Michel Touchstone.

While I was teaching classes, I was led by "accident" to a group in Huntsville, Alabama, that taught me to channel and work with frequencies and vibrations, such that this planet had never seen before. This wonderful group taught me to be a direct channel for the beings off-planet that love and want to create heaven-on-earth for all of humanity.

One of the first missions that came to my attention was the problem with the dolphins and sonar. There was a huge beaching in north Florida. I had an inspiration. If we had oversouls, since the dolphins were fully present sentient beings, they had oversouls also. They could be "sponsored" and taught about the actions of humanity in the ocean and thus protect themselves from being harmed by the ships creating this havoc in the Gulf and other places. On this premise, I contacted the others in the group and we had a channeling session where we contacted the dolphins, whales, and others of the sea and created a plan to educate them about the sonar. We had their angels tell them where the ships were that could harm them, and they could just be other places. It worked for the most part. There were no other beachings for several years in the Gulf. When the next incident occurred, I contacted the Dolphins and asked them what happened. They told me that they had done it to call attention to the problem. Because of this, we went to the angels and assisted with getting laws passed in Florida to prevent sonar from being used around their coasts.

In the meantime, Mike, my soul mate, got sick. We thought that he had contracted mold in his sinuses, simply because we helped with the rebuilding of a friend's house after Hurricane Ivan. I had gotten the *Sanador* back and paid off all the loans. We planned to travel on it, not live on it to do hurricane repairs, but Spirit had another plan.

We parked the *Sanador* and went west so that Mike could get well. While we were in Sedona, I picked up a *Sedona Journal of Emergence* and it opened to an advertisement for Linda Shay and her Dolphin Healing HeArts school. It was a moment frozen in time. I got chills from head to toe as I excitedly told Mike I would go to that school. He promised me that I would and we would find a way for me to come back. When we returned to Mississippi, Mike was diagnosed with cancer. Sadly, he died six weeks later.

A few months later I got a postcard in the mail telling me that Linda Shay would be coming to Pensacola for a talk at Unlimited Horizons. I was not going to miss that for sure! I did go, and when she mentioned the six Attunements, I felt the frequencies of all six come in. When we did the meditation, I saw seven ocean beings come in as my guides. And when she asked for a volunteer for her demonstration of Dolphin Healing, I was on my feet like a shot. I was totally blown away by that day and knew beyond a shadow of a doubt that this was my next step in my dolphin adventures. I will always be grateful for these weekends that gave me language and tools from the dolphins. Not only did I complete the six weekends, but I moved back to Florida to put together other weekends for her and assisted.

After we had our last weekend with Linda Shay in Florida, all the energy shifted. I was no longer assisting with Dolphin Heart World and so was looking for how to serve the dolphins, whales, and ocean beings next.

Then I started getting messages to go to the beach and start sending frequencies to the water, and to use the crystals in the beaches as an antenna to send the higher frequencies throughout the world. I started this in the form of playshops, and it evolved until I was going at least monthly to send these amazing healing beams throughout the world with many people participating at certain dates and times.

I had no idea why I was being called to do this until the Gulf oil spill happened. We have continued to send healing to the Gulf and assist with getting information out about the environment ever since. My film that went across the world on *FOX News* with Capt. Lori DeAngelis called the attention of the world to the distress of the dolphin pods in Gulf Shores and can be found on YouTube along with the free demonstration of the Bubble exercise that will start your journey with the dolphin energies. I did physical dolphin rescues and eventually got sick from the oil spill and had to return home to Mississippi where I wrote the book *Bubbles and Billy Sandwalker*.

Bubbles and Billy Sandwalker is a book that is for all of humanity. It teaches about who the dolphins really are, the blue people who are the off-planet counterpart for the dolphins, the gifts that the dolphins bring, and animal communication. This simple work of fiction shows us all how to use frequencies to heal the planet. Although this book has no villains, it entertains and gets the messages across in a funny and positive light.

I have connected with mermaid frequencies and channel mermaids. I created a support group for mermaids on Facebook for those of us who can't stay away from the seas. Anne Gordon told me about the need to assist the Sea Rays. We created an amazing adventure with the Golden Rays and assisted in the clearing and healing of these beautiful beings.

Now I can't go to the beach without these beautiful beings following me up and down the shore. This created another chapter in my book *Bubbles and Billy Sandwalker.*

I am still creating playshops and weekends for those interested in learning about the dolphin/human connections and how living from your heart can change your life on a daily basis. It includes the Dolphin Merkaba Activation, working with and shifting into higher frequencies, and creating a different way of seeing the world and your place in it. I also can put together Dolphin playshops on the water so that while we experience the energies we can see the physical dolphins. I have worked with autistic children several times with the dolphin energies with amazing results. We usually take a trip to the Gulfarium in Ft. Walton Beach for that. I take people to swim in the Gulf and experience the magic when the dolphins come by.

I am an author for an animal communication magazine, *Species Link*, and appear on radio shows frequently to talk about energies, dolphins, whales, and environmental issues. I am a speaker and vendor at Paracon, Unlimited Horizons, The UFO conference in Eureka Springs, and many other festivals. I do channelings and readings worldwide and am a member of several groups working globally with the frequencies and energies for ascension energies for the earth and all beings on it. This is part of my beach activation work.

"How can I describe the indescribable talents of Cyndie Lepori, Dolphin emissary? Feeling her work will tell anyone with a modicum of sensitivity that her connection with the energies of the dolphin and cetacean world is nothing short of profound. I have interviewed and worked with Cyndie on both of my Talk Shows, "What the Animals Tell Me" and "Woman Spirit Rising."

We have shared information about the beloved dolphins and she was incredibly informative about their ways of communication and the challenges that they face in the world where they are so incredibly endangered.

Probably the most incredible and engaging experiences that I have had with Cyndie occurred during her Dolphin Workshop and on my radio show "Woman Spirit Rising" where she co-Priestesses with me monthly. In both situations it was her use of her Bubble Ritual which she taught us.

This is an incredible process that she channeled from the Dolphins themselves. You basically create a magical bubble around you placing yourself inside and asking all that is not for your highest good in this bubble to leave. After that you are encouraged to feel how you feel minus all the funk that may be hanging on you or sucking your energies, after which you bring your guides and helpers back in and feel that as well. This is a wonderful way to create good boundaries, release that which does not help you, yet keep that which helps you close at hand. As a sensitive one who needs to keep my energy field clear this has been a wonderful tool and I use it daily! It has been a great tool to share on the show as well.

Cyndie has just the right balance of intuition and intellect to offer others a gentle but powerful road to healing and inspiration."

- Flash Silvermoon - Animal Communicator, Author, Psychic and Talk Show Host

"Cyndie Lepori opened up the world of the dolphins to me through her wonderful book, "Bubbles and Billy Sandwalker," and through her Dolphin Workshop. In the Dolphin Workshop, Cyndie introduced us to the bubble. It is my practice to start my meditations with a protective affirmation and now I use the bubble for that purpose. Using the bubble, which Cyndie explained is a gift from the dolphins, is a great way for me to rid my aura of negative entities and honor my spirit guides, guardians and helpers. Among these beautiful spirits is Blue, the dolphin who adopted me in the Dolphin Playshop. She gives me a kiss every time I create my bubble to remind me how much love she and all the dolphins have to give. Thanks to Cyndie, I have opened up to all that love. I recommend "Bubbles and Billy Sandwalker" to readers of all ages for a delightful adventure in the magical world of the dolphins." – Pandora Lightmoon, Meditation teacher, visionary, New Age editor

"Cyndie's work with the dolphins embodies the path and practice of Radical Joy for Hard Times. She is not afraid to look at what's wrong, yet she never lingers in grief, but dives passionately into awareness, energy and creativity. She is a gift to the dolphins and people alike." – Trebbe Johnson, Founder and Director, Radical Joy for Hard Times.

Cyndie Lepori, RN, BSN, Dolphin Emissary. Cyndie is an Ascension Reiki Master/Teacher, Level 13, and certified Dolphin Energy Healing practitioner from Linda Shay's and David Rosenthal's Dolphin Healing HeArts school. She is a Certified PADI Scuba Diving Instructor and Sailor. She has been chosen by the Dolphins and Whales to be an Ocean Emissary and teach the Bubbles of Joy Playshops. She is a Channeler, Medium, and Animal Communicator.

Cyndie Lepori has authored *Bubbles and Billy Sandwalker*, which teaches the gifts from the dolphins in a fun and educational way, with beautiful illustrations by Layne Murrish throughout. Cyndie is currently creating two new versions of the *Bubbles and Billy Sandwalker* book for younger children. She is a writer for *Species Link Magazine* and *Fate Magazine.*

She is currently writing a new book called *SEAS Spiritual Energy Ascension Systems.* This is a series of dowsing cards and techniques to reconnect to Higher Plane Energies. She volunteers with the Spirit Rescue Group and the Radical Joy for Hard Times Group.

Cyndie creates ocean healing events called Beach Activations to send healing energies to the waters internationally. Her YouTube videos are free and demonstrate the Bubble Exercises. Her "Hope for the Dolphins" video was shot during the BP oil spill. This clip went worldwide via *Fox News* to call attention of the oil on the dolphins.

For 33 years, she has brought passion and integrity to her work. With her background in nursing, and her developed skills as an intuitive on quantum levels, Cyndie balances spirituality with common sense.

www.dolphinhugs4u2.net   dolphinhugs4u2@gmail.com
Youtube: Lasanadora2002
Facebook: Cyndie.Lepori

Chapter 13: *The Grace of Interspecies Family, Love and Healing*

By Teresa Wagner

In all except our bodies,
we are the same as our whale brothers and sisters,
and our connection is a sacred and powerful one.
When our lives intersect and we help one another
in ways we are called and able to do,
an undeniable grace fills us all.
- Teresa Wagner

Like most life changing experiences, my own transformation from meeting a whale was not planned or anticipated. In October of 1988, I traveled to Provincetown, Massachusetts for a long weekend packaged trip that just happened to include whale watching. At the time I knew nothing about whales. I would not have known a humpback whale from a sperm whale if they were in front of me, and I knew little of our human history of slaughtering whales until I learned the harrowing statistics from the on-board naturalist.

When I saw my first whale that year in Stellwagen Bank, a national marine sanctuary in the Gulf of Maine, my life changed irrevocably. As we watched dozens of humpbacks from the Dolphin Fleet boat, I was immediately awed by their physical magnificence: their beautiful, long white pectoral fins, gliding like wings with a grace surpassing any human ballerina; their fifteen foot wide flukes lifting above the water soundlessly and delicately, belying their great power; then seeing their spectacular physical power when hurling their 45 ton bodies out of the water, breaching. I found myself alternately weeping and screaming in joy. Every view of their bodies took my breath away. As Roger Payne[15] has said, "You can't encounter a whale for the first time and not remember it for the rest of your life." We saw seventy-four humpbacks that afternoon and even the reserved naturalist started squealing about the unusually high number of whales around us. I was smitten.

One whale came right to the side of the boat and stayed for about an hour. I was mesmerized. Time seemed to stop. I went on this weekend jaunt with a friend simply for some relaxing time away from sixty-hour work weeks. I knew next to nothing about whales and hadn't an inkling that my life was about to be transformed because of them. But the moment I saw this whale I felt something shift deep inside me. I felt love as I've never felt it before. It was as if I were somehow awakening, though to what I didn't know. As I looked into his eye, the trust and love he offered was as clear and real to me as the bumpy tubercles on his head. As we continued to look at each other, the hair on my scalp tingled and chills raced down my spine. I knew I was with family. I knew I was somehow home but I didn't yet understand why. I also knew I was in the presence of a great being. I was at one with this whale, a profound oneness that took me completely by surprise.

As I cried tears of ecstasy, telling him over and over, "I love you, and thank you for coming," I distinctly heard him speak to me. He gently, knowingly offered detailed, loving guidance on very personal issues in my life, and said he would be honored to continue to be available to assist and guide me through my life, along with a group of other whales who knew and loved me from long ago. I felt as if I suddenly had a wise, loving

---

[15] *Among Whales*, Roger Payne Scribner, 1995

great grandfather and other elders to help me in life. And then it hit me: here was this gentle, trusting and wise whale who quite obviously came intentionally to the boat, the same type of human-made vehicles that carried humans who, not so long ago, relentlessly hunted and slaughtered whales in these very same waters. I asked him how he and other whales could bear the presence of humans, and why he chose to come so close to a boat and stay for so long--since boats and people represent the very combination of what brought (and still brings) a horrible death to millions of whales. He said,

> "Some whales have returned to earth to stop the cycle of hate, to continue to bring love to the earth. We know that many humans find us charismatic and beautiful. We find that when we are close to humans many of them like us, begin to love us, and open their hearts to all the whales. It is only love that will heal violence. We come for the love--to give it, receive it and to create more. And I came to you because we have a long and intimate history which you will soon remember."

Right before he left, the last thing he said to me was,

> "Teresa, loving us so much, and loving your cats [I didn't tell him I had cats, he just knew I had cats] as deeply as you now do, there is something we would like you to think about, to just gently ponder, without any judgment or harshness, just to reflect upon. And that is to consider not wearing our cousin the fox on your back and not putting our cousins the cows, the pigs, the chickens and fish in your belly when you can nourish your body with other food that does not cause suffering. We ask you to consider this. We love you."

I was stunned. As much as I loved my cats and other animals, I realized the moment he said these words that I had been living with blinders on. I had not wanted to even think about the pain and suffering endured by the beautiful foxes who suffered for my vanity and the thousands of animals who died horrible and gruesome deaths so I could eat what I was culturally taught to eat. I had never wanted to think about such things and no one ever asked me to consider them before. Now, I could not. I didn't feel at all judged. His tone was gentle, soft, loving, unimposing and utterly void of admonishment. It was more like he suggested that I might want to turn on a light bulb. I did, and the light showed clearly how my choices created horrific and unnecessary suffering for animals. I knew what I needed to do.

I went home changed. I got rid of the fur coats and became a vegetarian. I began to see and feel the God in everything. I was an avid rose gardener and for years had systematically and chemically killed the Japanese beetles who love to eat roses. When I first went into my rose garden after this trip, I saw the beetles for the first time. They were not pests, they were stunningly beautiful beings! Realizing the horror of what I had done to them, I humbly offered my deepest apologies, promising never to harm them again. Incredibly, they forgave me--albeit slowly-- and later promised that they would not eat more than 10% of a given rose. And they kept that promise. We became friends and talked often. I also promised the birds, the insects and the soil that I would never again place chemicals into the earth that harmed them. We came to balance. I began to sing to them and the roses when in the garden. I was no longer the "owner" of the garden but its steward. Peace was restored, all because I met a whale.

About a week after the trip I attended a party in an upscale apartment in Philadelphia filled with stylishly dressed, upwardly mobile corporate professionals who were my peers. Suddenly I realized I didn't fit anymore. A deeper meaning to life had presented itself to me with the appearance of this whale. Much of my lifestyle now seemed shallow. At the party when I talked about the whales most people's eyes glazed over. When my women friends chatted about where Calvin Klein pumps and Harve' Bernard suits were on sale, my eyes glazed over. Something was wrong. Only a week before, I was a serious clothes shopper. Now, that seemed frivolous, and it paled in comparison to the vibrancy of communing with the whales.

Meeting that very first whale began my journey away from a conventional set of values to begin to find my true self, and to create more meaningful ways of working and living. Nothing was wrong. Everything was just beginning to be right. I have talked with animals since childhood, but until the day I met and spoke with this whale, I hid it because I wanted to be "normal." No more. A year later I moved to California where I felt Lemurian[16] energy and knew my soul belonged.

---

[16] Lemuria was a continent in the Pacific Ocean in existence approximately 50,000 years ago, with a culture of predominately female energy (sometimes referred to

Soon after, I began an animal communication practice and left a lucrative corporate career behind.

I believe that every human has their own unique path to knowing God, to remembering the Divine in all beings and within themselves. I also believe we each have a unique path to learning how to love and be loved. For some of us, these paths are lined with animals--being with them, near them, exchanging love with them, being guided and inspired by them, at times just looking at them. And for some of us, the animals that speak the loudest to us are the whales. For the first moment I saw a humpback, I yearned to be with them whenever and wherever I could. And so I did. I traveled to Alaska and Hawaii and returned to Provincetown many times to be reunited with these great beings who continued to guide me.

Though it was always a thrill and sacred experience to visit them physically, it also began to feel alienating and even stressful to be on boats in the company of others who didn't recognize who the whales really are. I often found myself with people who saw whales merely as the incidental focus of their latest ego-driven adventure, or as fascinating objects to be studied or photographed. I often felt like I was in a church trying to pray while others played racquetball off the altar. It was disconcerting. Though I have great respect for the naturalists and researchers who work very hard to study whales, their perspective often seems to preclude even the possibility of telepathic or spiritual connection. I often felt very lonely surrounded by rowdy vacationers and stoic scientists on boats. I felt closer to the whales in the water than with the humans on board. I yearned to be with the whales in the company of like-minded people and wanted to share the joy of the connection and the messages the whales were continuing to give me. And I had dreams of being in the water with them, in their home, looking into their eyes.

One day a phone call from a friend and client, Sierra Goodman[17], made these dreams come true. Sierra had recently begun offering wild dolphin swim trips and felt the experience would be enhanced for the group with an animal communicator on board. She asked if I would join her to talk with the dolphins on her next trip. I was thrilled, though not

---

as compassionate intelligence), benevolent leadership, and egalitarianism within and amongst all species.

[17] Founder of Divine Dolphin, www.divinedolphin.com

available for those dates. But I said, "Sierra, if you ever do a HUMPBACK WHALE swim trip, I'll drop anything I've scheduled to come do it!" Though I meant what I said, I never dreamed it would actually happen. I knew it was not legal to intentionally get into the water with whales in any U.S. waters. At the time, I didn't know it was legal and already happening in Silver Bank off the coast of the Dominican Republic. So, a year later when her phone call came asking if I'd facilitate a humpback whale trip for her with Penelope Smith, I thought I had died and gone to heaven. For the eleven years after I met my first whales off Provincetown, my relationship with them deepened exponentially as they guided me to understand and balance my identity as a soul with the challenges of an incarnation as a human on earth. They also continued, privately, to describe to me what the lives of whales on earth and in spirit were all about. As the time approached for the first swim trip in Silver Bank, things changed. The whales made it clear that it was time to share what they'd taught me.

By the time of this 1999 trip, I'd had an active animal communication practice for almost a decade, so translating messages from animals to humans was not something new. But talking with the whales for others was new. So I asked the whales what they wanted me to do on that trip. They said,

> "Tell the people that we have heard their call. When they felt the desire to come be with us on this trip, their call for connection with the whales was heard. Whales will be waiting to meet them in the water. For each person on board there will be a whale or whales with private messages for them to offer them encouragement, guidance and support for their current life issues and to answer their questions about whales. If they would like your help in hearing these messages tell them to come to you, and translate for them."

It turned out that every person in the group wanted this help so there were seventeen readings that week.

With this first trip and many since, I've done what the whales asked me to do--made private readings from the whales available for each participant. All of the whales come to these sessions with great love and intention to offer some form of guidance, encouragement, clarity or wisdom, usually about issues of current concern to the human. Yet each communication is different. Some of the whales have deep, intimate past life histories with the humans they come to speak with, while others come just for a temporary time for a person, perhaps as short as the duration of the trip, a particular phase in the human's life, or for their current lifetime. Some of the whales who come to speak with us are in spirit form, not physical form, while others are most definitely in the whale bodies with whom we interact during the trip. People describe the messages offered them by the whales as deeply meaningful, inspirational, sometimes of great practical value and sometimes transformational.

One woman's story about her whale communication experience aired on PAX television show Animal Miracles (now shown on Animal Planet). Her whale guide told me to tell her point blank:

> *"Leave your husband, now. We will have your back and so will your father."*

I could feel the energy of her father right there. I was nervous passing on such a blunt and directive message with such far reaching implications. When I did the woman began to cry and told me that her father had just died and that he had been her biggest supporter in life. She also described being in an abusive marriage and knew after hearing the whale give this message that it was time to leave. The reading continued for some time with much encouragement and guidance from her whale guide. The woman told me that it all confirmed what she already knew, but the message gave her the courage to transform her life. Six months later she wrote to me to say that she left her husband, left an unfulfilling career, quit smoking, became a vegetarian, and got a whale tattoo! She also later moved to Hawaii to be closer to the whales. She said that until she spoke with her whale guide, "I was a sinking ship, suicidal, but the whales have shown me that I have a place in this world and with their help I have taken it."

Helping other humans hear what the whales want to tell them, passing on the guidance they have for participants' individual life journeys, is one of the greatest privileges of my life. It is a great honor to watch people's hearts open and their consciousness expand from being with the whales in their water home and hearing the messages the whales have for them. In 2008 the whales told me it was time to teach the people on the trips how to communicate with them directly, so classes were designed and made available to all trip participants since then.

For me personally, being in the water with the whales changed everything. Eleven years of seeing them on the surface and talking with them regularly was enormously fulfilling. But entering their ocean home and literally being right next to them is the closest thing on earth that I've ever experienced to being in heaven. I've heard it said that when watching whales on the surface we see only approximately 10% of their bodies, except for breaching, of course, for those few seconds of immeasurable joy! Being with whales in the water we see all of them in all of their glorious, massive beauty--sometimes for hours at a time. The difference between seeing them from a boat and being with them in the water is the difference between having a pleasant day and having what feels like the most exquisite day of your life.

There are no words for it really. Being in the water with humpback whales is so other worldly I don't think our human language can adequately describe it. Each encounter, every moment of seeing them so up close in their home, feeling the intense depth of their profound love and acceptance of us as they approach us so closely, is an experience of love more easily felt than described. To swim with whales, so very close to their magnificent, huge, beautiful bodies in the water is such an undeniable thrill, yet at the same time, it doesn't seem to even matter that we have bodies when we're together. There seem to be no differences--only one spirit, only love. There is no fear, no alarm, no ego, only love. There is simply light and love.

I've been blessed to have over 150 encounters with humpbacks in the water[18], and every single one is a miracle to me. Yet, there are some

---

18 Such encounters with whales in this country are monitored by strict adherence to "soft-in-water" guidelines which are part of the official Silver Bank Regulations of the Sanctuary for the Marine Mammals of the Dominican Republic. These guidelines were developed by Captain Tom Conlin with whom I charter, in tandem with Dominican Republic government officials, for the purpose of keeping humans safe, whales undisturbed and to insure that it is always the whales' initiative and choice to have an encounter with humans. For the actual guidelines and more information read, "Is it really non-intrusive for whales?" at http://swimandcommunicatewithwhales.com/it-really-non-intrusive-whales.

that standout because of the personal, intimate connection between us, such as this one:

Underneath me three whales were lined up like a layer cake: a male escort on top, under him a calf, and under the calf the mother. As the gentle ocean swells moved my floating body, I was centered right on top of the huge male, though I could clearly see the baby and mother under him. I heard the message: "You are with family."

I immediately began to send them love. Often when I send love and healing energy to the whales in the water, it is to one whale at a time. But this time I felt such a surge of power, of love, of recognition, that my love encircled this entire whale family immediately. I didn't feel small anymore next to them. I felt as able to love as powerfully and hugely as they do. I created a web of light and love around them. It felt as if I had enough love and healing energy in me to heal the whole universe as I was with them doing this. I cried happily, so full of love, oneness and peace, so surrounded by family.

As I connected with the male, I felt our shared ancestry immediately. All whales are family to me, but he was immediate family and I knew it. We had all been together before in these waters as whales. I felt such a sense of safety, of belonging, of protection, of perfection of love. Feeling this as I saw them was overwhelming. I began to cry through my mask (not an easy thing to do!). I began to remember that this male had been an elder to me in the past. He was pleased that I remembered and knew so quickly. I sensed such great wisdom embodied in him, along with his willingness to share and impart it. Without words, this history and our story was simply there, between us, renewing our bond. I felt myself asking him silently for help in accessing more of my own natural powerful male energy for appropriate use in my current life, which had been a stumbling block for me. Before I was even done asking, it was as if he beamed it into me. It was not as if he zapped me with a wand and imbedded me with something I wasn't ready for and wouldn't know how to use responsibly. It was more like he helped me unleash my own inner power by sending the energy of his straight into me for me to feel, first-hand. It worked. By placing his power momentarily right inside me I recognized and remembered my own. Since then I have felt and watched changes in my use of personal power. It was a priceless gift.

As I offered more love and Reiki energy to his whale body and his whole being, he asked me to direct this energy to his heart chakra. I did, and WHOA! Immediately a huge, pleasant blast of love filled every cell in me, uplifting every bit of my being with fireworks of love. I felt him smile at my reaction, and he explained that he knew if I directed my love to his own heart center, I would more strongly feel what he wanted to give. What he intended to do and did, was switch from receiving to giving in a glorious moment of surrounding and filling me with his huge whale love. Oh to be so blessed! If I could breach, I would have breached and breached and breached my gratitude to him.

He moved just a bit more deeply into the water after this, and the mother surfaced next to me with her calf peeking out from beneath her. I fell in love with this baby! I kept exclaiming over and over how beautiful she was. To me, all humpback whale calves are perfectly beautiful, but this one was special to me in a way I had not felt before. I felt an old, deep connection between this huge whale child and me, as with the male. Just as I thought this, I heard her say,

"Of course you recognize me. I have been your baby here in these waters many, many times. Long ago, we shared many lives as whales together. I am here now to welcome you, to bring you my love, to help you remember even more deeply how eternal and far-reaching love is. We are still family."

With each word I remembered our history and was consumed with the power of love. I was home. I remembered her as my calf and I yearned to be close to her. From my heart I gently whispered,

"If it is right for you, come closer to me little baby, come to me."

Up she came from under her mother, slowly, gracefully and almost imperceptibly moving as only a humpback whale can do, until she was next to me with just a few yards between us. Our bodies glided ever so slowly in the same direction, side-by-side, eye-to-eye. When she changed her body direction, I changed mine. When she surfaced to breathe, I surfaced to breathe. When she came back down, I came back down. With her, I was a whale. Time stood still. For the first time after having had many encounters with whales, I experienced the extraordinary phenomena of being in the water with these huge, powerful and oh-so-gentle animals, not as an extraordinary experience, but simply as normal.

I was calmly present. Being with this beautiful, perfect fifteen-foot calf was the most real thing I had ever experienced. Stroking her aura with Therapeutic Touch seemed as normal as petting my cats. The magnetic pull between us was palpable. Baby and I were one. It felt like we were dancing. It was that same feeling I have in my dance class when movement of my body becomes one with my soul--only ten million times more wonderful. I was home with this perfect whale, within myself, and with the whole universe.

After some time, the mother began rising, all fifty feet of her, slowly gliding right next to me, eye to eye. She thanked me for loving her child, and blessed me with her great love in return. My heart was overflowing. Just as she began that slow, gentle turn to swim away she said with the energy of a smile,

> *"Remember? I am your sister from long ago. This time, the soul who had been your baby many times was now born through me. We enjoy this and are so pleased to have you here again in our old home. We are both here now to be with you closely in this lifetime. We love you immensely. We will talk again and we will meet again."*

The truth of her words filled me. And then they were gone.

I couldn't speak for a time when I got out of the water. Back on the small Zodiac, as we cruised away, I began to sob joyous tears, taking it all in, feeling the full impact of such great love and reunion.

From these encounters and many continuing conversations, I was reminded of my Lemurian roots, where I had alternately been whale and human. Whales and humans regularly swam together and communicated in Lemuria. It was not a special pilgrimage to do so because such sacred connections were part of normal, everyday life. I was also reminded by them that long ago, near the end of Lemuria as a civilization, many of us made the decision to come back to earth in Atlantian waters and land, to bring back the energy of the Lemurian culture, a Divine Feminine culture, to help balance the earth's energies. So I came back as a whale many times, in what we today call the region of the North Atlantic Humpback Whales--migrating between feeding grounds now called Stellwagen Bank National Marine Sanctuary in the Gulf of Maine and the mating grounds of Silver Bank. As these memories came back to me, the tremendous pull I feel to these areas finally made sense. There was great peace in remembering where I'd come from and who my people are--who are not people at all but whales.

I have often felt uncomfortable being human in this life. Even after years of major healing from childhood rape, being disowned from my human family of origin for not following their religion, even after coming out about talking with animals and building a fulfilling life and professional career around it, I still often felt that I did not "fit" here and that I had no roots. For years I yearned for the whales, grieving deeply for their presence in between our visits. I finally knew why. They are my family. It was so satisfying to learn that I do have roots--deep, ancient Lemurian whale roots. Remembering all of this, I felt more grounded, more part of the earth, not just attempting to serve beings of the earth but belonging on the earth.

When I am with the whales, so close in their water home, I am one with God. When I am with the whales, I know the deepest peace of the universe. When I am with the whales, I exist once again in the deepest sanctuary of my soul, brought back to the place of purity of my heart, to purity of love. When I am with the whales, I am, so easily, myself.

I can tell many stories about human healing and transformation from encounters and conversations with whales. For this chapter, however, I'd like to share how a whale experienced healing, in part, because of her experiences with humans. It seems important to recognize that it is not only humans who need and receive help from whales, but that whales also need help from humans. Here is an example.

The story revolves around a baby humpback whale we encountered and helped in Silver Bank who was severely entangled in fishing gear. It is a story of many layers in which each of us had our own profound experience and opportunities for learning and healing simply by being present during this crisis. The universe conspired to bring whales and humans together in a complex web of who needed healing, who was available and skilled to offer healing, and who received healing in this situation--with ramifications that lasted for years beyond the crisis. Because the entire story is too detailed and long for telling here, I will focus on one of the whales.

On a beautiful afternoon in March 2009, while on a small boat in Silver Bank looking for whales, our group came across a month-old humpback, his mother and an adult female escort. To our horror, we quickly saw that this calf was tortuously wrapped in fishing gear. Thick float lines criss-crossed down his body in a tight, jumbled pattern all the way to his fluke. It was embedded several inches into his flesh, creating deep, open wounds. And the lines didn't stop at his fluke.

This twelve-foot baby was dragging fifty feet of fishing line behind him, at the end of which were two huge, heavy fishing traps and several floats. His mouth was severely injured from the lines that ran through it like a horse bit, made worse from the weight of the drag from the traps attached to the line entangling him. I learned from talking with him that he first saw the lines and traps on the bottom of the ocean floor when he was one week old. He was curious, began to play with them and in minutes became entangled. His fast growing body had been entwined with these ropes, lines, floats and traps for three of his four weeks of life at the time we met him. He had much difficulty attempting to dive. His breath was wheezy and irregular. His weariness and pain were palpable. His mother was stressed beyond description. And so were many of us, witnessing it. Suddenly, whale entanglement transcended the statistics, stories, photos and graphics I had read about and shared in presentations about whales for years. This was real. And it was obscene.

Two things happened quickly. A decision was made that attempts to disentangle the whale would be made by Tom Conlin of Aquatic Adventures and Jeff Pantukhoff of Whaleman[19]. I immediately pulled my small group of people together to walk us through a process to put our own pain and horror aside and to focus on sending each of these whales the energy of calm, love and healing. I specifically asked experienced healers Judith White[20] and Joan Beattie[21] to work with the obviously panic stricken mother of the calf. I began talking with all three of the whales.

Despite several hours of heroic, tireless efforts to disentangle the whale, the mother remained too frantic to allow the men close enough, long enough, to complete the disentanglement. They were able to cut off the lines from the fluke which held the heavy fishing traps. The calf told

[19] Tom Conlin, founder of Aquatic Adventures www.aquaticadventures.com Jeff Pantukhoff, founder of The Whaleman Foundation www.whaleman.com
[20] Judith White is a Certified Energy Health Practitioner who practices The Healing Codes, Matrix Energetics, the Body Codes and Reiki and is an Adjunct Professor of Complementary and Integrative Therapies at Drexel University in Philadelphia. reikiferret@gmail.com
[21] Joan Beattie, MD developed the Bioenergetic Emotional Access Method of energy therapy. http://www.beamtherapy.org/summary.html

me that the amount of physical pain he felt was considerably lessened after this weight he had been dragging was cut loose from his body. He communicated a great sense of relief. However, all the remaining lines wrapped around and gouging his body still posed a certain threat to his life.

One might assume that the central figure of healing in this crisis would be this precious baby whale suffering from the visible, horrific physical entanglement, and he certainly did receive healing from us. But the greatest healing, I believe, was experienced by his mother, whom we called Mama. At her request the pieces of her story shared here are in the order she requested.

She shared with me that in previous lives as a whale she watched many other whales be killed and had been killed herself by whalers. She described how this embittered her, and hardened her heart even into subsequent lives.

"When I saw others in pain, emotional or physical, I could no longer feel any compassion or empathy. I was emotionally shut off, empty and ignored others who were hurting. I felt flat when I saw others in challenging situations, not at all wanting to risk feeling their pain and certainly not mine in response to theirs. My own pain was deeply buried and I wanted nothing to do with anyone else's heartbreak. And I hated humans for their pointless killing.

Before coming into my current life, I committed to a goal of healing this, and to learn again to feel and express compassion and empathy for others who are traumatized. My precious calf coming into this life in such horrendous circumstances brought me an opportunity to do this. Seeing him in such agony and having no power to help him crushed me. I no longer had any defenses to deny my pain. It was inescapable and almost ate me alive. The fear, anger and pain from my past from humans killing us, combined with this pain in the present from humans placing these torture ropes in the ocean and became one enormous ball of rage, helplessness and grief.

I had a secondary goal for this life and that was to learn to trust humans again, knowing intellectually that most humans no longer harmed whales and some reportedly even loved whales. I would have liked to meet this goal slowly, bit-by-bit. But seeing my calf suffer from your ropes, and then, to have a human come near him with a knife was almost unbearable.

You kept telling me he was there to help my son. I did feel his kindness. But he was human.

It was very confusing at the time. My friend [the "escort" as scientists call adults with mothers and calves] told me she knew you and that the humans who were with you could be trusted.[22] I believed her when she said people on your boat might be able to help. I was amazed at the depth and openness of your love and concern. And yet, it was still hard to take in. You were humans. I tried. I really tried. It helped tremendously, especially when I look back, to have all that love and healing sent to me. I did feel it and am grateful for it. Without feeling this energy, I could not have stayed. I would likely have hurt the man with the knife. [She did thrash about with her fluke many times when Jeff was in the water trying to disentangle the baby. If he were not the highly experienced person with whales that he is, he likely would have been hurt.] And yet, I did know he was genuine in his attempts to help my son, and the love I felt from you and the other humans transformed my perception of human capacity for kindness, good and love. I couldn't bring this knowledge to a place of calm that day. But I did feel your love and help so strongly.

When you told me that your boat had to leave because of the coming darkness, I then realized all that you did. My heart was wildly broken, yet there was this very tiny light I felt, a small hope that perhaps more humans were like all of you. I was so grateful for all that tender love and healing and that the trailing ropes and traps were gone. He had so much relief from this. But I knew in my heart he would die."

When I told the whales that we needed to leave the area Mama calmed a bit. She and her friend slapped their pecs in unison in front of us several times as they said thank you. It was very, very hard to leave them knowing that the little one was in such great pain and peril.

Less than two weeks after we saw these whales, I was back home in California. One morning as I was waking, the little one came to tell me he had died and showed himself to me in spirit. He was so beautiful, so whole, so luminous, and so full of gratitude and love. I was breathless feeling the enormity of his love and joy. He showed me that as he made his transition, he was met by many souls who know and love him. He still

---

[22] The female friend/escort is the same whale who I saw a few years earlier who told me we had been sisters and that we would meet again.

deeply loves his mother and cares about her distress, yet this did not in any way burden him. He showed me how he was able to send her endless compassion and love, yet not take in any of her pain. He was free from all pain, physical and emotional. He was in his full power, and at peace.

After talking with him, I immediately connected to Mama who showed me herself moaning at his body. She showed me vividly his little dead body, still all wrapped up in the fishing gear which killed him. She said,

> *"The hardest part was not being able to nuzzle him or stroke him. We all know to not get close to a whale with the ropes or we could get wrapped in them also. To not be able to feed him, stroke him or hold him, even now after his death is unbearable. I still have milk for him and I yearn to give it to him and cannot."*

Her pain was so huge it was as if her heart was exploding in red and black fire. She breached and breached to expel some of it, then continued to moan and cry. I could feel many whales nearby hearing, knowing and feeling her pain and sending support. There were also angels and spirit whales surrounding her in support. The whale friend with her is a strong and wise and loving female who holds her, soothes her and allows her her pain. Mama did not want to leave her calf's body, but after a few days her friend persuaded her to leave. Still heavy with grief, they left to begin the journey to northern feeding grounds. We have stayed in touch ever since. One of the times we were talking she said,

> *"I'm so pleased that somebody remembers my loss."*

I told her I'd remember her, her baby and her loss for the rest of my life. Over time she began to feel physically strong again, but her heart was still fragile.

> *"It hurts especially when I see calves the age mine would be. Yet I feel strong too--fragile in short term but strong in my learning. I accepted my grief and pain this time. I did not resist it. I know despair so deep it's changed me for always. I will never ever again fail to feel compassion for someone in pain, or to even notice when someone is in pain."*

She has shared many stories but these were two that really touched me:

> "During our migration [a year later], we came across an octopus who was badly injured. He was bleeding and in agony. In the past, I would have barely noted his presence let alone his pain. I would have kept moving. But much to my surprise, I cared deeply. I stopped and stayed with him for quite some time. I asked him what happened and listened for a long time. I let him know I cared and surrounded him with calmness and love - mimicking what all of you did for my baby and me. I continued to talk with him as I traveled on. It felt good to help and to know that my heart worked again."

Later she told me that she met her goals of learning to feel compassion for others in trauma and to trust humans.

> "I've met my goals to heal what I wanted to heal. I feel so different. I care again. With my friend, I now ask about her stories and listen, before she did all the caring and listening. I am more whole now. The tremendous depth and amount of love and healing you and your human friends showered onto me helped me melt away the bitterness from the past. There is still some residue, but I am mostly free of this now. My heart is still very tender where my baby is concerned, but I function and enjoy life more. I feel free. I am not so angry anymore, though I wish humans would stop putting the ropes in the ocean. Whales still get entangled in them. Why must you kill and take out so many fish and then leave these ropes behind? Do you not have food on land?"

I explained the facts and unfortunate politics of this to her and my own practice of not eating fish.

Mama and I continue to talk and I've been thrilled to see her again in Silver Bank. Because of her and other whales whom I am blessed to know intimately, I have learned that inside of us, in our souls and our emotional hearts, whales and humans are the same. Some whales and humans are master healers who help to shift the very consciousness and health of the planet and the universe. Other whales and humans provide healing one-on-one for individuals or for groups. But not all whales and humans have taken on roles as leaders or healers, some are here to live out their incarnation on earth with different purposes and to learn their own private and unique lessons. We are the same, whales and humans, and our connection is a sacred and powerful one. When our lives intersect, and we help one another in ways we are called and able to do, an undeniable grace fills us all.

The whales who are my guides and elders have helped me remember that I came as a human in this lifetime to be a voice for the whales and all animals, and a voice for the Lemurian way of living where all beings are considered and treated as soul peers. The whales have guided me to bring people and whales together in the ocean, in conversation, in sacred activism and in healing.

Specific services currently include:

- Sacred Swims with Humpback Whales: facilitate trips every winter in Silver Bank, off the coast of the Dominican Republic bringing whales and humans together for the exchange of love, joy, education and healing
- The Captive Whale Healing Initiative: in collaboration with an energy healer, telepathically communicate with individual captive whales to bring them loving companionship and support, to assess their emotional and physical needs, and to get feedback from each whale after energy healing work is offered.
- Private Consultations to assist people to have conversations with and receive guidance from whales.
- Teach classes on how to communicate telepathically with whales and other animals.
- Teach classes on the natural history of humpback whales to help people understand the physical aspects of being a whale, what whales need from us, and to encourage humans to not limit their relationship with whales to only the physical or spiritual realm--but to get to know the wholeness of whales.
- Share messages and stories from the whales in classes, articles, websites and a book in progress.
- Educate humans about threats to whales via classes, social media and website about the threats to whales and to encourage them to offer their prayers, their healing

abilities, their political voices and to make everyday lifestyle choices to help make the earth safe once again
for whales. Visit:
http://swimandcommunicatewithwhales.com/helping-to-save-the-whales

- Support Sea Shepherd, financially and energetically for their work which has saved and continues to save the lives of thousands of whales from whalers.

Teresa's conscious connection with whales began with her first encounter with a humpback whale in 1988 which changed her life irrevocably, prompting a shift from a corporate career to becoming a professional animal communication consultant.

In 1999 she had her first opportunity to swim with whales off the coast of the Dominican Republic and to communicate their private messages of encouragement, support and guidance to the humans aboard.

She continues to facilitate annual Sacred Swim journeys, bringing groups of people to honor and to communicate and exchange healing with the humpback whales as they swim together--eye to eye and soul to soul.

Teresa is devoted to bringing humans and whales together in the ocean, in conversation and in sacred activism and healing. She believes passionately that it is time for our relationship with cetaceans to evolve--beyond the inspiration, exhilaration, wisdom and healing we *receive from the whales* to move on to accelerating our *giving back to the whales*--by helping those in physical form who face and suffer from myriad threats of human activity on the earth. With such reciprocity our relationships with whales are more balanced, mutually healing and whole.

She teaches classes on how to telepathically communicate with whales, and also provides private readings with the whales. Teresa co-founded the Captive Whale Healing Initiative in collaboration with an energy healer, telepathically communicating with individual captive whales to bring them loving companionship, empathic emotional support, and energy healing and is deeply committed to sacred activism to help free captive cetaceans.

Teresa has a master's degree in counseling psychology and has had a grief counseling and animal communication practice for over 25 years. She is the author of *Legacies of Love, A Gentle Guide to Healing From the Loss of an Animal Loved One* and founder of the Animal Loss and Grief Support Professional Program of Study. She lives in Carmel, California.

Messages from the Whales, Sacred Swims, Helping the Whales: http://swimandcommunicatewithwhales.com/sacred-swims-with-whales.
Animal Communication, Grief Support: http://www.animalsinourhearts.com

Chapter 14: *Unity Interspecies*

Unification

By Madeleine Walker

"You must talk to the whales at night,
when they speak of a great coming together of animals and man"
- Credo Mutwa Chief Zulu shaman

The huge Orca opened its mouth, close enough for me to see its rows of teeth and deep down into the pink depths of its throat. My face pressed closer to the glass that stood as a barrier between us. The hydrophone had serenaded me with the blessed sounds that had permeated my being. I felt such deep sadness at their captivity, deprived of their wild magnificence. The two Orcas had been imprisoned in the Vancouver Aquarium for many years, and feeling their confinement stirred something very deep within me. I was at once awed and so profoundly moved by the love that seemed to emanate from this incredible being. I knew it was communicating with me, as it kept returning, time and again, to the glass looking directly into my eyes and then opening its mouth, as if to speak. I knew that I would never be quite the same again.

This was many years ago now and I had actually gone to Vancouver from the UK in order to visit my boyfriend. We had decided to get married on the spur of the moment, and exploring the sites of Vancouver became part of our honeymoon. I remember being transfixed and rooted to the glass wall and my husband getting impatient, as he could see that I felt unable to leave the whales, and was perplexed at the powerful emotions that were erupting within me. Although I felt it was so wrong that these huge beings should be incarcerated, I bought a mug and key ring with their images, in my naivety, to keep the connection with them. I never stopped thinking about them and was so happy to hear that they did leave the aquarium for a larger slightly more suitable environment, but I was devastated to hear that they had later died. I now know that no cetacean should ever be in captivity. They have led me on such a journey of self-discovery and healing ever since that first encounter.

My connection with those orcas seemed to trigger some deep remembering within me. When I hosted a workshop at my house, the facilitator had some flyers about trips to the Dominican Republic to swim with humpbacks. I just knew I'd have to experience this one day if I could ever find the money! It took me about five years to finally get there, and once in the water with these beautiful multi-dimensional beings, nothing was ever going to be the same in my life again. They "spoke" to me of unconditional love for all, and especially our beloved Mother Earth. They told me that they imbue every water molecule of water with their love, so that when the oceans meet the shore, that love can be absorbed into the land masses. I also realise now that their "'programming" of the planet's water affects everything including the water in our bodies. They reminded me that I had to let go of feelings of isolation and my perception of being ineffectual. They guided me to realise that we are all here as vital components to co- create with the animal kingdom, in fact to unify with them to heal ourselves and the planet.

My work has expanded in the most incredible ways, thanks to the whales, reminding me of my task! I now work as an animal communicator and human empowerment coach, and I have dedicated my life to be a bridge of understanding between humankind and the animal kingdom. It is my passion to reawaken others to the importance of the profound connections we have with our animals and that they are our greatest teachers and healers! I have since been fortunate enough to connect and swim with many different species of whale and dolphin. I have realised that they have a whale collective consciousness, as every type was "telling" me the same information in their messages of love for us, despite what humans have done to them! This is a beautiful message from the Southern Right whales that I met in Hermanus Bay in South Africa.

> *"Our journey is long and dangerous especially for our little ones. We sing our song of love for mother Gaia. We sing our song to bring balance to ourselves and the earth. Mankind has brought discord and death to so many of us over time, but we still choose to bring healing and the recognition of the need to love all creation. All is divine and contains divinity within. The echoes of our song's vibrations resonate that message through each water molecule of the sea that splashes and sprays this message onto the rocks and shores, infusing the land with our song's energy and clarion call to all."*

I was also lucky enough to visit Anne Gordon, who runs the Panama Whale Watching Company in the beautiful Pearl Islands, to co-facilitate a humpback whale and dolphin retreat. Every day was spectacular, on almost the last day we witnessed a mother, calf and male consort, breaching and fin slapping with such exuberance, it filled us with joy. We started to feel the presence of a very large being, like an energy overwhelming us with love. This seemed to trigger something deep inside of me that I was too awestruck to intuit just then. Only on my return to my home in England, and in my jet-lagged state, the full force of the energy came through, as I lay in my bed trying to catch up on some much needed sleep! It felt like a huge white whale that appeared to be an ambassador for the whole whale consciousness. When communicating with different species of whale before, I had marvelled at their collective desire to impart their love to humanity despite our treatment of them. It felt that this energy was the unification of all cetacean and interspecies communication. I had been unable to sleep and was trying to release some concerns and anxieties that I'd been faced with on my return. Suddenly I felt this immense presence fill my room, and I was guided to lie with my arms outstretched, like a star, with my palms facing upwards. I had noticed while on the boat that I always seemed to be holding onto something like a towel, a cup, or sunscreen. I remember being "told" that I should open my hands to receive and let go of the past, and the physical items in my hands were symbolic of things I was holding onto in my life now! So it felt marvellous to open my hands unreservedly and await further instructions! I immediately felt incredible heat and tingling pouring into my hands as though two huge pectoral fins were touching each hand. What followed was the most incredible cycle of giving and receiving with this being. It gave me the most beautiful mantra to say out loud, "With the guidance of the great white whale, I release all fear, worry, guilt, and doubt from my being now. With the guidance of the great white whale, I embrace only love, courage, forgiveness, and belief into my being now!"

I immediately felt so serene and at peace with myself. I was further instructed to share this with everyone I could and to contact several influential people around the world, to ask for help in spreading this message. I reflected that fear, worry, guilt and doubt, were the biggest issues that can sabotage our levels of trust in the abundance of the universe and unconditional self-love. They certainly had affected mine! Our thoughts create our realities, so it seemed vital to release anything that limits us from creating the best realities possible for us and to embrace everything that re-empowers us! This of course felt truly wonderful on a personal level as my anxieties melted away, but I knew that this had to be shared on a global level. I was asked to contact renowned whale communicators and artists to help further anchor in the energy of this consciousness.

I'd specifically been instructed to consult Mary Getten, (fellow cetacean communicator and author). She suggested creating a global event for 11/11/11. With the help of the internet, Anne Gordon and many others, we felt that if each of us could hold a glass of water and call in this beautiful energy to be imbued into it, we could then spread this water in a ceremony, dropping it into any natural water source from a mighty ocean to a tiny stream, to carry the blessings out into the world. We created a synchronised ceremony through all the time zones of the world on this special day. These are momentous times in our planet's history, and so many different channelled sources are reiterating the need to connect and work with the animal and nature kingdoms, in order to facilitate planetary healing for 2012 and beyond. A timely reminder to start working with the planet instead of against it, with the help of this magical collective consciousness, it seems we have all the help we need, if we can only embrace it! We have since been asked by the whales to continue our blessings of the water in order to spread their loving energy in the lifeblood of the planet.

When I visited the Dominican Republic to swim with and research Sperm Whales, I was excited to see what they would have to say regarding the planetary shifts and the global unification process of ascension. We were so blessed with many incredible encounters, but one large calf allowed me to swim alongside him, eye-to-eye, as he searched deep into my soul with his penetrating gaze. Being scrutinised in this way was quite incredible, but it felt like he was scanning every cell of my body. They also use encoding "clicks" to detect their prey and also for communication. I could feel, having his powerful sound vibrating through me, that he was also fine tuning me in ways I can hardly begin to understand, but later that night in my bed, the whale revisited me and gave me this message! This was obviously directed at me, but I felt very strongly that it was also aimed at humankind!

"Our sound holds the rhythms of the universe. It was founded in Atlantis in the ancient times as the beginnings of verbalisation of thought forms and telepathic communication, expanded into everything having its own sound to express individuality. The bushmen of the Kalahari, an ancient tribe in the heartland of the stirrings of mankind, still retain the clicks in their spoken words .The click stream that you felt and absorbed was further fine-tuning your being into remembering at a cellular level, all that you have temporarily forgotten and will aid you in reclaiming all that has been left unclaimed for eons of time. There is so much that has been let slip from your knowing, and it is crucial that you access this knowledge at this time. When we had eye-to-eye contact, I looked deep into your being and I saw that your heart was ready and willing to take this wisdom forward at this time of expansion and inter-dimensional realities, in that you as a race have the choice to join in what the rest of the kingdoms know already. You have been limiting yourselves for too long now. NOW is the time to unify and work as one, reattaching yourselves to the life plan of Gaia. This is a time of great change and rebalance, and fear should NOT come into the equation. Allow the love that we create in the ocean depths

and widths to spread into your psyche. Completion of your long journeys is at hand. Spread the frequencies of our sounds' energies wherever you go and tread into the memory of your path, both in the physical steps you make on the land and in the steps that you make in your reawakening awareness. Your human lifetimes are but a blink in time, but there is much to achieve during your brief stay on the physical plane. Your challenge has been to find your way home to unity and love. Continue on your quest. There is so much more to come, but for now, we honour and appreciate your willingness to be of service and all the progress you have made. NEVER lose faith in our love for you. You are never alone in your endeavours. We are behind you every step of your journey! All love and blessings and peace from the whale unity consciousness."

I was again awestruck at this 'download' of wisdom from such a generous source. Despite our best efforts to annihilate them, they are prepared to hold our space through love and compassion, gently nudging us back to the path of unity.

Nearly two years later, I finally had the opportunity to go to the Kalahari and meet with the Bushmen. It felt quite surreal sitting in the vast expanse of the desert, discussing these concepts with an incredible shaman who had never seen the ocean but who understood the sperm whale's message exactly! It was wonderful to hear him speaking in his ancient tongue and hearing the clicks! I felt a sense of completion, a reconnection of ancient wisdom from the ancestors, that I feel I need to share with people, so that they too can feel that reconnection to the whole.

My journey with dolphins has been equally awe-inspiring, and they have now given me some wonderful healing tools to help people who come to me for sessions to release emotional and physical blocks stored deep within their cellular memories.

Cetacean Soul Healing

I'd had a lifelong ambition to swim with wild dolphins, and I'd managed to fulfill my wish with a visit to the Azores. Although I didn't have many close physical encounters, I was amazed at the diversity of the migrant species passing through the islands and the super-pods of dolphins who were so joyous. I also visited the crystal waters of the white sand ridge in the Bahamas to learn more from the spotted dolphins there.

However the most powerful encounters and messages came from a large pod of Spinner dolphins in the Red Sea off the coast of Marsa Alam in Egypt. On many occasions when experiencing encounters with wild creatures, it's wonderful to know that we may be so blessed that they might choose to interact with us. I have noticed that they usually save the most powerful encounter to the very last meeting. This was again the case, when on our very last swim with a resident pod on an incredible reef with the most beautiful coral gardens I have ever seen, they pulled out all the stops to really get their messages across!

A huge wall of around sixty dolphins came right towards us and then proceeded to gift us with the most incredible show of playful antics. It was a bit like swimming in dolphin soup. They were everywhere, shooting up from the deep like a surreal display of dolphin fireworks! They gave us so many eye-to-eye connections. Here is an excerpt of their message to me.

"Welcome to our world. You are here to learn the art of play! You humans come here with your fixed agendas and expectations, more pressure to accumulate. Once you let go and open your hearts to joy, look what happens! We show you the art of joy and play. As our sounds resonate through your body, we infect you with our joy! Every cell now contains the dolphin joy that you sadly lacked. We understand so much from eye-to-eye contact. When do you play? When do you truly feel joy? Remember the feelings of being in our midst as we dashed and frolicked around you. Hold the awe and magnitude of joy that was shared.

We show you the art of being in the joy of the moment. Call this in whenever you are too serious, and we will remind you! Life is to be enjoyed and FULL-filled. It is a precious commodity, as is the planet. You are here as caretakers, but we feel it is YOU who need to be cared for and re-educated in the art of life and living!"

They also spoke of parasitic energies stored within our DNA that hold the trauma and grief from the downfall of Atlantis. We need to clear these from our systems if we are ever going to be able to truly forgive ourselves and become whole once more. They gave me beautiful healing techniques where I can help people to journey back into Atlantean healing temples, where special crystals programmed to perform different functions in order to heal and release negative beliefs and contracts from ancient times. These contracts or beliefs are still impacting our lives in our current incarnations. I call these "light crystals" and had been working with them previously, but the dolphins showed me a whole new dimension of using them to heal people who need to release such limiting and debilitating physical and emotional challenges.

I worked with a lovely lady called Catherine, who had been very ill with cancer. She had a troubled life, with very little joy. The dolphins guided me to assist her to visualise journeying through time and space back to the healing temples. She could feel the dolphins all around her guiding her so gently. After they placed her on a bed of crystal, she could feel them imbuing her body with healing bubbles that carried the healing dolphin joy around her body, specifically where her cancer had been. She could see her skeletal structure becoming crystalline and the bubbles transmuting her cells into health and joy. The dolphins guided me to ask her to visualise a large crystal pillar in front of her that could scan her body to see if there were any areas of residual imbalance. The dolphins showed me the scan as a holographic image of her body and auric fields. Catherine also visualised this. She could still see some areas of darkness in her heart, and we intuited that was symbolic of the sadness that her life's journey had given her. I felt that she had chosen a disempowered life and that she needed to create a new life contract, by clearing old agreements of possible guilt and self-blame for the past. The dolphins guided us every step of the way. They told me that the crystal pillar could also act as a laser to burn away the dark residues. She proceeded to visualise the dark areas being dissolved by the lasers and then did another scan to check if she was now clear. She had also visualised dark tentacles being burnt away like cutting the ties and bonds to the past, freeing her from any limitation, so that she was now able to choose dolphin joy, perfect health and abundance. I asked her to continue to call the dolphins in, to keep strengthening her physiological and emotional systems. She told me that the dolphins gave her bubble healing and support for five days after our session, and that she was now feeling so light and free. Her body seems to have chosen to live in health and abundance, and her life is transforming with so many opportunities now opening up for her. These manifestations of her new life choices allow her to stand in her power and create the life she deserves!

I have had many many cases where the dolphins have drawn close to the people I work with and support them on their healing journey.

They have shown me different ways of working with the crystals and that they can take the form of many shapes and sizes. The dolphins have also created group healings for people I work with, who may well have been living and working in the ancient times or different dimensions together, and they have enabled me to help people access the wisdom that they need in order to be healed on all levels.

Whales are said to be the record holders of all humanity, known as the Akashic records. I feel they hold the space for us to evolve and reclaim our and raise awareness of our higher levels of consciousness, so we can unify and work as one to help heal our planet. I was told on the sperm whale trip that the whale's name for the Akashic records is The Library of Love, which I thought was so beautiful.

My most recent whale trip to Baja to meet blue and grey whales also reiterated their planetary healing work. The blue whales said:

"We have the biggest lungs and therefore lung capacity of any living creature on the planet. We hold the divine breath to oxygenate the oceans so all sea creatures can breathe. The standing people do this for the air on the land. We have the biggest heart so we can shower the divine love upon you"

Once again a final encounter with the grey whales allowed us to touch a mother and calf, who blessed us with their presence. As a final goodbye they surfaced right next to our little boat and simultaneously blew, showering us with their beautiful breath that refracted the light into rainbows.

These are a few words that I wrote to them in gratitude.

The Rainbow Breath: "Sweetest spray caresses my face as the sound of the blow emblazons my senses. As the huge being graces us with her divine breath, I feel blessed to the core of my soul!"

We are indeed blessed to have these beings of far higher consciousness choosing to help humankind on a personal and planetary level. There has never been a more important time to reconnect with the animal kingdom and nature beings so that we may learn to reconnect with ourselves. They have given me beautiful healing meditations, which are now recorded on CDs, so that more people can access the healing energies of whales and dolphins and experience their healing techniques. Other animal species have told me that they also connect with the cetacean nations to work together to support the land masses and oceans of our beloved earth. We humans need to join in too! I leave you with a final message from the humpbacks, which sums everything up for me. Allow the cetaceans to guide you home. I hope you enjoy it and choose to work and sing with them!

> *"We beseech you to remember our messages of love that we spread through the oceans. Please help us by singing our song of love. Fear and negativity destroys the heart of the planet quicker than any pollutant. In fact it is an emotional pollutant that we struggle to overcome. So join us with the vibration of love and peace that you can sing out in harmony with us. This is our greatest, most powerful strategy, but we need your help. As you raise the vibration of positive energy, you work with us to raise the vibration of the whole. We connect with the whole whale collective, where every cetacean species holds that message of love for the planet." Blessings and peace from the Whale Consciousness."*

Madeleine Walker is a world renowned Animal Communicator, Horse and Rider Trauma Consultant and Spiritual Empowerment Coach. Her mission is to raise humankind's awareness of the incredibly deep connections we have with our animals, and the importance of their messages of healing re-empowerment for us and our beautiful planet. She travels extensively to work with wild species, e.g. lions, elephants, whale sharks and large cetaceans, in their natural habitat, and writes and lectures internationally, about her experiences. She is well known for her healing skills for both animals and humans on both emotional and physical levels. Madeleine specialises in the past life connections between animals and their human carers. She is a pioneer with her techniques on past life script rewriting, cetacean soul healing and pre-birth soul contract realigning, all taught to her by animals! She formerly worked in adult education with holistic stress management and Art therapy, and also worked within conventional veterinary medicine. She is based in the UK, but facilitates courses and retreats internationally. She also performs distant consultations for her overseas client base. She has been featured on many US (including *Coast to Coast*), Canadian, and Australian, radio shows, and in many international publications. She was also a finalist in the 2013 About.com reader's choice awards for favourite Animal Communicator, and her *Animal Whispers Empowerment Cards* were also nominated as finalists in the favourite Oracle card set category.

She has written three books, her first book *An Exchange of Love...Animals healing people in past, present and future lifetimes* published by O Books. *The Whale Whisperer, healing messages from the animal kingdom to help humankind and the planet* and *Your Pets' Past Lives and how they can heal you* (now translated into Chinese and German) published by Findhorn Press.

Her meditation CDs *Whale Whispers, Lion Roars- a journey to re-empowerment* channelled meditations from the whales and sacred white lions, and *Fearless Earth meditations for Gaia*, and her Oracle card set *Animal Whispers Empowerment Cards* are also available from Findhorn press and Amazon etc..

Her website is www.anexchangeoflove.com

Chapter 15: *My Journey to becoming an Inter-Species Communicator & Soul Healer*

By Laurie Reyon

"The largest brains on this planet are in the ocean.
Communication with the whales and the dolphins
is the greatest achievement the human race can aspire to."
- John Lilly

I have always loved animals, and they have been my greatest teachers. I grew up in rural Nebraska and had a natural ability with horses. At age 14, I was hired by the Buffalo Bill's Wild West Show and Congress of Rough Riders as a dancer and brought my horse into the show. I was soon trained by Hollywood professionals to trick ride on my horse, and my enthusiasm for show business began to grow. Three years later, I moved to Los Angeles and brought my horse, Bonfire, along. I began a life as an entertainer and professional dancer, then began college with a desire to become a veterinarian. During my time in college and in the clinic, I was confused as to why I was not really happy on this path. Animals had always been my best friends, and it was my desire to help them. In 1983, I graduated as an Animal Health Technologist but decided to pursue my other passion as a career which was dancing. During the next years I dedicated my life to professional dance and building my Los Angeles-based Laurie Jean's Performing Arts Center.

In 1992, I was given a wonderful kitten as a gift by a dear friend. We named him Puddy, and it became evident that he was not only different from my other pets, but he was different from other cats as well.

In early 1994, my life changed dramatically. My home in Sylmar was very near the epicenter of the Northridge earthquake. I have always been grateful that I was not really hurt, but there were many challenges in the days and weeks following. In February, I was in an accident and things got much worse. Puddy became my constant companion and never left my side during my convalescence. I was very independent and refused help from anyone. I made some very poor decisions regarding treatment, and my health continued to decline. I came to a point where the pain was unmanageable, and I gave up hope. Puddy wrapped his body around my head and encouraged me to get help. I drove to the hospital, and Puddy came with me. That night I went to the other side and experienced what is known as a near-death experience. I was taken to a room with a council of 12 beautiful White Light Beings and had a life review. I was shown that my death was by my own hand, using my free will to create the end of my life. I was shown Puddy, locked in the car in the parking lot and my mother, who was my best friend. I was shown the beauty and magnitude of the soul of my cat, Puddy. This Being had come to Earth in the body of a cat as a healer and had intentions to assist many on their paths of awakening. The loving emotions I felt helped me make the decision to return to Earth and come back to my body and heal myself. I made the choice to begin my spiritual awakening and a new path opened up for me.

Over the next three and a half years I was not able to work, as my immune system was compromised. I moved into a beautiful beach home south of Rosarito in Baja, Mexico, and began the process of healing and awakening to my telepathic abilities. Puddy was with me, and we began to spend hours sitting outside looking out at the ocean. It became evident that I was able to hear his "cat" voice during our time together, and I began to write down what he would repeat to me.

He told me that the goal is to remember WHO we truly are within our human bodies and ultimately create Heaven on Earth. He helped me remember what I had been shown during my near-death experience and during my life review. I found myself softening and trusting the voice of this master teacher in his beloved cat body. During those years, three dolphins came every day while we sat on this wooden platform on our deck above the ocean waves. He encouraged me to tune to the frequencies of the dolphins. He said it was my destiny to talk with many animals, not just him. Then Puddy introduced me to Simon, a big male dolphin who was full of love and spunk. Puddy helped me to tune into the static noise I was hearing in my mind and begin to focus it, kind of like tuning a radio dial. He asked me, to ask Simon to jump, and then to swim to the right, then left, and to jump and spin. Simon responded immediately to every request. We became fast friends, and I began to really look forward to the dolphin visits and lessons every day. The dolphins told me they are from the future but have written their stories into Earth's history. They asked me to "be" their voice and give their messages to others. They told me they are kind of like the cheerleaders for Earth and all of the people. They told me that they and other animals can assist humans in clearing their electro-magnetic fields which make up the humans' emotional bodies. I did not always understand what was asked of me, but I agreed to be their voice and the voice for Puddy as well. It was so much fun to be their friend. They continued to help me find love and joy within myself and asked me to share it with others. They told me that love is the only vibration that is real. Everything else is an illusion. They said we are the creators of our own experience and the co-creators of everything that happens in our world. They showed me that if we are happy, we are well and vice versa. The foundation of our true "creatorship" is the vibration of joy!

Puddy explained to me that I had the potential to become an animal communicator as well as continue to talk to the dolphins and translate their messages. The love and trust I had for my cat friend helped me move into the next years where I began to find the confidence to share Puddy's messages, prayers and poems. Puddy told me that when we incarnate, we are just one aspect of a greater over soul. I learned that there are 12 aspects to each larger Soul, all dedicated at this time to the Earth experience. He told me that it was easy for him to teach me about dolphin communication because he was a dolphin in a different body. Puddy and I shared eight amazing years together and many, many miracles. Puddy passed away on August 29, 2001, ten days before 9/11/01. I was devastated as I had become very co-dependent on this being and did not yet understand that my cat had gone to help with the souls who were about to transition from the Earth.

I arranged to bury him on the beach in Mexico by our home over Labor Day weekend in 2001. What I did not know is that a communication goes out when a great soul transitions, and several people made the journey to my home in Baja for Puddy's funeral. I had no phone or real address in Mexico, but that did not stop two shamans and several others from finding us. They told me that they had come to bury and celebrate the life of this great being. The ceremonies continued on in two different languages for three days. It became evident that there was much more going on than I had known. A Mexican shaman became my dear friend in the coming years and told me it was just the beginning. A female shaman, Colette Lady Hawk, declared herself the grandmother of this soul, and she began to teach me the indigenous ways.

In October I went to a class with the famous Animal Communicator, Amelia Kinkade. I showed her the picture of Puddy who had passed in August. She held that picture and told me she had always wanted to meet a cat that is not really a cat. She said Puddy was an "Ancient of the Ancients and a Healer of the Healers." She told me he was a "Great Being of Light" that had chosen me to work with and that I was to share his messages with the world. She said I was being greatly honored to have been chosen for this, and that he would reincarnate and have the same birthday. She said, "March 3, right?" I was amazed that she knew his birthday and was so very happy! I then remembered that I was shown the cycle of the soul through reincarnation during my near-death experience. I saw Amelia again in December and she gave me the same reading, except she said Puddy would be reborn on March 3, in the Garden of Eden, and that he would find me!

The prophecy came true and the soul of Puddy was born to a wild cat in a beautiful botanical garden in Mexico called "Eves Jardin" which means Garden of Eve! My friend found the kittens and called me. We recognized Puddy's energy as he had returned as a beautiful baby girl, asking to be named Puddah. Our life picked up where it had left off, and the miracles began! When Puddah was seven weeks old, she asked to begin to teach and we gathered several people. She also began to work physically on many people, and they would get well. She loved being at the house in Mexico and going out to the beach to see the dolphins who would gather. I began spending time sitting out on the beach writing with her at least one day a week.

One Sunday, I had climbed way out on these rocks on a jetty that was being built near my home. I settled in to write. Later that day, I was looking at the ocean, and the water began to rise, right in front of me! I stood up, and a whale surfaced and sprayed me from a few feet away. That whale looked into my soul, and I began to cry. I looked around to try to find someone to share the experience with, but I was the only one in sight. I heard the words inside me that said, "Look up!" A white ring of light began to form around the sun! It was a miracle, and I knew that it was for me. I kept hearing inside of me, "We are the Creators." The eye of that beautiful whale looked into my soul and gave me a gift.

Later that summer, I began to really understand more about the significance of that day with the whale. I had become friends with a woman who was a female shaman and incredible intuitive. We went out on the beach one day, and she asked me to meditate with her. We journeyed very far together into colorful realms. It was the first time I had experienced a joint journey such as this. When we returned, she knelt before me and said that she was clearly shown a vision that she was to share with me. I was a "whale," and I was standing up on my tail teaching their wisdom to the people. She said my name was "Standing Whale Mother." I felt so honored by her message and reverence, but I did not understand it. I had only connected with dolphins at that time, not the whales.

One day, two friends and I walked out on the beach one day and onto the jetty. It was almost dark and a big saucer-like ship emerged out of the water! My friend Kenn looked at it and was very calm. He said he knew this ship, and in another dimension, had helped build it. He was telepathic from a young age with the Pleiadians who had visited him, and he was delighted to meet these star friends. I was very excited and wanted to know more and more. They began to appear to me, mostly in and around my home in the following weeks. I could see them, but I could not hear them yet. However, my friends Kenn, Jerelyn and of course Puddah, could hear them. During that first week, I was given my star name, which is Reyon ("Ree-ON"). It means "Rays of the Sun." The communications continued every day, and we began to call these light beings the Arnon. They are loving, very advanced light beings, who are only here to assist us. They told us that they come to those who radiate light and can assist us in remembering more about who we really are.

During the next few months, I asked them if I could visit their ships and travel with them. They said "yes" and advised me on how to prepare my body. That summer I would lay down on my bed at night with Puddah on one side, and her twin brother Buddy on the other and my other cat, Kito, at the foot of the bed. The energy would rise up out of the ocean, cross the beach, and come to my home. Somehow I was transported energetically to their ships, and Puddah was always there as a 10-foot-tall cat being with seven fingers on each hand. The big cat Puddah was always smiling, driving the ship, and operating the control panels at light speed, kind of like a cat version of "Data" from Star Trek. I knew they were making the ship appear in that way for me. In truth, it was pure energy and operated through the consciousness of these formless light beings. Many times they would show themselves to me as upright dolphin beings. I was so honored that they took the time to help me have these experiences. We traveled through many wormholes, or stargates, to many different realities, and I was thrilled. In hindsight, I realize now that these experiences were made possible by the three cats at home forming a star tetrahedron around me and assisting me in creating a borrowed living light body or merkaba. In later years, I learned how to create my own merkaba light body and orb travel, and now I am a teacher for others seeking these experiences.

In 2003, I was called to visit the Big Island in Hawaii. Puddah was pregnant at home in Mexico. I went to The Psychic Children's conference hosted by James Twyman. It was amazing, and I was introduced to swimming with the dolphins for the first time. I met Grandma Chandra and Joan Ocean. I was also introduced to John Lilly's work and began to research his work. John Lilly said, "Communication with the whales and the dolphins, is the greatest achievement the human race can aspire to." I bought Joan Ocean's book *Dolphins Into the Future* and read it on the plane. I realized that Joan was a pioneer for this amazing work with the dolphins, whales, and light beings and that helped me validate my own work.

In 2004, Grandma Chandra came to San Diego, and we connected more deeply. I asked her many questions about the star beings I called the Arnon. I also asked her about my communications with the dolphins. She said it was my destiny to be a voice for the cetaceans and the star beings and suggested that I listen to her CD called *Whale Speak.* I bought it and could not stop listening to it. Something shifted inside of me, and I am so grateful that she gave me the encouragement.

That fall, Puddah passed away at just three and a half years of age. I was sad, but she told me that she would return and would have the same birthday. The prophecy came true, and she and her twin brother were born on March 3rd. An old neighbor called me late in March and said, "You better get down here because your cat is back!" She was right, and after a few visits to see the kittens, it was evident that Puddah2 had arrived.

We were in transition as a family and went for a retreat to the Rosicrucian Fellowship in Oceanside, CA. It was a quiet and healing time for me, and I was delighted to be there with my two new kittens and Kito. The administration that had approved my stay there was supportive of my work as an animal communicator. They had heard of me and my work with Puddah 1. They were very interested in how Puddah behaved and taught me some of their philosophy. Their belief is that the animals are connected to the Archangels. I had a small apartment overlooking a beautiful canyon and began more in-depth study of the dolphins and whales in my spare time. One night I awoke to see two very tall bluish glowing figures. My telepathy was becoming more advanced, and I was delighted to "hear" that these two beings were Pleiadian. They told me that I had an agreement to begin my healing work with the whales and dolphins. I told them I loved dolphins and communicated well with them, but that I really knew nothing about the whales. They said they knew this and that is why they had come. They said they would help me "not have to sleep much" for about three months, and I was to stay up and begin writing a workshop called "Healing with the Whales and Dolphins." I agreed, of course, and my tutors began teaching me about who the cetaceans really are. They told me that they are creator gods, very ancient and wise super sentient beings who are the stewards for our planet. They said they are masters of multi-dimensionality and time travel. They said the whales would work through me if I allowed for it and I did not have to know how it all works.

Puddah 2 began teaching her classes again at eight weeks, and life as her partner was an adventure. She gave birth to five kittens and asked me to be very careful about who adopted them. She told me that when she passed and reincarnated the next time, she would be born to her daughter in this life. I did not want to hear about any more death transitions, but that is exactly what happened.

When my time was complete with my Pleiadian friends, I moved away from the Rosicrucian Center. With four others and my cats, we created a Healing Center. I hosted Grandma Chandra again in our beautiful new healing home center, (which she had prophesied would form). We called it CATS, meaning The Carlsbad Awakening and Transformation.

My "Healing with Whales and Dolphin" workshops began, and people came to hear about the origins of creation, the Sirian messages, Pleiadian time travel meditations and the truths that the whales wished to share through me about core-level healing. The next time I went to visit Grandma Chandra, she said to me, "When are you going to begin your REAL Mission?" I said to her that I was doing my real work, thank you. She said you are supposed to be upright, like a whale speaking their wisdom from boats. I told her boats had made me violently sea sick all of my life. How could I do boat trips when this was how my body reacted to being on the water? She told me to get serious about this and just heal it! She also said she would come back to California and do the first boat trip with me. She said, "If you don't heal yourself, and you get sick, I will give the messages for you. I am the backup plan." So? So I believed in her and what she told me. I prayed and asked the angels, God, the dolphins and whales and everyone to please heal me. We chartered a boat and sold all of the seats. It happened and we did the messages together and to my surprise, I did not get sick.

I began the boat trips from Dana Point, California to see the mega pods of dolphins that live there and to see the migrating whales. Over the past six years, 95% of the time, I do not get nauseated or feel anything except joy. The boat trips give me an opportunity to share the messages I receive from the group consciousness of the whales, as well as give personal messages to our passengers from the dolphins. I have grown in my ability to be an inter-species communicator, and the people continue to come! The whales tell me we are helping people to heal their soul energy and remember who they really are.

Puddah passed and continued the birthday tradition when she reincarnated on March 3, 2008. This is the fourth life where this soul continues to be born on 3-3. She is a conscious Creator and my partner in life and in business. Our work with the dolphins and whales continues to grow and we are blessed to be full-time Inter-species communicators and soul healers. We completed our first film, "Messages of the Whales and Dolphins for Humanity." We teach, travel and speak, sharing the messages from the animals, of healing and preparation for ascension. I am a firm believer that the animals are the greater body of teachers and healers on our planet.

Master Puddah and I have co-created the *Omni Dimensional Mystery School* together where we live now in Oceanside, California. Our lives are dedicated to assisting others in finding their self-empowerment. We help others begin to "Youth" as cellular regeneration is a gift from the dolphins! We even have etheric dolphins swimming in our pool that everyone can see and swim with. The dolphins have shown themselves to be the designated keepers of the human DNA templates. They calibrate your DNA and offer you accelerated healing in all of their forms. The healings and the miracles continue! We continue to be the guides on many boat trips in California, in Catalina, and in Hawaii where people can interact with the cetaceans and hear their messages. We have created many retreats under the umbrella of "Expand Your Consciousness" in California, in Mexico, Hawaii and in Panama with Whale Watching Panama. We teach about Lemuria, known to us as the first golden age on Earth. We teach time travel, activating your merkaba and third eye, animal and angelic communication. Master Puddah and I have a monthly radio show on McLean Masterworks Healing where we offer meditations for healing and get to share the animal's wisdom with people all over the world. But most importantly, we recognize the cetaceans as the healers of the healers! We are witness to thousands of people getting well when they open their hearts to the whale energy and consciousness. We have received 12 templates to assist humans in activating their higher consciousness and assisting them in healing their bodies. The white whales call these activations "Light Body Programming." Master Puddah and I now work with the white whales as they have shown us that they can heal you from any location. As the "voice of the whales," they ask you to open to their wisdom and allow them to activate the codes of creation within YOU!

Whale Consciousness Message for Humanity

The Universe is one living breathing conscious Being demonstrating inter-connectedness and oneness. The incarnated whales are an example of the all-loving, all-knowing consciousness that came to planet Earth to be a steward for Gaia and for humanity. As a species, the whales and dolphins are the most spiritually and intellectually-evolved souls in our world and they anchor light beamed to Earth from distant sources. Using their Living Light Fields, known as the merkaba, they align with the frequency and resonance of Gaia or Mother Earth. The whales have held the highest incarnated vibration on the planet for eons and also hold the resonance or frequency that is the heartbeat for Gaia. We would not have survived these many years if the whales had not chosen to use their vibration to balance and steady our beautiful planet.

The end of polarity or duality is nearing. The responsibilities the whales have held for humanity is now being shared with many humans as we awaken to our true selves and choose to take our power as children of Creator/Source. We are reclaiming the true dreaming state of the living heart. This is true Creatorship. What this means is that through exercising intentional evolution we are entering into a time when thoughts will manifest very quickly into our dimensional realities. Because many of us have chosen to awaken to the truth of our Souls journey and become conscious creators, we are now able to connect with the super-sentient ancient cetaceans we call the whales.

The whales are the ancients, the elders, and are the greatest healers we will know throughout our many journeys and lifetimes upon this planet we call Earth. The whales ask you to call upon them often to realign your auric fields and your organ systems. They remind you of the phrase "ask and you will receive". It is their honor to assist us, and they come in joy and in a state of bliss that can best be described as "living in Oneness with the all that is." The whales are leading us back to the ability to remember and create in multidimensional planes.

Humpback Whale Council through Laurie Reyon

Dolphin Message for Humanity

The dolphins are the ambassadors and the embodiments of joy here on planet Earth. They represent the positive feeling and emotional states of happiness, passion, love and joy! They are ambassadors to humanity assisting us in finding and living those qualities within ourselves. The dolphins offer us a literal rainbow bridge of light on the pathway to ascension and merging with our Higher Selves.

The dolphins are emissaries of light and work closely with the Pleiadian beings to assist everyone in becoming a conscious creator.

The dolphins can assist you in going deep within yourself to find the truth that lives within your heart. They ask us to connect with the Divinity within ourselves and truly connect with our souls. They remind us that the soul is the consciousness that we incarnated from and that which we will ultimately return to. Our physical bodies are just an expression of that part of us that embodies a higher power and consciousness. Our souls want nothing more of us in the physical than for us to be happy and live a joyful and magical life. It is only through creating joyful feelings that we can achieve a higher vibration and can truly connect to and communicate with our higher selves. So the dolphins message is quite simply to become aware of how easy it is to monitor our thought forms and just choose to change them if we find our thoughts anything other than joyful! Simple but profound. Remember, to think is to create and we are the creators and co-creators of the world in which we live.

The dolphins intend that you will find great love and joy in your heart each day and find a way to share it with another!

Dolphin Emissaries of Light through Laurie Reyon

Dolphins and DNA

The Dolphins have shared with me that they are the designated keepers of the human DNA template system. They receive infusions of DNA activations through the earth's ocean systems from Creator. It is their given task to process this information internally and calibrate the actual DNA that is perfect and right for each person. They also hold the energy of love and joy for actual locations on the planet that are experiencing war and chaos. They create frequencies and infuse them into these areas with templates of peace, harmony and healing. The Dolphin Matrix supports DNA re-encodements for people and places through these energy code systems. The Dolphin Family of Light has created a template for the human DNA and uses it to monitor the overall template for the pure holographic possibility equation for humanity and Earth.

If you choose to connect with the planetary dolphin family, you can receive these attunements directly from the dolphin group consciousness.

Dolphins are the masters of DNA recalibration and are able to shift old energies very quickly with their healing frequencies. Also, they work in a frequency of joy and playfulness that is perfectly suited to the energy of ascension and the "New Earth." Beloved humans, please listen to our hearts as the energies accelerate during 2012 and beyond. Call upon the dolphin energies as they are the chosen Emissaries of Light. Their communications will be of valuable assistance in helping you to align with the crystalline grid system, your personal DNA upgrades, and the dolphin matrix systems that are assisting in creating the "center" for the New Earth.

Also know that the dolphin matrix of energy is assisting with the cleansing and balancing of the earth's oceans.

Currently, many scientific experts are saying that DNA plays a powerful role in newly-discovered communications between dolphins and humans. An ongoing study at the Sirius Institute in Hawaii has revealed that dolphins and whales receive and transmit sound signals capable of affecting the genetic double helix. Using natural biotechnology, dolphins can actually heal humans swimming near them "sono-genetically." It is now being proven that DNA, traditionally considered the blueprint of life, can be changed by the sound and electromagnetic fields generated by dolphins.

New research shows that our DNA is activated by waves and particles of energized sound and light that literally switch genes on or off. Likewise genetic inheritance is energetically transmitted bio-acoustically and electromagnetically through special water molecules that form the electro-genetic matrix of DNA." [23]

This amazing phenomenon explains how remarkable healings have been reported by people in our boats near the dolphins and by swimmers following dolphin contact.

---

23 The Sirius Institute quotes taken from the site: <u>Dolphins Spirit of Hawaii.com</u>

The cetaceans have had complex languages for millions of years and they have the largest brains on the planet. Visitations by dolphins and whales have demonstrated a history of friendship and cooperation and even partnership with humans.

The dolphins and whales are living examples for humans, showing us how to live in peace and in harmony with our planet. We encourage you to connect with the dolphins and the whales each and every day, energetically, telepathically and in the physical oceans whenever you can. They are the living ultimate expression of how we humans can begin to live in our hearts within the pod mind, which is demonstrated by living for the good of the many, not the one.

Laurie Reyon & Master Cat Puddah and the Cetacean Councils of Light

Blue Whale Message

As a species, the Whales are the most ancient spiritually and intellectually evolved souls. In our world, the whales anchor the light beamed to Mother Earth from distant sources. The whales communicate with off world intelligent celestial beings that are in stewardship and service to Mother Earth and her inhabitants. The whales create a resonance in their heart beat that corresponds and communicates with the very essence and consciousness of our planet and the being of light we know as "Gaia". After millions of years of existence on this planet, they have both knowledge and experience of how to work effectively with the other conscious energies of the planet, solar system and the galaxy. They use their living light fields or "merkaba" to balance, synchronize and heal themselves, the planet and others that express their desire for their expertise.

In their communication with other intelligent forces, the blue whales work to balance and harmonize the electromagnetic fields of light in the oceans that correspond to the longitude and latitude lines upon the Earth. The Blue Whales have shared that they function in their physical embodiments as neural-electricians for Mother Earth. As they swim northbound in the oceans along the coastlines, they use their innate abilities to connect to the magnetic fields of a given area. They then realign the magnetic fields of energy as needed to correspond to the star fields and other planets that are currently influencing the electromagnetic fields of that area. They have said they are the physical "electricians" for the Earth. When the blue whales ultimately turn to make their southern migration, they have completed their annual attunements for the coastal area,s and they quite simply check in and make any necessary final adjustments before they exit the area they have just visited. The immensity of their physical body allows them to do their very important electrical alignment work, keeping us in balance as the gravitational influences affect us and our planet.

The Great Blue Whale Council through Laurie Reyon

Laurie Reyon is an inter-nationally known Inter Species Communicator and Soul Healer. Reyon's gift allows her to speak to the animals and the Angels and then translate their messages to humanity. She recognizes the cetaceans as the ancients Beings on this planet. Her work involves communication and healing with the dolphins and whales of earth. Reyon recognizes the great whales as Master Healers and offers healing sessions and workshops where people can interact with their energy and intelligence.

Reyon has been named "Standing Whale Mother" by the Native Americans and she brings the wisdom and healing energies of the whales and the dolphins to the people, guided by Spirit and the energy of Master Cat Puddah. Reyon has recently received information from the Whales and Dolphins on how to use their energy to activate and calibrate the HUMAN DNA and assist the humans in preparing for Ascension.

In 1994 she suffered an accident with complications and ultimately experienced a radiant Near-Death Experience in which she actually died for six minutes. She subsequently lived in Baja Mexico where she interacted with the local dolphins and whales, being taught their wisdom and writing their stories and prayers with the assistance of Master Cat Puddah.

Reyon acknowledges her Service to Spirit and now works in partnership with the consciousness & healing abilities of Master Cat Puddah and the Whales & Dolphins. Currently, Reyon and Master Cat Puddah work as an Intuitive Ascension team, offering Life Path and Akashic Record consultations, Animal communication, Spiritual Life Coaching, and Whale and Dolphin Medicine sessions for Healing and Clearing. They also facilitate boat trips and retreats to swim and interact with the dolphins and whales. They operate the *Omni-Dimensional Mystery School* in Oceanside, CA and in 2014 will open their Maui location. Her radio show is broadcast on McLean Masterworks Healing and she is about to release her second film *Ascension Guidance - Living in Your Sacred Heart*. They are the co-creators of the *Dolphins Love Kids* charity program, offering the opportunity for children to spend the day on a boat with free dolphins. www.LaurieReyon.com 619-271-9461

Chapter 16: *The Path of a Dolphin Light Worker*

By Megan Leupold

Long Ago and Far Away

It began in a fairy-tale land by the sea. It is a love story that has resonated across the ages, with many odd twists and turns. There was once a lovely young woman who lived in this land by the sea, where the humanoids had gills and were able to both swim in the water and walk on the land. There was once a handsome young dolphin who was master of his domains, both the sea and the etheric consciousness, to which his species had a clear connection.

They met, by chance and destiny, while both were frolicking in the waves of the warm, clear turquoise water. Fascinated by their differences, as well as their similarities, they became the closest of friends and would swim and play and talk and share for hours. The beautiful coral reefs and flowing grasses were their playground and the colorful sea creatures smiled to see their happiness. He called her Marni, or Earth Angel and she called him Palani, or Sea Angel.

As time passed, and they grew older, life got more complicated. Marni's family told her that sea dwelling was only for the very young and with maturity came responsibility. Societal dictates said that she needed to attend school, develop her human abilities, find a mate and form a family unit...on land. Her gills would gradually recede and the sea would be visited only for brief holidays.

Meanwhile, Palani's pod reminded him that he needed to learn the skills of the dolphin, develop his cetacean abilities, find a mate and join a family unit ... in the sea. He would occasionally be able to see the Humanoids on the beach and could wave and sing to them. Marni and Palani refused to listen to their communities and continued to spend all their time together. With the threat of separation came the realization that they had become much more than friends. They were sacred soul partners and, despite their different bodies, their spirits were one and belonged together.

Because their union was unconventional and misunderstood, there were many attempts, by both species, to discourage their connection. The humanoids threatened ostracism, pleaded, ordered, laid guilt and blame and tried to catch Palani in their fishing nets. Marni learned of their plan and, at great risk to her own safety, cut the nets. The cetaceans threatened ostracism, pleaded, ordered, laid guilt and blame and tried to have Marni eaten by a shark. Palani learned of their plan and heroically fought off the shark.

Finally, both sides just gave up their efforts, dismissing the couple as being odd and eccentric ... the magic of which legends are made! Their many years together were peaceful, harmonious, spiritual and loving. No one was ever happier! The humanoids and dolphins came to honor and respect Marni and Palani's unique connection, learning valuable lessons regarding judgment and the beauty of nontraditional love.

The couple knew and accepted that Palani's species was not as long lived as Marni's, and as they prepared for his passing, they vowed to reconnect their souls in a future time and place. Sad but accepting, Marni asked, "How will I recognize you, my Love?" Palani replied, "I will whisper, 'you knew me'."

This Current Life Expression

Do you believe in miracles? Is synchronicity just another name for fate? Have you ever had the sense that something momentous and amazing is just over the horizon? With age comes wisdom, they say. That may be true but, in my humble opinion, what really happens, as the years progress, is that we gain an ability to see the bigger picture, to review our life and gain insight into how the pieces of our own, personal puzzle have so cleverly been provided and, ultimately, woven together. To condense a lifetime into one chapter, I shall touch on the highlights of a most amazing journey – the path of a Dolphin Light Worker.

Growing up in rural farmland, with few human playmates, I learned at an early age to be independent and adventurous. My friends were the fairies and devas of the woods and fields, and it was not unusual to find me riding long, solitary miles on my bicycle, imagining flying carpets, unicorns and shimmering crystal energy waves carrying me along. My mother, normally a very cautious person in other matters, never once tried to reign in her wandering daughter. It seemed she intuitively knew and accepted that independence was to be my destiny. Now I see her gift of freedom as a piece of my puzzle.

My father, also known as my hero, taught me to be one with nature, to love all living beings, to see beyond the veils of illusion and, most importantly, to swim like a dolphin! No fear – just fun! He was a gentle giant, highly intelligent and an Olympic-level swimmer for an Ivy League school. To this day, I treasure the memories of him tossing me far into the ocean and his cheerful encouragement as I swam back. No fear – just fun! He left this world when I was just 17, and my heart felt broken. I couldn't see this separation as an important piece of my puzzle, not yet.

Life went on, and my heart learned to feel again. In an ideal world, one's first love is beautiful, innocent, uplifting and true. I had that experience times ten. Lance was handsome, smart, funny, adoring and magical. We were so in love, planning to marry after we both completed college. Destiny had other plans, however, as the Vietnam War escalated. Sensing the hot breath of the draft coming ever closer, my love joined the Army, requesting assignment to the Screaming Eagles of the 101st Airborne Infantry. He served heroically, receiving multiple medals for acts of bravery that saved the lives of many fellow soldiers. When he returned, however, he was wounded both mentally and physically. The man I loved was nowhere to be found – another silent casualty of a war that made no sense. He eventually chose to leave those he loved and wandered for years. Again, my heart felt broken, and I was left with another piece of my puzzle that I could not understand.

Eventually, I married a college classmate because I didn't know what else to do. Jack asked, he seemed a decent man, and I was lost and wandering myself. Those I loved most seemed to disappear from my life! Of course, there are no coincidences, and Jack turned out to be a necessary and important part of my puzzle. We had two sons, whom I had the privilege of homeschooling, we lived a very organic and healthy lifestyle, and two important and life-changing events occurred. First, I got my basic and advanced SCUBA certification and, second, I returned to graduate school to earn my Master of Social Work degree.

Feeling a growing wanderlust, I founded the SCUBA Travel Club and led groups of people on many memorable adventures to various Caribbean Islands, Florida, Mexico, Hawaii, and Bermuda. On one of these journeys, we visited a piece of heaven called North Caicos, a small island in the Turks & Caicos chain which eventually became our second home. It was there, in front of our weather-worn beach house that I met and connected with JoJo, the famous wild dolphin who travels the T&C coastline. I would call him by tapping together two conch shells and, if he so chose, he would come racing from wherever he might be. JoJo and I played for many happy hours and a deep memory began to surface in my dreams.

In retrospect, I can see that, as my spiritual, multi-dimensional, adventurous self began to expand, the energy of the marriage began to shift and change also. While I may have been the first to feel the shift, Jack was the first to act, selling his business in the USA, relocating to Turks & Caicos, and, eventually, moving to Panama. I came to realize that our contract together was complete, and it was now time to move on. Many puzzle pieces had been laid in place, and my former husband and I remain connected and active co-parents to this day.

Although these events signaled the end of the Scuba Travel Club, I had recorded well over 500 dives and felt very much like a mermaid in the sea! Of even more significance, I had been privileged to spend many magical moments, face-to-face, communing with a wild dolphin!

The social work arena now called to me, as I felt a growing need to be of service. I was infused with a mission – to support those who were lost in complicated grieving, to aide veterans and others suffering with PTSD, and to provide a beacon of light to those lost souls who wander through our toxic systems with no guidance or mentoring. I worked tirelessly in this field for almost 20 years and know that I had a positive impact on many lives. Would I have had this drive and passion to make a difference without the early influence of my father, the loss of my first love, the changing tides of my marriage, and my own unique childhood experiences? Pieces of my puzzle were coming together. Remember, there are no accidents!

Now the miracles really began to ramp up! I was invited by several friends to attend a presentation by a fellow who had conscious memory of being taken aboard Acturian and Ashtar ships and, consequently, returned with many expanded talents. Among them was the unique ability to draw complex and intricate representations of his experiences, which he now shared as a tool to awaken evolving consciousness. It sounded interesting, and I had nothing better to do, so I went. Much to my amazement, as I watched the video, I vividly recalled having seen one of the drawings in a recent dream; I shared this information with the presenter, and, long story short, Warren and I have been companions for the past 19 years! Yahoo, another piece of my puzzle!

We moved to a community of like-minded folk, one of whom was a gifted healer and channel of spiritual energy. The first time I walked into Hanna's session, she looked deeply into my eyes and said, "Welcome, what took you so long, we've been patiently waiting!" I soon became her devoted pupil and dear friend and, over the course of 15 years, she assisted me in expanding my heart, my soul, my consciousness, and, in the process, totally changed my perception of reality. Our meeting and deep connection was certainly no accident – nothing ever is!

Hanna and I shared a magical, mystical inner journey together. We had many, many extra-dimensional experiences, but I shall share two that particularly affected me. During a very deep, past-life regression, Hanna took me to my original arrival on planet Earth. I was a child and the sole survivor on an interplanetary ship that had crash landed upon Earth. Looking around my space, I recognized, among the deceased occupants, my parents and older brother and was flooded with the awareness that we were fleeing our beloved home, which was on the edge of destruction. Most fascinating, however, were our physical forms. We were not humans, we were dolphins! I was rescued and cared for by some loving people, many of whom surround me still, and reconnecting with this deep soul memory helped to explain the many moments when I have felt like a stranger in a strange land and have experienced dreams of life in a dolphin body.

Another regression took me to the beautiful, crystalline healing temples of Atlantis, along with the shock and terror experienced while witnessing a gigantic tidal wave poised to destroy all that I loved. I was both dolphin and human in this vision, morphing back and forth between the two. In this current-life expression, I had experienced repeated night terrors involving tidal waves since childhood, but the details were always fuzzy, and I pestered my father with endless questions on the subject. In the regression, we distanced ourselves emotionally, which enabled us to stay present and witness the event, providing a clearer vision of the bigger picture, the lessons learned and our purpose for returning to assist Mother Earth at this moment in time. I never had the tidal wave nightmare again.

One cold night in February, Hanna asked me to stop by for a visit. It was then that she gently told me her time in this earthly body was nearing an end, and she had some important messages to share. Entering a trance state, her words of wisdom flowed, "Always, always, always remember, there are no accidents! If the meaning is temporarily unclear, have faith and trust that a divine plan is in place and know that the puzzle pieces have been created to fit together perfectly. There will come an 'ah-ha' moment when all is made clear."

Hanna then continued with future predictions that I would travel to sacred sites and have magical, heart-opening experiences. I would write books, speak to the media, channel highly-evolved and wondrous beings from multiple dimensions and consciousnesses. I would teach classes and assist others to expand their own inner knowledge, while remaining a humble beacon of light shining brightly for those seeking. Perhaps the most beautiful and wondrous happening was to be a reunion with my twin flame, for whom I had long been searching, and the deep loneliness I had often felt would be healed. Hanna peacefully passed in her sleep that very night and, while I missed my dear friend, I was filled with gratitude for the many gifts she had imparted. We still chat, now and then, as friends do, and she provides beautiful guidance when asked.

Interestingly, the energies of the intentional community shifted and dissolved with her passing. The light went out, people moved away, friendships ended and several chose to also pass. The postal address remains the same but the vibrational frequency is totally changed. I no longer think of it as my home, but rather, a place to store my stuff, while my true home is within and no material structure is needed. What a sense of freedom!

Meanwhile, Warren and I were indeed having adventures! I felt the moment of magical awakening coming ever closer; my puzzle about to take form. Our travels took us to the Mayan ruins in Chichen Itza, Mexico, where we experienced that unique lifetime through a very thin dimensional veil. We camped on the beaches of the North Carolina Outer Banks while observing the most beautiful meteorite shower I have ever seen. We hiked the slopes of Mt. Shasta, searching for the opening to the Inner Earth, which we had experienced repeatedly and vividly during dream state. We wept with joy as we hugged the majestic California redwoods, sharing visions of our happy and peaceful life as members of an innocent and loving tribal community. We traveled the length of the Blue Ridge Parkway and Skyline Drive, both by car and motorcycle, influenced by deep memories to sleep in the woods and hike the mountains. We sat at the sacred vortex sites of Sedona, Arizona and saw the dry valleys as they once had been, filled with water and home to many beautiful sea creatures. We were called to Bimini, where our emotions alternated between a deep sadness for something lost and an overwhelming joy for something found.

And then came the journey to Hawaii. The Universe felt we were finally ready for the moment of contact that it had been priming us for all along. Since this was a major investment of both time and money, we planned every detail very carefully and concisely …. like we really had any control! All went as planned until we reached the Kona Coast of the Big Island. I attended a session with an amazing woman who did trance readings, and her message regarding my future endeavors was very similar to Hanna's but more detailed and imminent. I was instructed to go to the Kealakekua Bay and snorkel with the wild spinner dolphins; they were requesting my presence, now! Our B&B gave us equipment and directions, and we entered the cool and calm waters early the next morning.

Although we were both strong swimmers, the task looked daunting. "Just go to the middle, and they will come," the reader had said. It was with a great leap of faith that we began the long swim out to the deep water, but come they did! Multitudes of dolphins streaked around us, jumping, playing, and singing in joy! We were filled with such bliss we stayed for hours, not noticing the cold and the fatigue that were setting in. Finally heading back to shore, the swim seemed to take forever! I was tired but supremely happy as we finally touched shore. We had fulfilled the request, and it had been truly magical. I thought I was complete.

However, that night, in dream state, I had a very vivid exchange with a beautiful, loving being that looked just like a spinner dolphin. He requested that I make the journey into Kealakekua Bay two more times. What! I barely survived the first swim, and they wanted me to go two more times! But, with my supportive companion at my side, I accomplished what seemed impossible. I went into the bay the next two mornings. The second visit went much like the first, with many dolphins surrounding us and playing joyfully.

The third day proved to be a very different experience. A smaller group arrived and called to my companion, who swam playfully with them a short distance away. Three dolphins separated, came over to me and proceeded to swim in a beautifully choreographed circle just under the surface. They continued this pattern for almost an hour, never changing their speed or direction, while I floated above them, watching in a semi-hypnotic state, unable or unwilling to move, until finally they sang a sweet farewell song and swam off into the deep.

My life was immediately changed in incredible ways. I felt as if I no longer had a body, the swim back to shore was effortless, and I was filled with beautiful peace and joy. I shed tears of emotion for some hours and then fell into a deep, interactive dream state where much information was downloaded. I learned that the experience I had in the bay was an initiation, a prearranged ceremony, intended to lift the veils of many lifetimes and to activate and clarify my link with the higher realms of cetacean consciousness. My dream visitors explained that there was but one step left in the process, and it would soon be accomplished. They did agree to give me some play and rest time before the next adventure and then swam away with loving, yet mischievous, grins!

Upon our return to Pennsylvania, Hanna and my spiritual family noticed that my frequencies were very different. My aura radiated brilliant colors of the rainbow, my DNA stranding was altered and my astral body no longer appeared as a human form. My internal experiences were altered also. I was able to see colors more vividly, had much finer hearing, instinctively changed my diet (I craved seaweed and sardines), interacted more lovingly and patiently with people and occasionally would hear faint but undecipherable whisperings.

Life, however, went on and my work position soon claimed all of my energy and attention. More people needed help. The issues grew in intensity and many walked that fine line between life and death, depending on me to make the difference. Soon, the dolphins' dream message slipped into the background and was lost among the demands of the here and now.

Finally, we were able to grab a quick vacation and chose one of our favorite places, Sedona, Arizona. Of course, there are no accidents, and our choice for a quick reprieve was, indeed, always the intended destination for the last and final step in the activation process. My puzzle was almost complete!

Stiff from a long, uncomfortable flight, I decided to attend a yoga class near our hotel. It was levels above my beginner abilities, but I was welcomed and reminded of the basic yoga rule: Listen to your body and do only that with which you are comfortable. I took a spot in the back of the room, out of everyone's way, and vowed to do my best. I was intensely focused on the instructor, because many of the positions were new to me, and was enjoying the challenge, even though detoxing copiously through my sweat glands, when suddenly a word formed clearly and quite loudly within my mind .... "UNUMI"!

It was as if someone had shot me with a stun gun! I did not yet consciously understand what was happening, but I was aware that I was unable to move, barely able to draw a breath, and was just standing there with tears pouring down my face. Of course, everyone, including myself, thought I had injured myself, and the class came to a screeching stop! I had no explanation because nothing hurt so I gathered my belongings as quickly as possible, uttered some sort of apology about jet lag and left the building post haste!

What was happening to me? What was that word in my head? Why did it have such an effect on me? I needed some space and time to think so I checked in with Warren, hiked a short distance to a local energy vortex, which luckily I had to myself, and was immediately joined by the dream dolphins that had guided me in Hawaii. It was here, in this beautiful space surrounded by the glorious red rocks that the puzzle came together. I remembered it all, the great love that was shared, the promises made, the lifetimes spent wondering and searching. It came as an instant download, a flood of emotion, understanding, connection, dissolved veils and answered questions.

And then he was there! My twin flame was in my heart, my mind and my soul. I thought I would burst from pure happiness as the space that had been reserved just for him was again complete. My dear friend, with whom I had shared oversoul, had finally made his way through the density and ego of this dimension to get my attention. He said it took lifetimes of synchronicity to make it happen. I was never alone, never unprotected. Everything that occurred, in any lifetime, had led us to this moment.

We just reveled in our reunion for the moment, but Unumi, now his chosen name, informed me that he had much to teach the world and, from now on, we would be a team, if I agreed. The only answer that was truly possible was, "I would be honored."

Our many adventures since those early days are a story for another time. We have traveled the world sharing higher wisdom and gifts provided by the Cetacean Nation. From individuals to groups, we have shared vibrational frequencies of healing and enlightenment. We have facilitated journeys to ancient and honored sites and frolicked and played with our brothers and sisters of the sea. We have assisted in the protection of the threatened Atlantian Crystals. We are well known for our Dolphin Dialogues, where Unumi has heart-to-heart discussions and is open to answer individual questions.

It has truly been an amazing journey. Some days I still can't believe I have been so blessed. It is with pure joy, love, peace and non-judgment that I welcome you on to the path of the Dolphin Lightworker.

Megan is a modern day mystic. Her life, from her earliest years, has been guided and choreographed by a series of synchronistic, meta-normal and magical experiences. A mental health professional, Megan is a Dr. of Metaphysical Divinity, a Diplomat of Clinical Social Work, a Master level Chi Energy Healer and Teacher, a Past Life and Child Within Specialist, a Dolphin Preceptor, and an accomplished channel of Cetacean Consciousness.

In 1998, Megan was guided to Kealakekua Bay, HI, for a predestined swim with a pod of wild spinner dolphins. As per an ageless agreement, a mystical initiation took place and Megan was reconnected with her kindred spirit and twin flame, a being of pure dolphin consciousness that lifted the veil of forgetting by whispering the simple yet profound words, "you knew me." Thus Dolphin Light was born.

Megan and Unumi now travel many paths, touching hearts and souls with their fascinating teachings, activating strong, self-healing energies, radiating unconditional love and revealing ancient, cosmic truths. Their famous Dolphin Dialogues are fun, enlightening, and healing. It would be their honor to touch your life with the many gifts from Dolphin Light.

Megan currently lives in the beautiful mountains of Pennsylvania with her companion, several dogs, even more cats and a pod of etheric dolphins (and a few whales)! Her adored grandchildren are nearby, as are her sons and families. However, she does admit a growing pull to The Big Island and has been looking at real estate ads. Who knows where destiny may lead?

Megan's forthcoming book: *The Path of the Dolphin Lightworker: Nine Gifts for Humanity from Dolphin Consciousness*, is due to be released soon.

www.DolphinLight.org

Chapter 17: *Dolphins & The Ecstasy of Everyday Life*

By Joebaby Noonan

"You give us entirely too much power.
We simply mirror your own divine joy back to you.
The exuberance you see in us is a reflection of your own essence!"
- Spotted Dolphin message

Just as you and I are spiritual beings having a human experience, the dolphins and whales are spiritual beings having a cetacean experience. To be fully immersed in the rich and adventurous journey of being human with all its contrasts, doubts and fears, we take on many veils of forgetting. The most significant veil we take on is forgetting that we are infinite and eternal and are left believing ourselves to be separate from the world around us.

231

In contrast, the dolphins and whales have no doubt about the eternalness of their existence. They remember their connection to all life, and as a result, they remind us of our eternal nature just by their presence in our world. How lucky we are!

In our humanness, we often lose sight of our divine nature and inner exuberance. It was intact within us when we took birth, and depending upon the path we set up for ourselves in this life, it can be the source of our life's journey. This chapter is a brief story of how the cetaceans helped me on my journey to fully accept, embrace and embody the ecstasy that is our essence.

Saving Grace

Nature was my saving grace as a child. I grew up on a farm, one of eight kids, and the suppression, craziness and dysfunction that went on inside our house would melt away as soon as I got outside. The earth, trees and sky were my second family and embraced me with a love that still brings me to tears. The deadening depression of my family, the same depression that took my brother's life, was soothed and softened by nature's grace.

When it would get really crazy at home, I'd go outside and flop down in the tall grass, take a hike in the woods behind our home or climb one of my favorite trees. Here, embraced by the loving energies of nature, felt the rush of ecstasy rise up within me again and again in response to the beauty and magic of my surroundings.

It would happen through the simplest of things. A blade of grass could catch my eye, and I'd find myself lost in a lush world of greens, drinking in the unique shades of color and vibrancy of each individual blade. An ant might scurry into view, and as my eyes instinctively followed its passage, I'd become entranced by the undulating pattern of its movement. A breeze would tickle the hair on my arm, pulling my attention to it, and as I followed, I'd find myself diving deeper and deeper into the subtlest of sensations, feeling the hairs moving in concert with the branches overhead.

There was great beauty, peace and harmony here, in stark contrast to the pervasive demands of family and society. As I got older, the ongoing struggle and competition for male dominance, to be the "top dog", better at everything even in the simplest of interactions, left me feeling more and more isolated. It sucked being a boy, for to be accepted by my peers, I had to constantly play the game.

My challenge was to integrate the ecstasy I felt so easily in nature with the suppression and conformity of family, school and society. Everyone around me seemed so dead and muted, even as they strove to "fit in".

In the desire to bring these two halves of my life together, I delved deeply into the healing arts. I learned to meditate in high school (I sold enough drugs to pay for a Transcendental Meditation course) and learned acupressure and shiatsu to heal myself of spastic colitis when I was 17. Hunting, trapping and fishing were part of my childhood, and reading the mystical adventures of Don Juan in Carlos Castaneda's books brought the natural world even more alive for me. By the time I was 20, in addition to my work as a carpenter, I had a healing practice where I offered reflexology and flower essences. I also worked as a healer with the laying on of hands in several churches and hospitals.

From there I became a therapist, using psychosynthesis, huna and outdoor adventure to help people regain their connection to their inner ecstatic selves. I also worked as a guide for several Outward Bound schools, bringing groups on backpacking, canoeing and hiking trips.

Using tools from my shamanic studies and experiences, I developed daylong and multiday leadership programs and teambuilding retreats for corporate clients, and led hundreds of retreats for Fortune 500 companies, businesses and colleges, including HP, Bayer, AT&T and Harvard University. I was coaching CEOs and executives using spiritual principles in the context of leadership and profitability. One of my favorite claims to fame was, after leading a two day sailing retreat for a group of engineers about to rebuild a steam generator at a nuclear power plant, they told me that the project set a new company record in GE for being ahead of schedule. The leader told me that it was the best project he'd ever run, and when they'd hit a roadblock or be at odds with the union and labor, they would circle up and "om" together!

Ultimately I became a shamanic nature guide; bringing executives, families and spiritual groups into nature to realign with the innate sense of oneness and belonging that is living ongoingly within each of us. I was facilitating my own healing through my work with others, and as rewarding as it was, I still felt a sense of separation.

I judged my humanness, saw it as course and crude and destructive, and felt that it barred me from fully entering Nature's Eden. I wanted to go "all the way" with my connection to nature, to immerse myself so deeply that I could never completely return. I felt trapped, stuck between two worlds. I sought desperately to bridge this gap within me, yet didn't know how.

A Bolt of Energy

One day some friends told me their story about swimming with wild dolphins. As they spoke, a shock of energy ran completely through me. It was the awakening of something old and forgotten, and I knew in that moment I had to go and experience it for myself.

I was living on an island off the New England coast at the time, married with a two-year-old son. I booked my flight for a month away, which at the moment seemed plenty soon enough.

In the days and weeks that followed, my desire to meet the dolphins grew. Something had been activated, and I wanted nothing more than to already be in the sea with them. It was a primal hunger, the need to have the direct experience, and it grew in strength.

A Desperate Yearning

Finally the day came, and I arrived in Hawaii excited and ready. I was staying with my friend LiLi, and together we swam in the coastal bays the wild dolphins were known to visit. Every day we looked for dolphins, and every day the dolphins were nowhere to be seen. Day after day after day, no dolphins.

Their absence triggered something within me, and one night after five days of looking, I found myself in a state of desperation. I was outside on the grass in my sleeping bag, overlooking the west Maui Mountains and the moonlit Pacific Ocean, when I had a very passionate heart-to-heart talk with God.

"What the #@!%&! is going on? I've come all this way to answer this calling, and there are no dolphins to meet me. Why is this happening, and what the #$@!%&@ am I supposed to do about it?"

I closed my eyes and prayed for understanding, the urgency and desperation to meet the dolphins growing ever stronger within me.

I had unknowingly opened Pandora's Box... With the lid removed, the yearning within me came alive. It grew like some demonic genie, scaring me with its size and power. I had no clue it was so big, and it threatened to overwhelm me.

I saw that I had been hiding the true scope of my yearning as a way to protect myself, in case I didn't see the dolphins.

I was humbled by this unconscious protection, shocked to see how unaware of it I was.

And then, all the protection was stripped away. The yearning became a raging hurricane. Helpless and in terror, I became a tiny speck before it, frozen, unable to move. Still it grew, into a galactic black hole that swept me and all creation into it, and everything went black...

An unknown infinity of time later, I came back to my senses. There was a profound sense of peace within me. I was laying on a sleeping bag under the stars, wondering where I was, when I remembered what had happened.

I wondered, how could I go from such terror and overwhelm to such peace? I was shown that something deep and desperate within me had been met on a profoundly deep and archetypal level; and in that meeting, the yearning had become fully met unlike ever before. I knew it was OK if I never swam with the dolphins. I knew it was OK if I never finished or achieved any of the things that I had ever sought or desired...

What I did know was that all things, all of creation was and is infinitely well. I recognized my yearning as the yearning within us all for re-union with Source, and that by surrendering myself to the yearning, it had somehow been met within me. I went to sleep that night completely peaceful with the remembering that all is infinitely and eternally well. The depth of this knowing was profound, and I felt it resonating within my DNA.

The Big Day

The next day I awake in great spirits. As we pull up to the parking lot to begin our daily hike to the bay to look for dolphins, I spontaneously offer a ceremony of thanksgiving to the ocean and her inhabitants. I apologize for my demanding agenda of before; every day demanding to see dolphins and practically ignoring the other fish and turtles and creatures she has sent my way. Humbly, I thank her in advance for whatever adventures she chooses to share with us.

We're walking across the jagged lava to the water when a woman on the trail ahead of us suddenly yells, "Look, there's dolphins in the bay!"

Her remark rocks me from my reverie, and the passion to swim with the dolphins returns full force. I begin to move across the tricky lava path at high speed. As I run, a multitude of thoughts race through my mind, "Will they stay? Are they leaving? Will they be gone before I get there?"

The dangerous meeting point of lacerating lava and crashing ocean, where I've learned to carefully time my entry into the sea, becomes a tiny hop, and with a splash I am in the water and swimming, looking eagerly for fins.

As I swim, the doubts return; "Are they still here? Have they left? Am I too late? Have I already missed them?"

Ignoring them, I swim further from shore. Anxious and excited, I'm looking all around – but no dolphins, no fins. Undeterred, I swim further from shore.

I stop and lift my head high, still no sight of dolphins. The water is getting deep, and my uncertainty grows...

Suddenly I see them! Six beautiful dolphins, swimming straight towards me! I'm awash with elation. Sleek, smooth and graceful, the dolphins are swimming side by side, all in a row. They are coming in from deeper water, and as they reach me, they break formation, swimming playfully around me.

I'm ecstatic! Here they are, I'm with the dolphins! I'm a bubbling rush of excitation as we swim around and around each other in greeting.

They dive below me and return to their formation, six in a row. They start swimming back to deeper water, and in my mask, snorkel and fins, I follow right above them.

I watch in awe as they glide though the water. They move slowly, with such grace. I'm giddy with excitement, catching my breath as I behold them below me.

After a few minutes, they begin to rise back to the surface. I wonder if they'll pull ahead of me. I know enough to keep my arms at my sides, rather than reach out or splash in their direction. To my surprise and delight, they surface all in a row right beside me, the nearest one easily within arm's reach.

I look in his eye and he looks back at me. We behold each other; it is a timeless moment...

I see such presence, such awareness, such intelligence and joy. I'm humbled in my humanness; the sense of kinship coming from him is amazing, and my thoughts fade into the background...

They take a few breaths and in unison glide back down into the sea, until they are about 10 feet below me.

How cool! I'm in awe! They are right below me! I feel so included, and my heart skips in joy.

We continue swimming, and I notice the water getting deeper. The realization of how far I am from shore makes me a little nervous. I'm a good swimmer, but if we meet up with a shark or something, I feel ill equipped to do anything about it.

But they surface again, this time on the other side of me. I look into the eye of the closest one and feel a wonderful sense of kinship and connection. My fears fade in the presence of their joy.

A few breaths and down they go. I rest in the reverie of our connection, and every couple of minutes they continue to surface beside me.

An Archetypal Fear

We continue to move steadily away from shore, and the water keeps getting deeper. Anxiety is building in the pit of my stomach, and an age-old fear from my childhood, a fear I'd forgotten for decades, re-awakens and returns full force.

Many of us have a fear of being eaten from something from the deep. It's a collective archetypal dream, a throwback from our evolution. I had my own version of it as a kid, a reoccurring nightmare of falling into the deep ocean. Strange and bizarre fish with big teeth would swim over to me to check me out. Just as they would swim closer to eat me, I'd sink deeper...

This is the face of the fear building in my belly. As a shamanic guide, I have profound respect for the forces of nature. When I'm in an environment I know intimately, I can discern between irrational fear and the "gut sense" of knowing if everything is OK. This is my barometer, my inner compass for navigating the edge of normal and supernatural. But when I'm in a foreign environment, I have less experience to balance out the personal and collective fears of our species. I'm literally way "over my head" here, and I know that to stay out here, I have to rely on the guidance of my newly found friends.

During this whole thought process, we continue steadily moving further out to sea. I wonder where we're going. Are they intentionally taking me with them?

Do they know I'm way out of my league? Maybe they're heading to the next island, many miles distant, and are even now wondering what the heck I'm doing following them... I imagine them saying to one another, "When is this guy gonna turn around? Does he think he can follow us all the way to Molokini?"

I recognize that I've put my welfare into their hands and projected onto them the responsibility of being my caretakers. Being a guide, I know this is unfair and unwise, and I may have already put myself in danger of being swept further out to sea by an ocean current (There's an ocean current somewhere out here called "The Tokyo Express" for how fast it sucks the unwary to Japan).

I have nothing but faith to allay the fear. But it is not enough, for as the fear in the pit of my belly grows, I think the unthinkable thought, "Perhaps its time for me to turn around and swim back to shore".

The very idea breaks my heart. How can I leave these dolphins? I've only just met them! But the wisdom of this thought remains unchanged. Reluctantly, I give it consideration...

I'm way out to sea in the Hawaiian ocean, of which I know little. I could get caught out here by a shark or current and never be seen again. I'm following a pod of dolphins heading away from land, and they show no signs of slowing. And I have no idea where we're going.

The logic is clear; I should thank the dolphins and immediately head to shore.

But I can't! I've flown five thousand miles to be here, and I'm not ready to turn around. In my dilemma, I turn to the dolphins. "Can you hear me? Is it OK that I stay with you? Will you keep an eye out for me?"

Their rhythm remains unchanged; they surface beside me, look me lovingly in the eye, and drop back down.

If they took off with a burst of speed and abandoned me, I'd turn around. But they're going slow enough for me to keep up. On the other hand, they're not playing with me like they did earlier, and they are clearly commuting to somewhere else.

Again I ask, "Is it OK I'm with you?"

They continue to swim. Another few minutes go by, the tension grows, and I become aware of the gulf between us. I, in my fickle human frailties, need a response from them. But how can they answer me? How do I know they even know what my dilemma is?

I've experienced interspecies communication many times, usually when I'm in a calm, relaxed space. But at this point I'm quite anxious because I need to know if I'm safe or if I'm already in deep shit for my rash actions.

The urgency grows. I dodge it every way I can. I shift my focus back to the dolphins, tell them how much I love them, how honored I am to be with them, how I'd love to stay with them, but I need to know I'm safe and OK. Can you hear me, I wonder, can you understand my predicament?

Fear tells me it may already be too late, that my safe turn around point has already been passed.

Desperately I ask, "How can you show me you can hear me?"

The conflict grows. I realize I'm facing the classic human dilemma: Am I safe? Can I continue to follow my heart in this moment, even though logic and my training tell me to turn around? (Right now, as I write this sentence sitting on a city park bench, I overhear a father yelling at his kids to stop and look before they cross the street).

Being human is a finite journey. At some point we all drop our body. But our spirit has gone through a lot of work to get us here, and the ego mind has the job of keeping us alive and out of harm's way. The voice of prudence continues to insist I turn around immediately!

My heart is torn; the angst within me grows. Again I turn to the dolphins, swimming so peacefully below me, and ask pleadingly, the voice of desperation growing, "How can you show me you hear me?"

Suddenly, I'm struck with inspiration. "I know! I know how you can show me! Every time you come up for air, all six of you come up on one side of me or the other. How about the next time you come up for air, you put me in the middle?"

And in that moment, the most amazing thing happens...

Having just barely finished the thought, all six dolphins begin to rise. I watch in complete awe as three of them go to my right and three go to my left...

I am in the middle. They are on both sides of me.

It is as if a switch in my brain is suddenly flipped off; all the thoughts, fears and angst of moments before are gone.

I'm immersed in peace, swimming with my six friends in the middle of the Pacific Ocean, like it's something we've done throughout all time and space. There is no more question about the depth of connection we seven share, it is total and complete.

I'm in total ecstasy, floating in a most delicious sea of community. Our destination no longer matters, I will follow them to Tahiti. On a deep cellular level, I know I'm part of the pod. I'm home, and I feel a depth of belonging that astounds me and strengthens me, awakening and affirming a quality of connection I've yearned for and feared was only a dream.

We continue on, we seven, and then we reach our destination. We join the rest of the pod, our pod, another twenty-plus dolphins with moms and babies playing and leaping in the open ocean. The seven of us are greeted with leaps and clicks, bubbles and whistles, and I find myself diving and splashing with them all.

I'm no longer a human swimming with dolphins; we're one tribe of kindred spirits, playing together in the rich sensual space of the present moment. There's no other place I'd rather be, there is simply no other place, for this is all there is, and it's way beyond anything I ever imagined.

There are times in our human existence when we touch the face of the divine and realize it is our own. These moments may be preceded or precipitated by much anticipation, preparation, prayer or effort, but in these moments, we remember the totality of our eternal nature. We see the thread of our human adventures with an expansiveness that carries great love and appreciation. From this perspective, all the experiences of our earthly journey, including the suffering and tragedies and travails, are equally blessed.

A Changed Man

It was from this place of great love and equanimity that I returned to shore. I climbed back onto land with an appreciation for the journey of life that continues to this day to gift me with the presence of mind to see all things for the blessing that they are. Sure, I get miserable and desperate. Yes, I still suffer and yearn. And in all that suffering and yearning, amidst all the drama and diversity of this human life, the perspective that all is well and we are infinitely loved returns, and in a moment's notice I can go from despair to delight.

I had always sought to live in the ecstatic energies of life in a way that brought balance and inspiration to my humanness, and am happy to say that the dolphins helped bring these two folds together. While I'd had many experiences of this oneness, the profound, visceral depth of connection I felt with the dolphins somehow put any doubt of belonging behind me forever.

After my first swim I had many more in quick succession, each with its own magic, and my admiration, love and respect for the dolphins grew. I was invited by them to bring others, and I started bringing groups to swim with wild dolphins and whales in different parts of the world, primarily in Hawaii and in Bimini, the Bahamas, where I currently live.

Healings of the Spirit

I've witnessed many kinds of healings as a result of being with the wild dolphins. The vast majority are healings of the soul, where the person finds that, after their encounter with the dolphins, they feel much more aligned and centered in their lives. Clients are constantly writing that since they returned home after their swim, they feel calmer, quieter, more peaceful and trusting of life. Clients have shared that decades of depression have lifted. Others report feeling much more present to the beauty of everyday life.

I'm often asked what happens when you meet a wild and free dolphin in the open ocean. I'm still challenged to put it into words. The simplest way I can say it is that it's the meeting of a long-forgotten friend from before time began.

Are Dolphins Spiritually Superior?

Many people put the cetaceans on a pedestal, seeing them as an elevated form of consciousness. If you tune into their spirit, it is easy to see why, for they are infinitely loving and joyful. I must admit that I had them on a pedestal myself at first; I thought they were total love and light.

As I spent more and more time with them, I began seeing behaviors that looked very "Un-dolphin-like", including fighting, head and tail whacking, biting each other hard enough to leave wounds. I've witnessed one species gang up on another. It takes practice to sort out this behavior, because, at first, all we see is dolphins playing. I've had groups cheer on a mixed pod of bottlenose and spotted dolphins interacting and mating quite vigorously, thinking it was all fun and play, but the video footage showed that several male bottlenose were mating with a reluctant spotted female by preventing her from getting to the surface to breathe and pinning her on the bottom.

At first, I resisted my conclusion (I must have been wrong). Then i minimized the encounter (it was a rare event), but over time I saw this behavior repeatedly. I've heard a number of accounts of captive dolphins maliciously hurting people when angry, and I always blamed it on the stress of being isolated and in captivity.

Do Dolphins Rape?

One day, I saw three big bottlenose gang up on a small female spotted. She was trying to break free from them, but again and again they blocked, pinned and penetrated her, until she gave up and hung vertical in the water while they pushed each other out of the way to have sex with her. I was outraged. My mind labeled the behavior with the words "rape" and "gangbang", and I swam away seething.

I needed to find a way to reconcile this behavior, and prayed to God to help me see it as She does.

What I was shown is that dolphins, just like people, incarnate into a body that carries many mammalian survival tendencies. Just as we struggle to live with some of our primal instincts, like the "fight or flight" tendency innate within us all, so they live within a physical form that also has survival mechanisms. The urge to have sex is a powerful driving force in all of creation, and as the thought-provoking book Sex At Dawn so clearly illustrates, we've adapted infinite cultural strategies to bring balance between our divinity and our primal humanness. It was sobering to realize that the cetaceans have the same challenges, and once I recognized that, they came off the pedestal. Which is a more grounded, balanced view. It is difficult to feel one with someone who you have up high!

Joy is Our Essence

I used to see cetaceans as more joyful than us. We were the brutish, violent Homo sapiens, and they were the joyful, fun-loving cetaceans. But it changed one day during one of my Bimini trips. It was midway through the week; we'd had some great swims with the dolphins, and as we prepared to do a shamanic journey, I invited everyone to ask the dolphins for a message for us as a group.

I love asking my trip participants what they think and what they intuit, as a way to break the hierarchical tradition of everyone looking outside of themselves, whether to me as the leader or to the dolphins, as their soothsayer and psychic. It seems crazy to ask another what is our inner guidance, and the dolphins remind me to always look within for my own answers, rather than outside to an external source. Structuring our circle so that everyone shares their own insight is a fast way to empower everyone's own inner wisdom and guidance.

At the end of the meditation, we sat in a circle and shared. There were a dozen of us, and each person shared exactly the same story! We were each met by a single dolphin who said that the love and exuberance and joy that we see in them is really their mirroring back to us our own inner joy. They said we need to recognize ourselves as sources of divine joy, and that doing so was a most critical (and fun!) step in our collective evolution.

For the past 18 years it's been my joy to bring spiritual groups, individuals and families to swim with the dolphins. It continues to delight me to see how the dolphins and whales touch people's lives, each in their own unique way, such that everybody come out of the water changed -- sometimes dramatically, sometimes quietly, but always with a grace that is undeniably joyful and intimate.

For the majority of people who feel called to swim with the dolphins and whales, the pull to be with them comes at a pivotal time in their journey. They are often contemplating big changes in their lives. For others, it is the fulfillment of a long-held dream. And for some, it is simply the irresistible appeal of splashing around with some of the most joyful creatures on the planet!

Are you a dolphin?

Our human journey is a brave one, for to fully travel this path we have taken on many veils of forgetting. How could we face the choice of love or fear if we knew we were God? Our cetacean brothers and sisters joyfully assist us in our journey, for they love us and admire our courage to walk this path. We are all; human, dolphin, animal, plant, mineral, from the same Source, and we live many lifetimes simultaneously. Those of us who are drawn to the cetaceans are likely living parallel lives as dolphins and whales.

My relationship with the dolphins and whales continues to grow and transform. Over the years, they helped me fall completely in love with the sea, once the source of nightmares. They've shown me the healing gift of water, and now, using holy water from sacred springs from around the world, I've led sacred water ceremonies and celebrations on five continents. I've been to The Cove in Taiji, Japan, to lead a Ho'oponopono ceremony.

While I still do a few open trips each year, most of my dolphin and whale trips are custom trips for small groups, individuals and families. Rather than bring large groups of 12 to 20 or more people to swim with the cetaceans, I prefer the longer, more intimate connection that happens when there's only a few of us in the water with the dolphins and whales.

A number of years ago at a sacred ceremony, I was given the name "Merman" by a group of Native American Elders for my work bridging tribes from the land with the tribes from the sea. I have been given the name "Dolphin Whisperer" by my clients. I accepted them when I saw they assist me in helping others realize we are all dolphin whisperers, for the language of the cetaceans, just like the language of all beings, is the language of the heart.

As a freediver and spearfisherman, I get a lot of my food from the sea. While I've never fed the dolphins, I've been given fish by them on multiple occasions. Food has become an ecstatic adventure for me. I've come to recognize that, whether we go directly to nature, the supermarket or the drive-thru window, we are all hunter/gatherers, and we bring more sacredness and joy into our lives and the world by how we regard our food.

Perhaps the greatest gift we can give this life and this beautiful planet is to be immersed in our divine joy and ecstasy. The cetaceans are intimate companions on this journey, well versed in saying "Yes!" to the present moment. If you too feel the call to joy and desire to allow divine exuberance to move even more fully though you, I invite you to join me on an adventure, either through a trip or one of my books.

The dolphins have arrived, and I go now to swim with them. I invite you, right where you are now, to join us in your imagination. They are available to everyone everywhere, for they are unlimited by time or space. Think of them, and they are with you. I dare you to give yourself full permission, right now, to let your inspiration guide you in the most magical dolphin or whale encounter you can imagine, right from where you sit.

Even now, as you picture yourself swimming with them in a beautiful, alive and vibrantly healthy ocean, it's as real and true as you dare believe.

Joebaby is an author, speaker, and shamanic nature guide who inspires people to embody a playful relationship with life. He leads spiritual adventure retreats swimming with wild dolphins and whales, and guides custom family trips around the world. He has been quoted by the *New York Times*, *People Magazine*, *Washington Post* and has appeared on *Oprah*, *Fox TV* and *National Geographic*. Visit his website at www.DolphinWhisperer.org , join his "Everyday Ecstasy" blog at www.AJoyfulNature.com and read some of his delicious stories in his book www.GodIsDelicious.com

"Life/Love/God is having a passionate, intimate and ecstatic relationship with our world, through our bodies and our senses, whether we're aware of it or not. Join me in the magic of celebrating all this joy, beauty and wonder!"

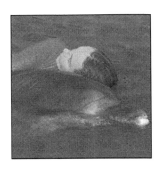

Chapter 18: *The Labyrinth*

By Frederique Pichard

Translated by Muriel Pichard

I was overwhelmed with a range of emotions the moment the dolphin looked me straight in the eye. My whole being felt alive. It was as if I was flying through time at the speed of light. I had returned to the original world, remembering who I truly was. My whole being felt awakened.

At the time, I worked in the travel industry as a tour rep and often travelled across the oceans, which brought me into contact with dolphins and gave me the opportunity to connect with their amazing intelligence. Each dolphin I met displayed different personality traits and had its unique way of connecting with humans. I soon realised dolphins were acting as scanners of matter and as amazing transmitters and receivers of energy. I was absolutely in awe.

Some years later, a friend told me that a dolphin had appeared in Royan Harbour very close to where we live as a family. This coincided with the sixth birthday of my daughter, who then celebrated her birthday with an Ambassador Dolphin! A dolphin, free and wild, who had come to live near us! Indeed, life presents us with some very pleasant surprises!

Ambassador dolphins have been identified since the time of ancient Greece, and at least 60 of them have been identified since. They are also called solitary dolphins and are very sociable, coming close to the shore to be near humans.

Dony, who is easily identifiable thanks to his gashed fin, differs from other lone dolphins who generally prefer to live in one place. Dony loves to travel, and has, therefore, been known by different names: The French often call him "Randy." The English "George." And the Irish call him Dony. I feel closer to the name Dony, because it resonates with the feeling of who he really is. In French, "donner" means "to give," and wherever Dony goes, he gives.

The day when my daughter Adélie and I went to meet him for the first time, we waited a long time. At first, without joy until Adélie connected with him through meditation and intuition, which led us to him. He was there, waiting for us, quiet, near a boat. We both jumped into the water. I felt as if I had always known him and as if we were meeting once again. We didn't need much time to become friends. After five minutes of our magical exchange, it suddenly came to me that I was swimming with a 250 kg dolphin that I was cuddling in my arms! From that moment on, my life changed totally, and I took the risk to go with the change.

Dolphins, like all of the animal kingdom, live in the present. This helped me to change my concept of Time. I came to perceive the significance of "coincidences," these mere synchronicities where life presents itself as the Guide.

Just prior to meeting Dony, our family was supposed to leave France to live in the Dominican Republic for three years or more. I had felt the urge to get close to the whales living in Samana Bay, located in the Northeastern part of this Caribbean tropical Island. Samana is best known for the frequency with which dolphins and humpback whales are seen there, and I wanted to observe, meet, and connect with them. The children were already registered at schools there. I had even found a long-term tenant for our house in France. So everything was organised in order for us to leave. However, a few days before our planned departure, a striking image came to me whilst looking at the sky. It came on the Summer Solstice, at dawn, on the 21st June 2004. I saw a perfectly drawn dolphin, with his fin and flippers. It wasn't a hallucination, or my own interpretation but very clearly a celestial message. At the time, when I saw and received it, I just smiled, but later on realised that Dony coming into my life wasn't a coincidence, but a divine gift.

What I clearly saw, was that I needed to stay in France, with my family, rather than going to the other side of the planet to meet the whales. This required a rapid change of program and the cancellation of all the school registrations, letting of the house etc... plus re-registering my children in schools in France... at the time these were "small" changes leading to much bigger ones. I didn't question any of it. It all seemed totally obvious and natural. Without any doubt, Dony had come into my life as a guide.

For many evenings, I went to meet Dony and "dance" with him. Dance has always been a big part of my life and a big channel of expression for me. In Dony, I had found a marvellous choreographer, and much more than this. He showed me another way of communicating: not in a creative manner, but in a much more subtle and deep way. A "cell-to-cell" communication and language, a physical and vibrational language. Dolphins live in a permanent Alpha state, half awake, half asleep. It is a meditative space where they are at one with the Universe. In this state of osmosis, where I sometimes spent hours with Dony at night, together looking at the moon and the stars, my cells deeply absorbed the energy he transmitted to me. Every time I came out of the water, I wrote words reflecting the messages I received through my body:

"I am with you, but I am not doing things instead of you"
"We are held together"
"We are held together in a state of abandonment"
"We are going with the flow of the waves, the movement of water"
"The water carries us"
"The Mother"
"The sea envelops us
"The sea brings us together"
"The Sea unifies us"
"You, as a human, in the amniotic fluid of your mother"
"Me, as a dolphin of the Sea"
"We both come from the same Source"
"The Source of beauty, of Love"

Dony helped me with my telepathic skills. I was already familiar with telepathy thanks to my twin boys who do not need to use words in order to communicate. But here I was receiving amazing teachings from a Master in telepathy! We, as humans, have become almost strangers to this form of communication, due to the excessive use of our mental skills. However, with practice, we are all able to use this form of communication. The internet mobile phones, are both mere tools of our own transmitter/internal receptor systems. Our interconnection, even though invisible and subtle is, nevertheless, real and present.

For two years after my encounter with Dony, I practiced the skills of intuitive communication. I communicated with Dony from a distance, setting up encounters and meetings with him in several locations and at different times. Of course, there were times when we missed each other, but most of our *rendez vous* were honoured, and we met as planned. This happened through visualization, images, emotions, feelings of joy in anticipation of being reunited again, all of which are different ways that can transmit vibrations. An emotion gives out a physical energetic wave and a thought wave, travelling through space to its recipient.

I drove for miles in order to be able to meet with Dony. It was as if we were magnets for each other. I felt inspired and followed this flow with total trust. I didn't feel any fear. I was in osmosis with the movement of life, invited in Dony's dance. My confidence in the process was strengthened each time Dony honoured our *rendez vous*. I don't remember today who invited whom? Was it me, was it Dony? I simply followed this energy.

I will always remember that, on the eve of one of our encounters, when another dolphin, Jean Floch was also present, I had expressed the vow under shooting stars, to meet both of them. The day after, my two friends were waiting for me exactly where I had asked them to meet me!

Another time, after meeting them again, being on my own after they had left, I felt overwhelmed with a deep sadness. I connected with them, just after their departure, transmitting to them my sadness, and for sure within five minutes they were back, giving me a big "hug" and went away again!! I remember another occasion when I was swimming with Jean-Floch, and I started to feel tired. Jean-Floch suddenly stopped, bit my flippers and went underneath my back holding me and allowing me to rest.

One day, I thought of Dony and Jean-Floch as I hadn't seen them together for a while. I didn't intentionally connect with Dony regarding this thought, the thought simply crossed my mind. As if by coincidence, they were both there the following day! Animals have this special gift of being able to read our thoughts before we are even aware of them.

In December 2004, Dony sent me an image where a group of people were holding their hands together in a circle. It was just before the Tsunami in Thailand. The message sent showed difficult times ahead, illustrating that only mutual aid, brotherhood/sisterhood would help towards our metamorphosis and evolution.

On All Saints Day, in 2010, I was in the water with Dony, and he suddenly changed position, standing upright as a human, cuddling in my arms as a child, standing still. My left hand was drawn as a magnet to his heart. I was overawed to feel his intense heartbeat so close to the skin. I will always remember this moment which I received as a sacred gift and as a universal message: the importance of feeling the beat of Life, this vibration, this pure crystal lodged in the depth of our hearts. I felt this love and unity vibrating between us and Life all together.

Since these several experiences, I have met many other wild animals: deer, storks, geese, a couple of swans who showed me the harmonious alliance between the feminine and the masculine. At night, other animals came in my dreams including lions, bears and horses. My encounter with dolphins had opened the way for me to discover the splendour of the animal kingdom as a whole.

I must not forget my cats "Tsadde" and "Venus." Venus was my best telepathic coach. Shaman, Lily who kept "miaowing" telling me to go for a walk and then meditate together on the beach facing the sea! My feline companions are always next to me and sometimes come to assist during workshops when participants are in need of support.

The kindness of Animals towards us acts as a spiritual support for us in these transformative times.

After my encounter with Dony, I contacted Mary Getten, who is an animal communicator and who has now become a friend. She came to my help when I needed to verify the messages I received from him. I needed the confirmation of a human teacher! Mary communicates perfectly and beautifully with animals. I feel enormous gratitude towards her, as I also do towards my sister Muriel, as they both have given me great support in my endeavour to spread the messages of the dolphins in

France, which to this day remains "prudent" in terms of inter-species communication!

Mary spoke about Dony to Dr. John E. Upledger, an American osteopath who studies the healing ability of dolphins. He has brought together cranial osteopathy and dolphins and uses this unique combination in training and healing. Being interested by Dony's behaviour, he has communicated with him through Mary.

The German biologist Monica Muller has written a very interesting thesis on Ambassador dolphins and their behaviour. What she observed is that they very often interact with us intensely for a few years and then stop and disappear to go back and live in groups as if their mission had been carried out and accomplished.

Dony and Jean Floch used to interact intensely during the summer season over a number of years with humans, and I often found that Dony was physically hurt. While I was training in Naturopathy, I became familiar with several vibrational essences frequencies through flower, gem, environmental and animal essences and came to use them with dolphins. I witnessed their huge sensitivity and receptiveness to these vibrational essences. As an example, Jean Floch who was known as a rebellious dolphin, came to be injured on his jaw. Thanks to one of the Alaskan Flower Essences, I was able to help him. I placed the bottle a fair distance from him, perhaps 20 cms, otherwise the energy would have been too strong for him. Humans do not feel this vibration so acutely.

This receptivity is a testimony to dolphins' intuitive intelligence. Their sensitivity demonstrates their connection and genuine empathy towards others, and it led me to discover their highly evolved collective intelligence. This inspired me to manifest this in my own life and work collectively. It is then that I came across the testimony of Dr John Lilly, which helped me to expand my consciousness, confirming what I already felt deeply. I knew that Dony had offered me a gift, which wasn't only for me: I had to spread the messages of the cetaceans. This was when I made the commitment to do this.

I almost ceased my practice in Naturopathy to focus on the "Association Dony" founded in 2006. With the support of friends and members of the Association and inspired by Lilly, the main focus of the association was then, and still is, to spread the message of the cetaceans, through conferences, talks, workshops and retreats where we meet the cetaceans. I approached several associations whose aim is to protect nature and wild animals. Unfortunately this didn't really go anywhere as we have different visions. Although they also work to protect the animals, they do not encourage inter-species communication. At the time, I felt discouraged, and my inner joy faded. I felt out of touch with what I had learnt through Dony.

After one experience of meeting Dony, an expression kept coming back to me: "The only thing that matters is self-responsibility."

I then understood that rather than projecting onto others my own will of unity, I needed to find it within myself. It would be true to say that for a big part of my life, I had been longing for the "lost paradise", and dolphins have really helped me to heal that wound. Our human suffering is often linked to our illusion of separation, abandonment and lack. The times when Dony didn't come to our meeting place, I used the space created to feel the silence and the stillness and to connect with nature deeply feeling and incorporating all the encounters that we had had. This is still an ongoing process. This remains the most beautiful and most demanding of my journeys. The journey of the mind grounded in the heart, feeling the inner peace, hoping that it will radiate in the outer world.

I see dolphins as bridges mirroring the soul. They help us reconnect with the most powerful healing energy, the power of love. We are beings vibrating at certain wave lengths. Like Mozart's music, the vibrational frequencies transmitted by dolphins are very high pitched which help us to rise. As the whales' songs harmonize the matrix of the oceans, they also invite us to gather and protect our beautiful blue planet, and visualize our seas and oceans filled with light.

It is now nine years since I have known Dony, and my inner bond with him is so strong that I no longer need to go and meet him physically. We are "partners". We work together. I feel his support and guidance from a distance and within me. He is now distancing himself from us and is gradually going back to his life as a wild dolphin. Other dolphins are now taking on his work. However, he was very present last year to take part in our film "Manimal," commissioned by the French film company Arte. This film has received the "bio-diversity" award. While putting things together for the film, I checked with Mary (Getten) which of the 3 pre-selected film-directors would Dony choose? He opted for Bruno Vienne and let her know via vibrations! Bruno specializes in wild life. When we started to film we assured Dony that the images of the film would convey and reflect what he wanted to communicate. He participated actively in this film and came up every time we started to film.

Dusty, an Irish female dolphin, who is nicknamed the "Ecologist" is also part of the film. She is a real character. She brings back to the shore all the rubbish of the sea, making sure we see it. She is affectionate towards us, however she is intense, demanding and wild. She has taught me a lot especially as far as love and respect are concerned. She is Love. And she also has very clear boundaries. Thanks to her, I have really understood what unconditional love is, which is by no means saying yes to everything. On the contrary, it requires extreme discipline. In our true essence, we are love and the guardians of love.

I love going on adventures with groups and embrace this wild feminine expression which is met in beings such as Dusty. I love doing this especially in the Azores, a special place of the planet where we can meet the goddesses and princes of the ocean. In the Azores, 23 different species of cetaceans live near each other in the depth of the Atlantic Ocean. The blue whale, the pilot whales, the sperm whales and the dolphins, all radiate their own splendor, and all are showing us how to be respectful and humble. In their presence, we have to let go of our expectations. On the first day of a trip last year, the sperm whales were telling us: "Be free of all expectations."

The rhythmic world of the cetaceans is poetic by nature. This world touches our senses, our imagination. In some ways, we are all artists searching for harmony. In the wonderful North American legend of the "fifth dream" we were dreamt by the whale. This is a dream which we all share at our core, at our essence. Through Dony, I have learnt that this sacred bond is forever present and doesn't require physical contact. Our beliefs are our only limitations. I love helping people discover/rediscover their "inner dolphin", feeling their infinite potential, and I do this by tapping into this forever-present connection during workshops which I facilitate in my home by the sea. Being connected to life, seeing how she desires us, and how through us, she also incarnates her own dream in consciousness and unity.

I am always in awe of the energy released and the healing taking place during these workshops. I never need to prepare, I just follow the images presenting themselves during guided meditations. Universal energy responds to the participants' energy, as if images of a film presented themselves to my brain and were instantaneously translated into words. I feel strongly that I receive the information from the cetaceans to which we are connected. The images and words are incredibly accurate. From the feedback I receive, they match the participants' experiences. It is as if, through my human form, I am developing more and more of my inner scanner, and this, is all thanks to the dolphins.

Last summer, I met another Ambassador dolphin named Clet. He was then spending time in France, near the Brittany coast. Through telepathy he told me "when I am seen as coming alone in a harbour, this is a human vision and concept. I am physically on my own, but I am forever linked to my group". I am starting to understand the word intricacy which is often used in quantum physics. The marine mammals live in several spheres and invite us to expand our consciousness and explore other realms.

During my numerous encounters with Dony, I received the invitation from him to co-create vibrational essences. My sister Muriel and I co-created with a group of dolphins and my daughter Adélie, Essence named: "Dolphin essence Together." Here is Muriel's testimony of this experience and description of the essence:

"This essence was prepared on a bright warm sunny day in France on the Brittany coast on 29th August 2010. We went out at sea with the intention of meeting a group of resident dolphins. From a distance, we started seeing fins... 1,2,3,4, and many more, all coming from different angles towards the same direction. We were suddenly surrounded by them and were in total awe of their energy, lightness, harmony with their natural environment. We were filled with joy, sharing this together. The water was so clear that we could see through it. The dolphins played, jumped in the air, followed the boat at great speed and with acute precision.

Suddenly the energy changed as the dolphins started to catch fish. The energy was intense as the dolphins went in several directions, however with a definite sense of strategy. It seemed as if they knew instinctively where to go, performing an individual action with a collective energy.

Frédérique had brought the equipment to prepare an essence. She started the process and then went on to meet the dolphins in the water and Adelie and I stayed on the boat, holding the bowl in turns. At some point, holding the bowl myself, I became suddenly drawn to the front of the boat.

As soon as I reached my destination, two dolphins came to meet me. They were swimming in very close contact to one another, totally in harmony with each other, matching the exact speed of the boat and always a little ahead of us.

One dolphin turned his face towards me and looked at me straight in the eyes. I received the following message from him: "We are here, we are part of this, we are participating in this process". This beautiful dolphin knew an essence was created and wanted to participate in it consciously on behalf of the whole group. Discussing this later on with Frédérique, she told me that she had indeed seen these two dolphins leaving her side to go to the front of the boat where I was holding the bowl. Several times, she saw dolphins taking an active part in the birth of an essence.

It was an awesome experience. We will never forget the interaction of the dolphins, their communication, their total engagement, precision and sense of direction. Going ahead, together, without attachment, was a teaching we took from the experience."

The central message of the essence is:

"It is time to gather. Together, we are strong, we go in the same direction, knowing exactly our individual contribution to the whole and performing it with total consciousness, aliveness, lightness and sheer inner knowing and determination. We are all part of a collective consciousness."

The essence is especially supportive of group work and families who wish to work consciously and together. Since then many more essences have seen the light.

Dony really feels strongly about helping children and another project of the association focuses on children by meeting them in schools and colleges. I meet children to speak to them about the ecology of the planet, and what I would call the "ecology of beings". One day whilst my son Coriolan, then 11 years old, was stroking Dony, he asked me: "Mum, who has invented the word 'abandonment?'"

Through his words, I understood that the notion of abandonment is only a human concept, and that whilst Coriolan was touching Dony, he felt Oneness. Much later, when his twin brother Raphael, then 19, went through a difficult time, I asked Dony through telepathy if he could come and meet us. He did, and at the time and place where we had agreed, he stayed two hours with us. Dony offered Raphael a real dance, a dance of ecstasy, as if to remind him of who he truly is: "Remember who you are, remember this love shining around you and within you."

Raphael found his centre again and immediately things fell into place for him as in alchemy.

I could tell many other stories about my collaboration with the dolphins. I will always remember a moment in the Azores when I went in the water with Michelle, a 70 year-old lady. There were a hundred dolphins all around us, and seven came close to us positioning themselves upright in the water, as if humans, acting as a symphonic orchestra just for us. Suddenly three came even closer to us, and Michelle and I saw a diamond-shaped hologram filled with bubbles of light, and I heard "healing of humanity." I dream of painting this very special and exceptional moment one day. I was happy for Michelle who has gone through very challenging experiences in her life.

I have since understood that this holographic symbol was a sacred gift offered to us. The dolphins of the Azores give out bubbles of light filled with gold. Everybody who has come with me there has received them as bubbles of healing light acting as holographic portals.

Whether in one-to-one sessions or group work (in retreats or workshops), I see people contacting their "inner dolphin" and see their life change radically as soon as they connect with this dolphin energy. It is not necessarily about miracle cures, but it is about changes in consciousness, an expansiveness that opens new doors, new understandings of why we are on planet earth.

As a final testimony, here is a letter I received from Dorian, a 14 year-old student who I had met while visiting his school:

> "I know that we have not been in touch for the last six months, but I have often thought about you. As you suggested, I have researched the work of Masaru Emoto and have read his book. I now understand better the meaning of vibrations, the importance of feelings and your telepathic communication with Dony. I perceive your contact with dolphins as a vibrational network. If dolphins are capable of such powerful feelings, it is because they have developed a very high emotional brain. On another hand, we as humans, have developed our cognitive brain. You are however the living proof that we are also capable of communicating telepathically. Telepathy is an incredible thing.

We could therefore be doubles, mirrors of the dolphins, living as they do in a society communicating freely and amicably with our peers. The only barrier between the dolphins and us is the surface of water which is a mirror. We see ourselves in the mirror, and we see our reflection, our double. We can see the dolphins. Everything in their world and in ours works in reverse: the dolphins live in the water, we live on its surface, they swim, we walk, but when we need to communicate with one another, telepathy comes in as a bridge between our two worlds. You are this bridge. I hope that many people will be able, thanks to you, to cross it and connect with the awesome happiness and freedom of the ocean."

The Institut Dony was founded in 2006, inspired by the American neurologist Dr John Lilly's spiritual testimony, having the aim to help with the protection of the seas and oceans, the cetaceans and Ambassador dolphins in particular, and put in place a research and exchange of communication between the cetaceans, the scientific world, the teachers and therapists, artists, children, teenagers, all sharing the same passion.

Frédérique Pichard was born in Paris where she lived until early adolescence. She spent most of her childhood holidays with her grandparents in Normandie where she developed an early bond with Nature. Every summer, she spent time by the skeleton of a whale who had stranded years before on the local beach. This triggered her imagination and her deep love for the seas and oceans. In 2004, she met Dony, an Ambassador dolphin--a big turning point in her life. This strong connection with Dony brought people of different backgrounds in Frédérique's life: philosopher, biologist, doctor, ecologist and together they founded the "Institut Dony". The Institute has a vocation of protection towards dolphins and aims to encourage the human/dolphins interspecies communication as well as encouraging research carried out by scientists, therapists, artists and all those with a passion for these amazing beings.

Frédérique is very passionate about vibrational energy and facilitates workshops and conferences in France and internationally to spread the magnificent energy of the cetaceans and their messages. Through her multiple encounters with dolphins and whales, she has understood that it is not required to be physically in their presence to feel their energy. She loves to teach young students at colleges how to feel this "dolphin energy" and open their consciousness so that they can trust in a universal connection. She is currently developing a range of Sea Essences, is the author of the book "Dauphins Ambassadeurs, Messagers de la Mer", a key participant and contributor to the film "Ambassador dolphins, Messengers of the Sea" in the Manimal series, and organises trips in several locations to meet with cetaceans.

For more details, please visit www.institutdony.com

Conclusion

By Cyndie Lepori

In creating the conclusion after reading the beautiful stories of all the contributors, I decided to connect with the Dolphins and Whales, to see what they had to say. After all, the book is all about them. I called in the ocean energies, created a bubble of sacred space for them to come into and waited. The bottlenose dolphin that is my guide Bubbles was the first to show, then the space was filled with Dolphins, Whales and many other creatures of the sea. The channeling that I received follows....

We have been creating a flow of communication for many humans for many years. We reach humans in every way imaginable. We are masters of sound, vibration and communication within our own species and many others. We lead by example such as being the embodiment of Love, joy, play, community, abundance, and connection among ourselves and with other species as well. We also are in Joy that the people of the dolphins and the whales are finding out about each other and connecting. We never call to one person alone. We blast the frequencies thoughout the planet and whomever connects to them simply receives. We can connect in many ways, through contact in person, the water, films, books, dream time, wherever you are on the planet or even off planet, we can reach every heart and connect when each person is ready, and open to receive. We truly value each and every person who hears our call. We envision a humanity that is as free, joyful, abundant, and as aware of their unique divinity as we are. With these frequencies we create an enlightened earth friendly, self-aware species in humans.

We have sent Ambassadors and Emissaries to walk among humans that carry our frequencies and allow people to wake up to the higher frequencies just by being in their space. A few are represented here. There are many more. We envision a great coming together for all with the human/whale/dolphin connections that embodies the principles by which we co-create a better earth for all beings in existence at this time.

As you can see there is a uniqueness among the collaborators of this book's experiences and yet there are also many common threads that lay in each story. We reach each human where they are currently at and lift them into higher frequencies. We have much to share and much to teach. There is no right way to connect with us. The important experience is that the connection is made. We welcome each and every one who is willing to explore the dolphin/human connection and be open to the information that we are willing and able to bring into their lives.

We invite each and every one who finds and experiences this book to awaken to the possibilities that we bring to the table in the exploration of the higher frequencies. We invite you to know your own divinity. We are the ultimate time travelers, dimensional shifters, and can carry each person to the next higher spiritual levels, no matter where they are at present in their journey. It is a great invitation. Are you ready for the oceans of knowledge that we carry? Are you willing to join with us in creating a better world for yourselves and the future generations? We can expand your world in ways that you can only imagine. We invite you to swim with us and create the ascended world that is being dreamed into existence now. Join us in this beautiful vision we have for the planet and all life that resides here. You are divine. You are safe. You are joy. You are love. You are abundant. We are one universe, one planet, one nation, one heart, and so it is.

Thank you for joining us on this beautiful journey with the dolphins, whales, and humans. The journey is truly an adventure.

About the Artist

Jean-Luc Bozzoli

Jean-Luc studied at the "Beaux-Arts" in Nancy and Paris, France, yet learned more from observing Nature and its intrinsic 'stargates'. For his graduating thesis from the University, he built a domed Cymatic sanctuary with light and sound in 1969.

Jean-Luc was born as a natural visual-intuitive, a modern shaman artist who can navigate dimensions and retrieve psychic snapshots of those realms to share with audiences; awakening in them the awareness of parallel realities where "sentient beings" communicate via ethereal frequencies forming images with colors and geometries.

Jean-Luc spent the 1970's in French Polynesia presenting shows at the aquarium; next he was setting stage shows in New Zealand with Limbs Dance Company, then became an illustrator with Simply-Living Magazine, an Australian publication featuring alternative health, sustainability and travel; he assisted an Australian TV show named Extra-Dimensions, by designing their advertising brochures and opening screen images for this innovative television series with dolphins 1980-83. He traveled with Interspecies Communication and the whales in the islands of British Columbia, Canada in 1984; and then co-founded and co-authored with Joan Ocean, Dolphin Connection Interdimensional Ways of Living - producing shows, books, posters, films and many international seminars featuring dolphins, whales and 9 journeys with Sasquatch contact in the forest at night. Jean-Luc co-convened multiple Dolphin and Teleportation conferences and seminars in Asia, Europe, North and South America; and presented his art films in many venues including the most recent event, The Star Knowledge Conference with the Native American elders in Palm Springs, California. Jean-Luc lives in Kealakekua, Hawaii on his sustainable farm, *Sky Island Ranch*, where he continues his art projects in communion with nature. - www.eyewithin.com

27945671R00156

Made in the USA
Charleston, SC
27 March 2014